HEIDEGGER'S
BEING AND TIME

Critical Essays on the Classics

Series Editor: Steven M. Cahn

The volumes in this series offer insightful and accessible essays that shed light on the classics of philosophy. Each of the distinguished editors has selected outstanding work in recent scholarship to provide today's readers with a deepened understanding of the most timely issues raised in these important texts.

Plato's *Republic*: Critical Essays
   edited by Richard Kraut
Plato's *Euthyphro, Apology,* and *Crito*: Critical Essays
   edited by Rachana Kamtekar
Aristotle's *Ethics*: Critical Essays
   edited by Nancy Sherman
Descartes's *Meditations*: Critical Essays
   edited by Vere Chappell
The Rationalists: Critical Essays on Descartes, Spinoza, and Leibniz
   edited by Derk Pereboom
The Empiricists: Critical Essays on Locke, Berkeley, and Hume
   edited by Margaret Atherton
The Social Contract Theorists: Critical Essays on Hobbes, Locke, and Rousseau
   edited by Christopher Morris
Mill's *On Liberty*: Critical Essays
   edited by Gerald Dworkin
Mill's *Utilitarianism*: Critical Essays
   edited by David Lyons
Mill's *The Subjection of Women*: Critical Essays
   edited by Maria H. Morales
Kant's *Groundwork on the Metaphysics of Morals*: Critical Essays
   edited by Paul Guyer
Kant's *Critique of Pure Reason*: Critical Essays
   edited by Patricia Kitcher
Kant's *Critique of the Power of Judgment*: Critical Essays
   edited by Paul Guyer
Heidegger's *Being and Time*: Critical Essays
   edited by Richard Polt
The Existentialists: Critical Essays on Kierkegaard, Nietzsche, Heidegger, and Sartre
   edited by Charles Guignon

HEIDEGGER'S
BEING AND TIME
Critical Essays

Edited by
Richard Polt

ROWMAN & LITTLEFIELD PUBLISHERS, INC.
Lanham • Boulder • New York • Toronto • Oxford

√

ROWMAN & LITTLEFIELD PUBLISHERS, INC.

Published in the United States of America
by Rowman & Littlefield Publishers, Inc.
A wholly owned subsidary of The Rowman & Littlefield Publishing Group, Inc.
4501 Forbes Boulevard, Suite 200, Lanham, Maryland 20706
www.rowmanlittlefield.com

P.O. Box 317
Oxford
OX2 9RU, UK

British Library Cataloguing in Publication Information Available

Library of Congress Cataloging-in-Publication Data

Heidegger's Being and time : critical essays / edited by Richard Polt.
    p.   cm. — (Critical essays on the classics)
   Includes bibliographical references (p.) and index.
    ISBN 0-7425-4240-8 (cloth : alk. paper) — ISBN 0-7425-4241-6 (pbk. : alk. paper)
    1. Heidegger, Martin, 1889–1976. Sein und Zeit.   2. Ontology.   3. Space and time.
I. Polt, Richard F. H., 1964–   II. Series.
B3279.H48S46613 2005
111—dc22

                                                    2005005337

Printed in the United States of America

∞™ The paper used in this publication meets the minimum requirements of American
National Standard for Information Sciences—Permanence of Paper for Printed Library
Materials, ANSI/NISO Z39.48–1992.

Contents

Acknowledgments

"WHY REAWAKEN THE QUESTION OF BEING?" is reprinted and translated with permission of the publisher from Jean Grondin, "Pourquoi réveiller la question de l'être?" in *Heidegger: L'énigme de l'être*, ed. Jean-François Mattéi (Paris: Presses Universitaires de France, 2004): 43–69.

"The Temporality of Thinking: Heidegger's Method" is reprinted with permission of the publisher from Karin de Boer, *Thinking in the Light of Time: Heidegger's Encounter with Hegel* (Albany: State University of New York Press, 2000): 66–69, 105–13.

"The Constitution of Our Being" is reprinted with permission of the publisher from Graeme Nicholson, "The Constitution of Our Being," *American Philosophical Quarterly* 36, vol. 3 (July 1999): 165–85.

"Heidegger's Anti-Dualism: Beyond Mind and Matter" is printed with permission of the author, Charles Guignon.

"The Genesis of Theory" is reprinted with permission of the publisher from William McNeill, *The Glance of the Eye: Heidegger, Aristotle, and the Ends of Theory* (Albany: State University of New York Press, 1999): 56–71.

"Being-with, Dasein-with, and the 'They' as the Basic Concept of Unfreedom" is reprinted and translated with permission of the publisher from Günter Figal, *Martin Heidegger: Phänomenologie der Freiheit* (Weinheim: Beltz Athenäum, 2000): 141–53.

"Subjectivity: Locating the First-Person in *Being and Time*" is reprinted with permission of the publisher from Steven Crowell, "Subjectivity: Locating the First Person in *Being and Time*," *Inquiry* 44 (2001): 433–54.

"Can There Be a Better Source of Meaning Than Everyday Practices? Reinterpreting Division I of *Being and Time* in the Light of Division II" is printed by permission of the author, Hubert L. Dreyfus.

"Genuine Timeliness" is from Daniel O. Dahlstrom, *Heidegger's Concept of Truth* (Cambridge: Cambridge University Press, 2001): 325–38. ©1994 Passagen Verlag, Ges.m.b.H., Wien; English translation ©2001 Cambridge University Press. Reprinted with the permission of Cambridge University Press.

"Historical Meaning in the Fundamental Ontology of *Being and Time*" is reprinted with permission of the publisher from Jeffrey Andrew Barash, *Martin Heidegger and the Problem of Historical Meaning*, 2nd ed. (New York: Fordham University Press, 2003): 162–76, 177–82.

"The Demise of *Being and Time*: 1927–1930" is reprinted and translated with permission of the publisher from Theodore Kisiel, "Das Versagen von *Sein und Zeit*: 1927–1930," in *Martin Heidegger, "Sein und Zeit,"* ed. Thomas Rentsch (Berlin: Akademie, 2001): 253–79.

"*Being and Time* in Retrospect: Heidegger's Self-Critique" is reprinted and translated with permission of the publisher from Dieter Thomä, "*Sein und Zeit* im Rückblick: Heideggers Selbstkritik," in *Martin Heidegger, "Sein und Zeit,"* ed. Thomas Rentsch (Berlin: Akademie, 2001): 281–98.

Introduction

MARTIN HEIDEGGER's *Being and Time* (1927) is indisputably one of the greatest works of philosophy published in the past hundred years. But the meaning and implications of the book remain the object of lively controversy, as does its author. Heidegger is the most discussed thinker of the twentieth century, and we can expect the discussion to grow in both quantity and quality. Since Heidegger's death in 1976, the ongoing publication of the *Gesamtausgabe*, or collected edition of his writings, has made dozens of his lecture courses and private manuscripts available. Along with newly published letters, these texts offer many opportunities to refine our judgments about his masterwork.

The combined mass of primary and secondary texts exceeds the reading capacity of any student of Heidegger. Where to begin, then? *Being and Time* remains the essential entry point to Heidegger's thought; it is the most thorough presentation of his earlier philosophy (before 1930), and even from his later perspective, Heidegger considered it a necessary path.[1] As for the secondary literature, this anthology offers a sampling of outstanding recent studies; some suggestions for further research are found in the bibliography. The dozen authors in this volume represent diverse nationalities, generations, and interpretive approaches, but all offer clear and independent-minded readings of major themes in *Being and Time*. Their topics include general methodological and ontological questions, particular issues in Heidegger's text, and the relations between *Being and Time* and Heidegger's later thought.

A Survey of *Being and Time*

The topic of Heidegger's book is Being *(das Sein)*—the basis for our understanding of entities *(das Seiende)* as such (SZ 6). Being allows us to make sense of what there is—to deal with and investigate all that we encounter, recognizing it as something rather than nothing. Being takes various forms: the Being of equipment, for example, is what it means to be equipment, or the basis for our understanding of useful entities; the Being of nature is what it means to be nature; and so on. But all the varieties of Being cohere, Heidegger assumes, so that we can ask what it means to be in general. Because it is not itself an entity, Being is a difficult, elusive topic: we cannot pick it up, perceive it through the senses, or subject it to experiments. However, we must already have some understanding of Being; otherwise, entities would make no sense to us. The trick to thinking of Being is to pay attention to the background intelligibility of entities—a phenomenon so fundamental and familiar that we ordinarily overlook it.

Heidegger wishes not only to put Being into words but also to investigate how it is possible for us to understand it in the first place. The thesis of *Being and Time* is that the horizon of Being—the context that allows us to understand Being—is time (SZ 1). "Time" here means our own temporality, by which we are drawn into the future, the past, and the present. The claim that time is the horizon for Being means that our temporality makes Being understandable, and thus makes it possible for entities as such to make sense to us.

To support this thesis, Heidegger must explicate our own sort of Being—what it means to be human. He refers to us as Dasein, literally "Being there." We are the entities who inhabit a "there," and even *are* the "there" (SZ 133). In other words, what is distinctive about us is that we operate in an open area, an illuminated field, in which beings can appear. (Earlier modern philosophy referred to this as our consciousness. Heidegger does not, partly to avoid traditional riddles about the relation between the subjective mind and external objects, and partly to point to a deeper field of meaning that makes consciousness possible.)[2]

Heidegger never completed *Being and Time* as originally planned. He published the first two divisions of Part 1, which interpret the Being of Dasein, but he was dissatisfied with the crucial third division, which would interpret Being itself within the horizon of time. This division was never published, nor was Part 2, which would have deconstructed the philosophical tradition on the basis of Heidegger's interpretation of Being. (Many of his later writings, however, are devoted to critical readings of the tradition.)

Division I of *Being and Time* as we have it begins with our ordinary activity. We do not normally contemplate entities, but are busy using and producing them. This everyday productive activity is a clue to Dasein's basic constitution: we find ourselves pursuing projects in particular situations; we are actively involved with the entities we encounter, including other people; we are not essentially neutral and disinterested spectators but are so engaged in the world (as a field of meanings and purposes) that our very Being can be called "Being-in-the-world." Furthermore, our everyday behavior is not distinctively individual but manifests an anonymous, average way of existing that Heidegger calls *das Man,* "the one" or "the 'they.'" In this way, Heidegger undercuts Descartes's influential view of the proper starting point for philosophy; instead of understanding ourselves by looking to the "I think," we have to begin with "one acts." By avoiding the intellectualist bias of Cartesianism, we can recognize that moods disclose our world, that we understand things in terms of what we can do and how we can be, that our grasp of things is never independent of language, and that we are normally absorbed in a web of concerns and commitments. This absorption is not the last word: we can be shocked out of it by the disruptive experience of anxiety, in which the meaning of our existence seems to drain away. But anxiety does not leave us with meaninglessness; it can give us a clearer insight into the essentially meaningful and engaged character of our Being as "care." Heidegger ends Division I with a discussion of reality and truth, tracing the traditional notion of truth—as a correspondence between theoretical judgments and objects—back to a deeper phenomenon of truth as Dasein's disclosedness (its way of being the "there") and the accompanying unconcealment of entities (SZ 220–21).

Division II explores further extraordinary experiences which, like anxiety, urge us to come to grips with our own Being. By facing my mortality, I can recognize that my Being is individual: no one else can relieve me of the task of living with the constant possibility of nonexistence. By owning up to my "guilt" (indebtedness and responsibility), I can recognize that my Being is my own: I must take over who I already am as I become who I am going to be. Death and guilt make "authenticity" possible, that is, a decisive and clear-sighted way of being oneself. Heidegger is now ready to interpret the Being of Dasein as temporality, which involves three temporal "ecstases": we are drawn into the future as we project possible ways to be, we are drawn into the past because we have been thrown into a particular situation, and we are drawn into the present as we become absorbed in dealing with the entities that surround us. Delving more deeply into temporality, Heidegger concludes that we are essentially historical: we are members of a community that continually draws on its heritage in order to work out its destiny. This temporal, historical happening of Dasein cannot be reduced to the superficial interpretation of time as a neutral timeline—the framework in which objects present themselves in a series of instants. Time, for Heidegger, is the marrow of our existence and the home of all truth; it is an incomparable gift that presents us with the inexhaustible challenge of being ourselves and attending to Being.

Even in its unfinished state, *Being and Time* is breathtaking in its depth and scope. It revives the ancient and medieval question of Being, challenges early modern philosophy, and draws on late modern trends such as the existential philosophy of Kierkegaard and Jaspers, Nietzsche's life-philosophy, and Husserl's phenomenology. But *Being and Time* is never a mishmash of received concepts; Heidegger's intellect and passion give it originality, unity, and direction.

Initially *Being and Time* was seen primarily through the prisms of existentialism and phenomenology, but with time it contributed to new philosophical trends such as hermeneutics and postmodernism. Some came to see Heidegger's thought as a world unto itself that had to be accepted on its own terms. As laudable as it is to try to understand a philosopher as he understood himself, the devotion of some pious Heideggerians has led to a jargon-ridden, esoteric discourse. In contrast, the past quarter century has seen the rise of "analytic" Heidegger interpretations that focus on precise reformulations of Heidegger's claims and arguments, often relating them to issues in contemporary Anglo-American philosophy. As Heidegger's most systematic work, *Being and Time* lends itself to such readings and rewards them; however, they run the risk of taking Heidegger's claims out of context. Today a balanced approach to interpreting Heidegger is gaining ground; this approach respects the need to combine an extensive study of his writings in the context of the Western philosophical tradition with independent reflection that takes Heidegger's thought as food for our own. Heidegger himself would surely approve of this attitude, which is evident in the critical essays in this volume.

Chapters in This Anthology

In the chapter that opens this collection, Jean Grondin asks, "Why Reawaken the Question of Being?" The question of Being is the driving force behind all of Heidegger's writings, but what drives Heidegger to ask it? And what exactly does it mean? Although the opening pages of *Being and Time* focus precisely on this point, Grondin finds that they do not provide an unambiguous solution. Is the question of "the meaning of Being" simply an attempt to clarify the concept expressed by the word "Being"? Or is it a more radical inquiry, a search for the ultimate significance of Being as a primal event? What gives the question of

Being its priority over every other question? Heidegger argues that the question is "ontologically" prior (§3) because some understanding of what it means to be is presupposed by all scientific inquiries into particular beings. But he also argues (§4) that the question is "ontically" prior for us as Dasein because our *own* Being is always at stake for us, always an issue about which we have to care. Grondin shows that the connection between these two types of priority lies in the fact that every understanding of Being is determined by Dasein's care for its own temporal Being. This care, however, usually takes the form of fleeing from the troubling burden of our Being—hence the traditional metaphysical ideal of a timeless, permanently present entity. Referring to recently published texts, Grondin argues that for Heidegger the task of bringing us back to the question of Being was in a broad sense religious. The question of Being attempts to recover the disquiet of the human condition as a fragile and fallible sojourn within the inexplicable unfolding of meaning and truth—a disquiet that is ordinarily anesthetized by the scientific and technological mind-set of our age.

In *Thinking in the Light of Time: Heidegger's Encounter with Hegel*, Karin de Boer considers two philosophers who try to do justice in their very ways of thinking to temporality and historicity. Our selection from this book analyzes the method of *Being and Time* on the basis of clues provided in *The Basic Problems of Phenomenology*, a lecture course from 1927 that takes steps toward the analysis of Temporality (*Temporalität*, or time as the horizon for Being) that Heidegger had promised to carry out in Part 1, Division III of *Being and Time*. According to *Basic Problems*, the three ecstases of time open "horizonal schemata" in which beings can become intelligible—including the schema of *praesens*, which provides the meaning of Being as presence. (For further details, see Theodore Kisiel's chapter in this volume.) De Boer carefully explains how *Being and Time* tries to think beyond *praesens*, incorporating pastness and futurity in its approach to Being. In traditional metaphysical thinking, the past takes the form of the a priori, understood as what is always and necessarily present; the future takes the form of a *telos*, a goal that is to be made present. Thus both past and future are traditionally understood on the basis of *praesens*. In contrast, Heidegger develops a new sense of the a priori as conditions that have "always already" been in place and thus have never simply been present.[3] Similarly, possibility in Heidegger is not what is not yet present, but a guiding, illuminating "projection" that cannot be exhausted by presence. According to de Boer, *Being and Time* never fully explains how these concepts apply to its own procedure—not even in the methodological (§7). Perhaps a philosophical method cannot be fully explained in advance of its results because the findings of the philosophy condition the method; because *Being and Time* remained incomplete, then, its method had to remain partly obscure. De Boer's elucidation of Heidegger's method, then, is not only a valuable prolegomenon to *Being and Time* but also a step toward seeing how the book might have been completed.

Being and Time is clearly a study of Dasein that is for the sake of studying Being as such. But the precise nature of this project can be difficult to grasp, as all the book's readers know. What exactly is the relation between Dasein and human beings? What exactly does it mean to call the ontology of Dasein "fundamental ontology"? When Heidegger writes that he is interpreting our "Being," our "'essence'" (in quotation marks), and our "constitution," do these terms have the same meaning? What are the relations among the basic concepts he uses to characterize us, such as existence, Being-in-the-world, and care? And why does "existence" seem to have two meanings, broad and narrow? In "The Constitution of Our Being," Graeme Nicholson patiently sorts out these issues. His interpretation focuses on Dasein's *Seinkönnen*, or "ability to be," as a "self-surpassing" that reaches out into possibilities. For Heidegger, in order properly to understand the Being of any entities we must first understand the self-surpassing character of understanding itself: understanding is never simply a present "state of mind," but is always a futural ability-to-grasp. This orientation to possibilities, argues Nicholson, cannot be reduced to the facts about our brain that are studied by naturalistic philosophers of mind. These philosophers assume that human beings are a special case of the physical universe; instead, from a Heideggerian perspective, the ontology assumed by modern physics is a special case of the understanding of Being that is involved in Dasein's ability to be. Heidegger, then, carries out a contemporary version of Socrates' turn away from "the things in the sky and below the earth" (Plato *Apology* 23d) toward the human world as the irreducible starting point of philosophy.

Charles Guignon's "Heidegger's Anti-Dualism: Beyond Mind and Matter" shows how *Being and Time*'s conception of Dasein challenges a dichotomy that pervades not only modern philosophy but also many commonsense modern assumptions about ourselves, our bodies, and our relation to the surrounding world. We often assume that action must be understood in terms of a distinction between two realms of being: inner, intending mind and outer, inherently meaningless physical occurrences. The dichotomy goes back at least to Descartes, who distinguished between two essentially different types of substance: thinking things and extended things. Guignon argues that Heidegger shows us a way beyond this substance dualism: for Heidegger, intentions and other so-called mental phenomena can be defined and realized only when they are expressed in a course of action in a meaningful world. Such expression involves projecting possibilities and being attuned to the way in which we have been thrown into a context. Here "projection" and "attunement" are neither purely mental nor purely physical; rather, they both emerge from and help constitute a shared domain of sense. Such phenomena are best described in terms of what Guignon calls an "event ontology." Citing the Zollikon seminars that Heidegger conducted in his old age, Guignon shows that Heidegger's opposition to substance dualism continued to bear fruit long after *Being and Time*. In these conversations with psychiatrists, Heidegger tirelessly expounds a nondualistic understanding of the body and behavior. A blush, for example, is neither simply a physiological process nor an inner, subjective state of mind; it is one way in which human beings can *happen* as embodied, engaged participants in the world. In his concluding pages, Guignon takes this insight further and suggests that a Heideggerian approach may help us overcome the dichotomy between facts and values, "is" and "ought": understanding Being-in-the-world can help us understand what it would mean to exist authentically and even to live virtuously.

William McNeill's *The Glance of the Eye* traces the theme of the *Augenblick*, the "moment of vision" or "glance of the eye," in Heidegger's thought as it evolves in dialogue with ancient philosophy, and Aristotle in particular. For Aristotle, the highest type of "seeing" is *theoria*, the contemplative insight into universal truths. But for Heidegger, theory depends on a more basic "seeing" that pervades our engaged activities in the world and that can reach a peak of acuity at certain authentic, decisive moments. In Aristotelian terms, it would seem that for Heidegger, *theoria* is subordinate to practice—that is, both *techne* (the understanding and know-how required by *poiesis*, or production) and *phronesis* (the practical wisdom required by *praxis*, or action).[4] However, according to McNeill in our excerpt, "The Genesis of Theory," a simple inversion of the classical hierarchy would be inadequate as an interpretation of Heidegger. Theory and practice are both made possible by a deeper phenomenon—the temporal structure of care. Furthermore, argues McNeill (in implicit opposition to many interpreters), Heidegger's initial accounts of how theory emerges from productive activity tell us "nothing . . . concerning the *ontological* genesis of cognition or theoretical comportment." Practice precedes theory chronologically, but Heidegger's description of this sequence is not yet an account of how theory is rooted in Dasein's Being. (Such an account is provided in SZ §69b, which McNeill interprets after the excerpt printed here.) McNeill's analyses have the merit of focusing on crucial claims of Division I while retaining the intricacy and subtlety of their connections to the rest of *Being and Time* and to the ancient tradition, which Heidegger studied with extraordinary attention.[5]

"Being-with, Dasein-with, and the 'They' as the Basic Concept of Unfreedom" is taken from Günter Figal's larger interpretation of Heidegger's thought as a "phenomenology of freedom." Here Figal elucidates Heidegger's difficult concepts of *Mitsein*, *Mitdasein*, and *das Man*. The main difficulty of the notions lies in their ambiguity: Heidegger's rather confusing terminology allows us to read his discussion either as a positive account of the ineluctably social basis of meaning, or as an attack on everyday inauthenticity—perhaps especially in its modern form. Figal insists that Heidegger is not merely propounding a cultural critique, but is providing a phenomenology of how the self and others become "explicit" and "inexplicit" in our behavior *(Verhalten)* and speech. My behavior involves other people in an inexplicit way, even if no others are currently present, because my understanding of what I am doing and the things I am encountering always implicitly refers to other actors and users: I am ineluctably "Being-with" others. Here Figal points out that even when we are actually present with others, it is precisely by remaining somewhat inexplicit, or holding ourselves "in reserve," that we enable each other to act: we refrain from inappropriate behavior, we let others have opportunities to participate in the current activity, and in this way we enter into work or play. All "Dasein-with" involves this phenomenon of "holding in reserve." As for the process of becoming explicit, or manifesting oneself as an individual, it too depends on a certain "otherness." As we can see from the use of phrases such as "I myself" (which implies "rather than anyone else"), selfhood is not isolation: it requires a contrast to others, who I must assume can be compared to me. For Figal, the "they" is Being-with as the context in which one can become explicitly "one-self." In this sense, the "they" makes all my behavior possible. Why, then, is the "they" the "basic concept of unfreedom"? Because neither Heidegger nor Figal is a behaviorist. We are not reducible to our behavior, even though we must continually make ourselves manifest by behaving in the world. More basic than behavior is *disclosedness,* and that is where we must seek genuine freedom and authentic selfhood. Authenticity is not a way of acting that is independent of others—that would be impossible—but a free way of being disclosed. (Readers might consider whether the distinction between behavior and disclosedness risks reinstating the sort of dualism that is criticized by Guignon.)

Heidegger's critique of the Cartesian notion of the subject and his view that the everyday self is "inauthentic" are sometimes interpreted as a dissolution of the first-person perspective altogether. (Such readings are often influenced by Heidegger's own later views; see Dieter Thomä's article in this volume.) To the contrary, argues Steven Crowell in "Subjectivity: Locating the First-Person in *Being and Time,*" the "I"—properly understood—is fundamental to meaning and human action as *Being and Time* portrays them. Drawing on speech-act theory, Crowell claims that Heidegger's account of conscience satisfactorily explains how we can successfully use the word "I." (Readers may wish to compare this aspect of Crowell's chapter to Figal's account of "saying 'I myself.'") The call of my conscience unmistakably singles me out as irreducible to my given milieu, my activities, and the things with which I normally deal. If there were no possibility of encountering the "I," no potentially responsible self, the intelligibility of the world would collapse; thus, argues Crowell, the first-person perspective is required for intentionality (the meaningful "aboutness" of our acts and thoughts). Taking some speculative steps beyond *Being and Time*, but drawing on the 1929 essay "On the Essence of Ground," Crowell then interprets conscience as calling for articulate justifications of one's choices. This reading shows how there can be a place for reason in Heidegger's ontology of Dasein. Heidegger is consistently antirationalist: he rejects the definition of man as the rational animal, and insists on a distinction between philosophical thought and reasoning. But to be antirationalist is not to be antirational: Heidegger acknowledges that we have reason, and never objects to its use within proper limits.[6] Crowell's reflections bring out the possible connections between Heidegger and Kant, who, after all, also tried to establish the limits of reason. Heideggerian conscience may provide an ontological basis for a broadly Kantian ethics, in which one takes responsibility by seeking to articulate the grounds for one's actions.

In his *Being-in-the-World* (1991), Hubert L. Dreyfus interprets skillful everyday coping, which Heidegger describes in Division I, as the basis of all intelligibility. Dreyfus's influential reading has done much to bring Heidegger into Anglo-American philosophy by building bridges to Wittgenstein, pragmatism, and debates on artificial intelligence.[7] The original edition of Dreyfus's commentary focused almost exclusively on Division I, but a new edition that is in preparation integrates Heidegger's explorations of authenticity in Division II. Like Crowell, Dreyfus now acknowledges that we cannot fully account for intelligibility on the basis of inauthentic everydayness; he reads Division II as passing beyond skillful coping to a level of action that can "disclose new worlds." His chapter in this volume—"Can There Be a Better Source of Meaning Than Everyday Practices? Reinterpreting Division I of *Being and Time* in the Light of Division II"—explains his general orientation. Using his phenomenology of skill acquisition, Dreyfus shows that risk and anxiety are necessary if we are ever to pass beyond the mere application of standards and take responsibility for developing our own abilities. Those outstanding individuals who have become masters of a cultural practice are the very people who are not easily satisfied but remain acutely aware of the inadequacy of all facile rules. Dreyfus suggests, then, that the encounters with guilt and death that stand at the center of Division II can be interpreted in terms of the synergy between dissatisfaction and ability. Our guilt, in Dreyfus's reading, is our indebtedness to norms that we cannot fully articulate and justify. Recognizing guilt undermines our complacency and brings us closer to achieving what Aristotle calls *phronesis*, or practical wisdom. Death goes still deeper: for Dreyfus, it is the lack of grounds not only for our shared norms, but for our very identity and that of our culture. Confronting death thus makes it possible to be born again, as in the Christian idea that one's life and world can be transformed in the glance of an eye. World transformers can change *das Man* itself—although in order to do so, they must draw on the resources of established common sense. Dreyfus leaves us with a goal that contrasts dramatically with Crowell's broadly Kantian ideal: rather than articulating the grounds for what we do, we can aspire to transform what we do out of a sense of its ultimate groundlessness. Such transformation cannot be based on an ultimate rule or standard but grows out of a long confrontation with the contingent intricacies of the world.

Daniel O. Dahlstrom's "Genuine Timeliness," from his *Heidegger's Concept of Truth*, lays out the main features of Heidegger's crucial interpretation of Dasein in terms of temporality. For Heidegger, the meaning of the Being of Dasein (or "the sense of the being of being-here," as Dahlstrom prefers) is to be found in temporality (or "timeliness"). But what is the sense of "sense"? Dahlstrom compares sense to the background of a picture or the accompaniment to a melody: the background and accompaniment do not normally seize our attention, but they provide the context that allows the picture or melody to stand out fully and effectively. Similarly, Dasein's timeliness is the normally unnoticed context against which our thoughts and actions stand out. But timeliness does more than that, as Dahlstrom points out: it makes all particular thoughts and actions possible in the first place, by virtue of the primordial "standing out" or "reaching out" that Heidegger calls ecstasis. Our Being reaches out ecstatically into the future, the past, and the present in an integrated way, so that time is not simply a linear sequence of "nows": at every present moment, we are appropriating who we have been for the sake of who we are to be. Our timeliness is limited by death—but this does not simply mean that we will run out of time someday. It means that it is always possibly impossible for us to be here; everything we do is done in the shadow of this fragility. Along with this fragile timeliness comes truth, the *disclosing* of timeliness as the meaning of "being-here." In this way, Heidegger's analysis of time undermines what Dahlstrom calls "the logical prejudice," that is, the assumption that truth is to be understood solely as a property of correct assertions or propositions corresponding to something *present* in some sense. If truth is understood in this way, then logic, as a study of inferential relations among propositions, necessarily takes the lead in philosophical analysis (as many philosophers would insist). But if propositional truth depends on a deeper disclosure and unconcealment that take place along with ecstatic timeliness, then logic must play a subordinate role in the analysis of truth.

In "Historical Meaning in the Fundamental Ontology of *Being and Time*," an excerpt from *Martin Heidegger and the Problem of Historical Meaning*, Jeffrey Andrew Barash investigates the thoughts on historicity (*Geschichtlichkeit*) with which the completed portion of *Being and Time* culminates.

Heidegger clearly intends to put forward a radically historical conception of Dasein (his later thought goes farther and concentrates on the "history of Being" itself). Yet this emphasis on history might seem to conflict with his attempt to establish universally applicable truths about the Being of Dasein. It might also be surprising to find historicity stressed by the same philosopher who, earlier in *Being and Time*, seemed to display unease with the power of cultural norms and of the anonymous "they." Heidegger rejects the long-standing historicist tradition in German thought, which looks to the evolving continuity of one's own culture as a sufficient source of meaning. His own position develops in dialogue with earlier "critical theorists of history" such as Wilhelm Dilthey, Wilhelm Windelband, and Heidegger's teacher Heinrich Rickert, who all tried in various ways to find stable forms or values within history. Like other members of the World War I generation, Heidegger is deeply suspicious of cultural stability and seeks truth in the individual who can sense the groundlessness of the tradition. This authentic realization does not, however, put the individual outside history. Instead, it is the source of an authentic historicity that faces finitude courageously. History, then, is more than the events and values studied by historians; it is our very way of existing—whether we do so authentically, or whether we evade finitude and allow ourselves to be absorbed in the entities that surround us. An insight into the historicity of existence can undermine the tacit sense of Being as enduring presence that is taken for granted, according to Heidegger, even by supposedly historicist thinkers.

Theodore Kisiel's "The Demise of *Being and Time*: 1927–1930" provides an invaluable overview of Heidegger's plans for the pivotal Part 1, Division III, and traces the process of frustration and disillusionment that would lead Heidegger to recast his thought in striking new terms. In his landmark study *The Genesis of Heidegger's "Being and Time"*[8] Kisiel has traced the composition of Heidegger's masterwork; the present chapter on its de-composition is a counterpart to Kisiel's *Genesis* and a compendium of his book in progress on this theme. Division III, "Time and Being," was to turn from the "temporality" *(Zeitlichkeit)* of Dasein to "Temporality" *(Temporalität)*— time as the horizon of Being. It would seem that in this delicate maneuver, Heidegger would have to avoid theoretically objectifying time and Being, as if we could observe them at a distance—for time and Being are intimately involved in our existence, making possible not only our theories but our relation to any thing or topic whatsoever. Yet in the lecture course *The Basic Problems of Phenomenology* (delivered in the summer semester 1927, immediately after the publication of *Being and Time*) Heidegger proposes a philosophical "objectification" of Being and tries to develop a theory of Temporality as a system of "horizonal schemata" that would explain the basic modes of Being. This may have been

Heidegger's second attempt to work out Division III, for as Kisiel tantalizingly reports, an unpublished 200-page document probably dating from 1926–1927 contains extensive notes in preparation for this crucial project. But Heidegger clearly came to see his attempts at Division III as dead ends. In *The Metaphysical Foundations of Logic* (summer semester 1928), he no longer thinks of philosophy as an objectifying science and speaks of "metontology" as a new way of thinking that would recognize the ineluctable situatedness of the thinker within beings as a whole. His next lecture course, *Introduction to Philosophy* (winter semester 1928–1929), opposes philosophy both to science and to worldviews, presenting philosophy as a provocation that inspires one to come to grips with one's own concrete existence. The entire language of "horizon" has now nearly faded away. Instead of beginning with Dasein's own Being and delimiting the general meaning of Being on that basis, Heidegger will decide by 1936 that we must begin with the "appropriating event" of Being itself and understand Dasein as a possibility that is required if that event is to take place.

The most influential interpreter of *Being and Time* has been, appropriately enough, Heidegger himself. As Kisiel shows, having nearly (but not quite) succeeded in formulating his philosophical position in *Being and Time*, Heidegger almost immediately began to critique and reinterpret this position. His self-interpretation is extremely valuable, but as Dieter Thomä argues in "*Being and Time* in Retrospect: Heidegger's Self-Critique," we must not assume that Heidegger should have the last word on his own work. Does the older Heidegger rightly state the goal of *Being and Time*? Does he explain in what respects the book failed to reach its goal, and how it should have proceeded? These questions are complicated by Heidegger's defense of *Being and Time* against external attacks. As his thought evolves and he tries to protect *Being and Time* against misunderstandings, Heidegger asserts that certain aspects of the book were "thought otherwise" than they were actually presented. What worries Heidegger in particular is a residual subjectivism that seems to linger in his masterwork. From the perspective of his later thought, Dasein must be understood as dependent on Being, not as an autonomous subject, but it may well seem that *Being and Time* offers us a way to rehabilitate and clarify the phenomenon of subjectivity rather than an escape from subjectivity altogether (compare Steven Crowell's article in this volume). In a dramatic move, the later Heidegger attempts to distance his thought not only from subjectivity but from humanity itself, presenting Dasein not as the essence of man but as a possibility for man. Yet he continues to insist that he is being true to the project he published in 1927. In order to test this claim, Thomä considers a striking line in *Being and Time* that speaks of the moment of vision as "a rapture which is *held* in resoluteness" (SZ 338). Here "rapture" suggests a centrifugal process that draws Dasein into the meaning of a situation, whereas "resoluteness" suggests a centripetal process of gathering meaning toward a quasi-subject; Heidegger's line implies a dynamic tension. However, Thomä shows that according to Heidegger's later explanations, both "rapture" and "resoluteness" mean "insistence" *(Inständigkeit);* the tension, then, has disappeared. Thomä concludes that Heidegger's self-interpretation does not do justice to his original intentions.

In closing, some comments on translation. Four of the chapters in this volume have been translated from the original languages. (I thank Julia Davis for her help in translating the chapter by Günter Figal, Daniel Dwyer for translating the chapter by Dieter Thomä, and Jean Grondin and Theodore Kisiel for help with their own work.) All the other authors have also, of course, had to make their own decisions about how to translate key concepts of *Being and Time* into English. Two complete translations of the book are available as models for such an effort. The 1962 version by John Macquarrie and Edward Robinson is meticulous and often felicitous, but there are cases where its terminology is awkward or inappropriate. Joan Stambaugh's version, published in 1996, is widely acknowledged to be more graceful, but it too has come in for its share of criticism.[9] In this volume, Nicholson's chapter and the translation of Figal's chapter use Stambaugh's terminology; others use Macquarrie and Robinson; still others have rendered Heidegger in their own terms. Some prefer "Being," others "being" (see Nicholson, p. 50). Heidegger's *Dasein* has been left untranslated (as "Dasein" or "*Dasein*"), hyphenated as "Da-sein," or Anglicized as "being-here" (Dahlstrom). The multiplicity of translations does not point to the inadequacy of any interpreter—in fact, it should remind us that genuine interpreting must remain open to different facets of the phenomena and competing conceptions of them. As for the challenging task of tracking this welter of expressions, it will be made easier by our index, where all the essential terms that are translated in more than one way are listed and cross-referenced in all their German and English versions.

Notes

1. "Author's Preface to the Seventh German Edition" (1953), in *Being and Time,* trans. John Macquarrie and Edward Robinson (New York: Harper & Row, 1962), 17; *Being and Time,* trans. Joan Stambaugh (Albany: State University of New York Press, 1996), xvii. My further references to *Being and Time* will cite it as "SZ" and use the pagination of *Sein und Zeit* (Tübingen: Max Niemeyer, 1953). This pagination is identical in the later Niemeyer editions; it is provided in both English translations and in *Sein und Zeit, Gesamtausgabe,* vol. 2 (Frankfurt am Main: Vittorio Klostermann, 1977).

2. For example, see Heidegger, *Zollikon Seminars: Protocols—Conversations—Letters,* ed. Medard Boss, trans. Franz Mayr and Richard Askay (Evanston, Ill.: Northwestern University Press, 2001), 225–26.

3. For an exploration of this theme in Heidegger in relation to ancient philosophy, see Thomas Sheehan, "*Das Gewesen*," in *From Phenomenology to Thought, Errancy, and Desire: Essays in Honor of William J. Richardson, S.J.*, ed. Babette Babich (Dordrecht: Kluwer, 1995).

4. For interpretations that stress Heidegger's subordination of theory to "practice" or "skillful coping," see Mark Okrent, *Heidegger's Pragmatism: Understanding, Being, and the Critique of Metaphysics* (Ithaca: Cornell University Press, 1988) and Hubert L. Dreyfus, *Being-in-the-World: A Commentary on Heidegger's "Being and Time," Division I* (Cambridge: MIT Press, 1991).

5. See especially Heidegger, *Plato's "Sophist,"* trans. Richard Rojcewicz and André Schuwer (Bloomington: Indiana University Press, 1997), introductory part, on Aristotle's account of the "intellectual virtues," or the fundamental ways of unconcealing.

6. On reason, one should also consult Heidegger, *The Metaphysical Foundations of Logic*, trans. Michael Heim (Bloomington: Indiana University Press, 1984) (the lecture course on which "The Essence of Reasons" was based), as well as the 1955–1956 lecture series *The Principle of Reason*, trans. Reginald Lilly (Bloomington: Indiana University Press, 1991).

7. For collections of essays influenced by Dreyfus, see *Heidegger: A Critical Reader*, ed. Hubert L. Dreyfus and Harrison Hall (Oxford: Blackwell, 1992); *Heidegger, Authenticity, and Modernity: Essays in Honor of Hubert L. Dreyfus*, vol. 1, ed. Mark Wrathall and Jeff Malpas (Cambridge: MIT Press, 2000); *Heidegger, Coping, and Cognitive Science: Essays in Honor of Hubert L. Dreyfus*, vol. 2, ed. Mark Wrathall and Jeff Malpas (Cambridge: MIT Press, 2000). For a criticism of the so-called analytic Heideggerian approach that is characteristic of a number of these essays, see Robert C. Scharff, "Rorty and Analytic Heideggerian Epistemology—and Heidegger," *Man and World* 25, no. 3–4 (Oct. 1992): 483–504.

8. Theodore Kisiel, *The Genesis of Heidegger's "Being and Time"* (Berkeley: University of California Press, 1993).

9. See Thomas Sheehan, "'Let a Hundred Translations Bloom!' A Modest Proposal about *Being and Time*," *Man and World* 30, no. 2 (April 1997): 227–38; Timothy O'Hagan and Giles Pearson, "The 'Alarming Task' of Understanding *Being and Time*," *International Studies in Philosophy* 33, no. 2 (2001): 131–37; Theodore Kisiel, "The New Translation of *Sein und Zeit*: A Grammatological Lexicographer's Commentary," in Kisiel, *Heidegger's Way of Thought*, ed. Alfred Denker and Marion Heinz (New York: Continuum, 2002).

1

Why Reawaken the Question of Being?

Jean Grondin

A Question That Is Doubly Fundamental for Heidegger

According to Heidegger, the question of Being is the absolutely fundamental question of philosophy, but also of existence itself. No one before Heidegger had truly defended this very strong thesis, but it has the advantage of linking the most primordial question of philosophy to the question that man is for himself, as soon as he finds himself confronted with the question of Being and its meaning. However, Heidegger's more complete and rather mischievous thesis is that the question of Being is one before which *both* man *and* philosophy tend to flee, for it is a destabilizing question, a question that tends to dissolve every certitude.

The oblivion of Being thus constitutes the point of departure of this anamnetic thinking (and all the great philosophies since Parmenides and Plato are philosophies of anamnesis, of recollection). The author of *Being and Time* (SZ)[1] seems to impute this oblivion to an inauthentic form of existence, but it is an oblivion that has dominated Western thought so extensively that the later Heidegger will eventually see it as the effect of a historical destiny, the destiny of metaphysics. But whether it be in the form of an explicit repetition of the question of Being in SZ, or in the form of *Andenken* ("thoughtful recollection") in his later philosophy, Heidegger's goal is always to call thought and existence back to their essential question, the question of Being.

The Readers' Irritation

The readers of SZ themselves have been disconcerted by the breadth and simplicity of this thesis. They have rather been fascinated by the power of Heidegger's reflections on time, death, anxiety, and the "they." Proceeding from these radical experiences of finitude, Heidegger's thought seemed to many of them to be largely antimetaphysical, so they did not immediately see the necessity of taking up again the question of Being posed by Aristotle. Most phenomenologists who have wished to extend Heidegger's philosophical efforts have expressly challenged the priority that he bestows anew to the theme of Being. This is particularly evident in Levinas, who asked quite early whether ontology was truly the fundamental discipline of philosophy—a critique of Heidegger that in fact took aim at the ontological ambition of the entire tradition, an ambition that was totalizing and, in Levinas' eyes, totalitarian. Levinas was followed by Derrida, whose thought of deconstruction was also, if not above all, a destruction of the question of Being. If Heidegger teaches us so very well to decode the language of metaphysics, does he not oblige us to deconstruct the question of Being itself—and the dream of a finally full presence of meaning or of the truth of Being (as *aletheia* or *Ereignis*), which Heidegger never gave up?[2] Jean-Luc Marion inherits this distancing when he speaks of Heidegger's "construction" of the question of Being. The author of *God Without Being* (1982) also tries to promote a "phenomenology without Being," founded on the idea of givenness, which he judges to be even more primordial than that of Being. This is all as if the very last Heidegger (the Heidegger of the *es gibt* and of its giving without reason) were turned against the Heidegger who had maintained the still all-too-metaphysical priority of the question of Being.

This critique of the priority of ontology in French phenomenology echoed an analogous suspicion that had long been formulated in Germany, even if its inspirations were often quite different. In some articles published in the late twenties, which are important since they were one of the first philosophical reactions to SZ, Georg Misch claimed to fear a relapse into metaphysics—that is, for Misch, a step back in comparison to Dilthey's historicism—in Heidegger's resurrection of the question of Being. Heidegger's most prominent student in Germany, Hans-Georg Gadamer, still spoke, it is true, of an "ontological turn" in hermeneutics, but he did not propose to revive the question of Being *per se*, but to emphasize the essentially linguistic nature of our experience of the world ("there is no understanding of Being without language"). So what inspired Gadamer was not the primacy of the question of Being, but the Heideggerian analysis of understanding and language. Summing up a rather widespread feeling, Klaus Held has spoken of a question whose evidence does not impose itself on the phenomenological gaze—for Being is never given as such in intuition—and which testifies only to the somewhat peculiar attraction that the thought of the Stagirite (if not Scholasticism) always exerted on Heidegger. And these were the most gentle critiques! Need we mention the more malicious and polemical ones? One thinks, of course, of Adorno, whose virulent and vitriolic pamphlets never ceased to stigmatize the jargon of the question of Being—a futile, crypto-mystical question that would betray, in his eyes, a flight from social reality, and that had not sufficiently meditated on Hegel's teaching that Being is equivalent to the uttermost void and the absence of thought. For his part, Ernst Tugendhat, an ex-student of Heidegger known for his rejection of the Heideggerian concept of truth, appealed to analytic philosophy in declaring that the question of Being had no object and remained without any real philosophical pertinence.[3]

A singular paradox: for all that the question of Being seemed primordial to Heidegger, it has seemed superfluous to the majority of his heirs—after a first, rather "philontological" wave that is somewhat forgotten today (Sartre,[4] Jaspers, Marcel, etc.). Is the question of Being essential to phenomenology and philosophy, or is it not? Is it, still more fundamentally, the most urgent question of human existence?

The Vigilance of a Question Is More Important Than the Answer

These criticisms did nothing but confirm in Heidegger's eyes that the oblivion of Being was endemic, even among his closest students. Exasperated, he asked in a letter to Hermann Mörchen: Dear friend, "can you name for me a single study that has truly taken up my question of the meaning of Being *as a question*, that has considered it critically, either in order to affirm it or in order to reject it?"[5]

For this, first of all, is the question of Being for Heidegger—the irresistible urgency of a question. *Nur dies*, "this only," one would like to add, borrowing a phrase from *Aus der Erfahrung des Denkens* (1947)[6] which faintly echoes the last sighs of Plotinus's *Enneads*: *monon pros monon* (alone toward the One). Heidegger encountered this question at the very start of his path, in the textbooks of his professor of dogmatic theology, Carl Braig, but also in Duns Scotus. He never ceased turning the question over, in every sense, in his life's work—which gravitates around a single unfinished book but which, with time, has taken on titanic proportions: 102 volumes are planned in the *Collected Edition* (GA), which Heidegger says in a draft of a preface presents only "ways, not works," whose sole aim is "to incite [readers] to pose this question in an ever more questioning way."[7]

As if it were more imperative to deepen the question itself, Heidegger always deferred the response to it. This "différance" first became dramatically apparent when the third part of SZ failed to appear—"Time and Being," where Heidegger had promised that the question of the meaning of Being would be "concretely answered" (SZ 19).

We have recently learned that Heidegger decided that the last writings to appear in the collected edition would be the "black notebooks" (*schwarze Hefte*) to which he consigned his most personal, and no doubt most revealing, reflections. We may have to wait a few decades for the completion of this edition before we can know the source of the unease that tormented Heidegger as he stirred up the question of Being. One can suspect, with Gadamer, that the unease was in large part religious.[8] The title of the hundredth projected volume of the GA already gives us a little glimpse of its contents: *Vigiliae*. This Latin title also reveals that, for Heidegger at his most secret, the space of thinking was perhaps not exclusively occupied by the Greeks and the Germans.

Striking evidence for this point can be found in a short autobiographical text from 1937–1938 titled "My Path Up to Now," which slipped into GA 66.

> And who would want to deny that this entire path up to now was accompanied silently [*verschwiegen*] by a confrontation with Christianity—a confrontation that was not and is not a "problem" taken up at random, but the preservation of the ownmost origin—of the family house, of the homeland and of my youth— and *at the same time* a painful detachment from it. Only someone who was so deeply rooted in an actually lived Catholic world can suspect something of the necessities that affected the path of my questioning up to now like subterranean seismic tremors.[9]

Heidegger himself spoke very little in public about these subterranean tremors, which he preferred to keep quiet (*verschweigen*), and it would be presumptuous indeed to wish to speak on his behalf. But one can at least try to understand in what way these origins could have led him to revive the question of Being.

The Formal Justification of the Question of Being in SZ

Why must the question of Being be revived at any cost? Although Heidegger seems to presuppose everywhere that it is the guiding question of philosophy as well as of our existence and our destiny, only occasionally does he try explicitly to justify this priority. Yet he does so in detailed fashion in his magisterial introduction to SZ, titled precisely "The Necessity, Structure, and Priority of the Question of Being." This text would deserve a rigorous commentary. We will only recall its lessons and its main "arguments" before returning to the question that concerns us—why repeat the question of Being?—which is not, perhaps, completely resolved by this text, which remains somewhat protreptic and general.

If Heidegger speaks of a necessity, structure, and priority of the question of Being, it is because these were hardly self-evident at the time. The period was still dominated by neo-Kantianism, although its authority had begun to ebb away in the 1920s—years marked philosophically by a powerful reception of Kierkegaard's thought, manifest in the work of Jaspers but also, and above all, in the dialectical theology of Barth and Bultmann. In what already amounted to a seismic tremor, the priority of the fundamental unrest of existence had already supplanted the epistemological and logical horizon that still predominated in the heart of neo-Kantianism—but also, Heidegger will discreetly maintain, in the heart of Husserlian phenomenology itself (whose most important textual manifestations were the *Logical Investigations* and the *Ideas Pertaining to a Pure Phenomenology and to a Phenomenological Philosophy*). Heidegger knew this "existentialist" wave well, and he allies himself to it in his own way in the introduction to SZ; but as if he had misgivings about it and its superficial nature (as Kisiel rightly insists), he takes more inspiration from Scholasticism and the predominant transcendental philosophy in his attempt to justify the *necessity* of expressly taking up the question of Being.

We must revive the question of Being, writes Heidegger, because its disappearance seems to be supported by three prejudices inherited from Scholasticism that deserve to be considered more deeply: 1) Being is the most universal concept, 2) it is indefinable, and 3) it is so obvious that everyone understands it spontaneously. Here Heidegger follows the classical logic of definition (*definitio fit per genus proximum et differentiam specificam*)—it is hard to say if he is doing so ironically or as seriously as can be, for it is a logic that he will end up deconstructing—and appeals to authors who were hardly part of the curriculum in the day of neo-Kantianism or Kierkegaardian existentialism: Aristotle, Thomas Aquinas, Hegel, but also Pascal. However, Heidegger does not truly refute these prejudices (in fact, he shares them); he is content to list them in order to "recall" the reasons why the question of Being may seem superfluous. Wherein lies the "necessity for explicitly restating the question of Being" (the title of §1)? It actually derives from the third prejudice, which takes Being to be a self-evident notion. This self-evidence may be only apparent, Heidegger suggests, for what we understand by this notion is far from being evident. It seems that it is precisely on this not-so-evident evidence that Heidegger founds the "necessity" of taking up the question of Being again: "The very fact that we already live in an understanding of Being and that the meaning of Being is still veiled in darkness *proves that it is necessary in principle to raise this question again.*[10] A strong but somewhat hasty conclusion, for what Heidegger says about Being here holds for many of our concepts, if not all. In fact, we all live within a certain understanding of friendship, of meaning, of happiness, and so forth, whose sense is also somewhat veiled in darkness, but this does not demonstrate the urgency of an explicit philosophical investigation of these notions. Why distinguish the theme of Being here amidst so many others? The question thus remains intact: why should we renew the question of *Being* at all costs?

What militates in favor of this necessity, as Heidegger will concede a few pages later, is above all the question's "venerable origin" and "the lack of a definite answer" to it (SZ 8–9). But this does no more than suggest the necessity of taking up the question of Being, inasmuch as the venerability of a tradition can itself be subjected to a destruction. One cannot, therefore, speak of anything more than a weak necessity, although Heidegger's considerations on the structure and priority of the question of Being will reinforce it.

In presenting the "formal structure" (§2) of the question of Being, Heidegger claims to rely on the structure that is common to all questions and that includes three constitutive moments. Here he takes up some trains of thought that he had presented in his teaching. In a course in 1923–1924 he had even distinguished no less than a dozen structural moments of every question! More significant is the fact that he had already expounded this structure without explicit reference to the question of Being.[11] In fact, the theme of questioning is quite longstanding in Heidegger's work. He dedicated one of his first lectures—to my knowledge, his very first lecture—to this theme: "Question and Judgment." Delivered in one of Rickert's seminars on July 10, 1915, this lecture was published only recently. It bears witness to the fact that reflection on the logical structure of questioning was one of the points of departure for Heidegger's entire inquiry. Very early on, the philosopher asked himself whether classical propositional logic was capable of grasping what the uncertainty of a question had in view. This meaning can be fully comprehended only on the basis of the very act of questioning, that is, only if one is seized by the question oneself.[12] This will also be true of the question of Being, as we will see: it cannot be comprehended unless one passes through the Being of Dasein, which will be introduced formally in SZ as the entity characterized, among other things, by its capacity to pose questions (SZ 7).

In every question, claims SZ, one can distinguish three moments:

(a) "that which is asked about," a *Gefragtes*; in this case—we intimate it, but without knowing anymore what we are putting into *question*—the *Gefragtes* is Being.

(b) "that which is interrogated," a *Befragtes*, that is, that to which our question is addressed; we will soon learn that this is Dasein and its understanding of Being;

(c) finally, there is "that which is to be found out by the asking," an *Erfragtes*: what is being asked, what one wishes to know when one poses the question, the meaning or point of the question—in short, the question behind the question.

What is one trying to know when one poses the question of Being? Heidegger answers: the meaning of Being. A mysterious formula, but it will receive a rather prosaic sense in §2: the point is not, we are assured, to bring to light the meaning of existence, but solely to elucidate what is comprised in the notion of Being by bringing it to conceptual clarity (SZ 6). Although Being is the object of a vague and immediate understanding, as §1 proposed, we do not yet have any clear concept of it (SZ 8). One could get the impression that Heidegger is presenting himself here as an analytic philosopher who is quite simply trying to clarify what one ordinarily understands by the concept of Being.

If this is the point of the question of Being, one would like to know the point of it all! Even after we have elucidated the formal structure of the question of Being, the meaning of our question—why should we revive the question of Being?—remains. Is it simply a matter of clarifying the meaning of the word "Being"? If so, what is the point? Following Heidegger's terminology: what then is the *Erfragtes* of the *Erfragtes*, the meaning of the question of the meaning of Being? One thing is certain: §2, devoted to the formal structure of the question of Being, does not really respond to this question.

Nevertheless, it has done so indirectly by making it clear—at the end of §2, and in the spirit of the 1915 lecture—that in this question, the Being of the questioner is itself affected by the question.[13] Very well, but how? One divines that the question is pressing for Dasein itself—if it is true, as we soon learn, that Dasein is the being (one would have to say "entity" to reproduce the German, but here the ambiguous English expression "being," like the French *être*, is better) for whom its own Being is an issue in this Being itself. Heidegger speaks here of the ontical priority of the question of Being, but he will not make this his theme until §4. As if further to defer any attack on this priority, which is the most primordial of all, Heidegger first treats the "ontological" priority of the question of Being (§3).

What Heidegger calls the ontological priority amounts to a *scientific* priority of the theme of Being. Heidegger's analysis takes an almost transcendental turn here, which at the time benefited from a blinding self-evidence, but to which Heidegger gives a more ontological inflection. Neo-Kantianism itself took the fact of science as its starting point and attempted to reconstruct its logical and subjective conditions of possibility. One will see that a similar line of argument leads Heidegger to emphasize the so-called ontological priority of the question of Being.

Every science, he explains, is interested in a certain region of entities. Here it makes use of fundamental concepts, which most often are drawn from pre-scientific experience, but which are not themselves any sort of entity or ontical thing. Rather, says Heidegger, they are concerned with the Being of this or that area of entities. The founding concepts of mathematics, of physics, or of the human sciences necessarily call for ontological reflection: "But since every such area is itself obtained from the domain of entities themselves, this preliminary research, from which the basic concepts are drawn, signifies nothing else than an interpretation of those entities with regard to their basic state of Being" (SZ 10).

However, it is not incumbent on the sciences themselves to proceed with this ontological clarification, but on philosophy, understood as the "productive logic" of the sciences. SZ thus attributes an ambitious ontological and scientific priority to philosophy. It is philosophy's task to elaborate the specific ontologies on which the sciences of entities are based. Husserl spoke here of regional ontologies.

But what interests Heidegger in §3, before these regional ontologies themselves, is *the priority of the question of Being.* For every ontological explication, such as the explication that philosophy is supposed to carry out for the positive sciences, ought to have first elucidated the meaning of Being. This clarification of the meaning of Being is consequently the first task of an ontology that wishes to be fundamental.

Ontological inquiry is indeed more primordial, as over against the ontical inquiry of the positive sciences. But it remains itself naive and opaque if in its researches into the Being of entities it fails to discuss the meaning of Being in general. And the ontological task of a genealogy of the different possible ways of Being (which is not to be constructed deductively) is precisely of such a sort as to require that we first come to an understanding of "what we really mean by this expression 'Being.'"

The question of Being aims therefore at ascertaining the a priori conditions not only for the possibility of the sciences which examine entities as entities of such and such a type, and, in so doing, already operate with an understanding of Being, but also for the possibility of those ontologies themselves which are prior to the ontical sciences and which provide their foundations. *Basically, all ontology, no matter how rich and firmly compacted a system of categories it has at its disposal, remains blind and perverted from its ownmost aim, if it has not first adequately clarified the meaning of Being, and conceived this clarification as its fundamental task.* [SZ 11]

Even if Heidegger claims to distrust a genealogical derivation, he is obviously defending the *ontological priority* of the question of Being by way of a reduction to ever more elementary levels of reflection. Prior to the ontical sciences there are ontologies that support them, but before these ontologies and founding them, a fundamental ontology should have cleared up the meaning of Being.

Ontical sciences	their task: the exploration of a domain of entities
Ontologies	their task: the elucidation of the fundamental concepts that circumscribe the mode of Being of these entities
Fundamental ontology	its task: the clarification of the meaning of Being as the "a priori condition of these ontologies"

The ontological priority of the question of Being in §3 points to this last level of reflection, which stands out as the most fundamental level in the philosophical order of reasons. Heidegger takes pains anew to specify what we should attempt on this level—namely, a clarification, once and for all, of "what we really mean by this expression 'Being.'"[14] If Heidegger reminds us of an analytic philosopher when he resorts to such formulas to defend the necessity of an inquiry into the meaning of Being, he presents himself somewhat like a transcendental thinker in §3 when he seeks to base the priority of the question of Being on the fact that it allows us to delimit the conditions of possibility of every inspection of an object and every scientific enterprise.

However, the reflections Heidegger devotes to the ontical priority of the question of Being in §4 demonstrate that the first fact for him may not be, as it is for the neo-Kantians, the fact of science, but rather the fact of a being that is overwhelmed by the care of its Being. "Ontical priority" means that the question (of the meaning) of Being is not only prior in the hierarchy of types of knowledge, but is also prior for a very distinctive *entity* called Dasein which is ontically distinguished "by the fact that in its very Being, that Being is an *issue* for it," according to the celebrated formula that Heidegger had already often used in his lecture courses.[15] This formula, of course, has in view the care that every individual is for himself, the care that will eventually sum up the entire Being of Dasein in §41. It is a disquiet that not only properly characterizes Dasein, but also pursues it in the most intimate recesses of its Being—as is confirmed by the fact that one of Dasein's greatest burdens will be to relieve itself of this burden, and thus to evade the all-too-vertiginous question that it is for itself. Hence Dasein's flight in the face of the question of its own Being. Dasein is thus most often there in the mode of being absent from itself. Heidegger sometimes speaks in this sense of a *Wegsein*, a Being-elsewhere, Being-far-from-itself—in short, a Dasein that is running away or that is not completely "there."

Dasein's oblivion of itself unmistakably derives from a flight in the face of its temporality or its mortality. This is a flight into inauthenticity, Heidegger believes, for it closes its eyes to the condition of every Dasein, the condition that provides the starting point for determining all of Dasein's projects. Authentic Dasein—a Dasein that is authentically there, instead of being elsewhere— would be an *entschlossenes Dasein* (a resolute or decided Dasein, we say, but the term *ent-schlossen* in its Heideggerian sense means above all "un-locked"). Such Dasein would be resolutely open to its own Being. This, according to Heidegger, is the privileged form of self-consciousness.

What Is the Connection between the Two Types of Priority?

In §4, this ontical priority of the question of the Being of Dasein is movingly and dramatically depicted, but one could ask what it has to do, after all, with the *Seinsfrage* which was in question in the opening sections. Until now, one may very well have had the feeling that it was simply a matter of conceptually clarifying what we understand by the term "Being" (§2) or of clarifying the ontological conditions of scientific procedure (§3). So let us ask directly: can we fully identify the question of the meaning of Being in general with the question of the burden that Dasein is for itself? Are they truly the same question? Isn't Heidegger confusing Aristotle and Kierkegaard?

Here it is appropriate to distinguish the perspective of SZ from that of Heidegger's later thought. The later Heidegger will be somewhat inclined to attenuate the question of Dasein's care for its Being, preferring to accentuate the event of Being itself, within whose opening *Da-sein* holds itself. The "Letter on 'Humanism'" will say in 1946 that the "there" of Dasein in SZ seeks only to indicate this clearing of Being.[16] The notion of care has now been reinterpreted somewhat to mean care for Being.

However, SZ could not be more explicit on this point: the ontical priority does not appear until §4 (thus rather late, and after the ontological priority), but this priority is clearly the priority of the care that Dasein's *own* Being constitutes for every Dasein. For each Dasein, its Being is itself an issue—Dasein's *own* Being-possible (*Seinkönnen*), which is awaiting disclosure (*Ent-schlossenheit* in the Heideggerian sense). So we must ask regarding SZ: what connection is Heidegger trying to establish between the question of the care of Dasein and the question of the meaning of Being?

Heidegger never states it in such clear-cut terms, but the nature of the connection that he is trying to establish leaves little room for doubt. Even if it is not discussed until §4, Heidegger clearly begins with Dasein as a being that is pursued by the care for its own Being—as confirmed by his early lectures on the hermeneutics of facticity. Death so deeply gnaws on Dasein in its Being that the *sum moribundus* (I am to die) incarnates its most intimate certainty, well before the *cogito*, according to a lecture course of 1925.[17] I am "here," but—curses!—only for a time. This too is meant by the title *Being and Time*.

But what is the link between this care, or this anxiety, and the more general question of Being as it has been posed in the venerable Aristotelian tradition? The connection consists in that, according to Heidegger, *every* understanding of Being will prove to be determined by this care for Dasein's temporal Being. Heidegger finds the most eloquent indication of this in the tendency to conceive of true Being in an "atemporal" way, as permanent presence. Heidegger develops penetrating historical analyses to show to what extent this reading of Being as *permanence in presence* has sustained the entire history of ontology, from Parmenides' eternally present Being, passing through the ever-identical Idea of Plato, the substance of Aristotle, the *ipsum esse subsistens* of the medieval God, up to the *cogito* that is set up as an unshakable foundation by the moderns.

On what is this singular privilege of permanence in the understanding of Being ultimately based, insinuates Heidegger, if not on a denial of the temporality of Dasein? To reawaken the question of Being is to bring to light this forgotten, repressed relation between Being and atemporality, and to ask whether the connection between true Being and time cannot be thought still more originally.[18]

What Is the Fundamental Experience for Heidegger?

We have spoken of a formal justification in order to characterize the way in which Heidegger "argues," in the introduction to SZ, in favor of the priority of the question of Being. It is a formal and a bit ceremonious justification that does not say everything, for the fundamental question can still be asked: why is it vital to resuscitate the question of Being? In order to bring to light the meaning of a polysemic word? In order to establish a fundamental ontology which could found regional ontologies, which in turn would found the positive sciences? Or in order to rethink the Being of man on the basis of the limit-experiences of death, of anxiety, and of the resulting call of conscience?

A little of all of that, no doubt—but what is Heidegger's truly first motivation? The text of *Besinnung* spoke of a silent confrontation with Christianity that accompanied the thinker's entire trajectory. Considerations of space prevent us from reopening the complex dossier that is the question of the religious in Heidegger. It has already been the subject of an abundant secondary literature, even before the publication of GA 60, which collects some lecture courses on the phenomenology of religious experience—indispensable, no doubt, but still rather elliptical.[19] We will simply try to sketch out the broadest features of the connection that there may be between this experience and our sole subject here, the justification of the question of Being.

Very early on, Heidegger was struck by an experience of Being as emergence (*physis*), presence (*Anwesenheit*), manifestation (*aletheia*), pure advent or event (*Ereignis*). But according to Heidegger, this experience is one that offers itself distinctively to man and even needs man, for without man this opening, this fulguration of Being would not take place. However, man does not control this fulguration. He is there (hence the term *Da-sein*), he belongs to it, for he himself is a sudden emergence, a rest-less unfolding in the opening of the present. This is Heidegger's fundamental experience. He recalls it in an interview with Richard Wisser in 1969: "the fundamental thought of my thinking is precisely that Being, or the manifestation of Being, *needs* human beings and that, vice versa, human beings are only human beings if they are standing in the manifestation of Being."[20]

It is also clear that what is at stake here is an understanding of Being as "time," but not as clock time. The time of Being—which the third division of SZ tried, yet still failed, to distinguish from the time of Dasein—would be attuned to Being as pure self-extending and self-unfolding, as simple advent or event. This is what the term "essence" (*Wesen*) comes to indicate in Heidegger, understood in a verbal sense and connoting a certain processual character. For *wesen* can also be a verb in German, which admittedly is very archaic in the indicative (*es west*), but whose form can still be heard quite clearly in certain compound verbs (*verwesen*, to decompose) or in the past participle of the verb "to be" (*gewesen*). Heidegger greatly loves this "archaism" (much like the archaism of spelling *Sein*, Being, in the obsolete form *Seyn*); it helps us recall that before our fixation on entities, there is and has always been a temporal "self-unfolding" of Being, an "essential happening" of Being that is neither a delimited thing nor an idea, but a surging in which we take part during the time of a sojourn imparted by Being.

Heidegger freely acknowledges that the emergence of Being is necessarily also the revelation *of something*, and thus of an entity that arises within presence and offers itself to a gaze.[21] This is how things come to pass. But the thinking he calls metaphysics is a thinking that is restricted too exclusively to the entities that present themselves in this way and that can be captured and grasped. The danger (another great Heideggerian leitmotif) is that now, entities tend to be grasped solely on the basis of this dominating gaze that is brought to bear upon them. This is what came about when Plato understood Being as *eidos*. Without realizing it, he placed entities in the perspective of a "supervision" from which the metaphysical will to explanation and control was born; the subjectivism of modernity was only the final avatar of this will.

If the fundamental experience for Heidegger is that of Being as a free unfolding, experienced as the "wonder of wonders," Heidegger also felt quite early on that a somewhat technical understanding of entities had gained strength on the trail of Platonism, which was taken up by epistemology ("Being cannot be understood except on the basis of its Idea, and thus, in principle, on the basis of the subjugating gaze that is brought to bear on it"). This technical understanding tended to erase the mystery and initial surging of Being, without abolishing it. One will object, no doubt, that Heidegger became interested in technology only later on. But this is not quite true. Ever since SZ, he asked himself whether the objectifying perspective of *Vorhandenheit*, which conceives of the thing as a *res extensa*, was the only way of envisaging the presence of Being. Still more fundamentally, his appeal to the early Christian experience of time ("the day of the Lord so cometh as a thief in the night"[22]) was already an attempt to disrupt the countable, reassuring time of clocks. In each case, the basic question remains the same: is the technical or objectifying relation to Being the only and truly fundamental relation? Does it not stem from an oblivion, or from the covering-up of a still more original experience? Heidegger has nothing against technology or against Platonism; he simply thinks that the construction of a Being that is immediately subjected to a rationalizing point of view may tend to obscure the experience of the gratuitous gift of Being, including our own, which emerges without a why.

Hence the basically quite simple Heideggerian idea of an oblivion of Being that has supposedly marked all metaphysics. The issue here is not some thesis about a theme that has unfortunately been forgotten in the textbooks of metaphysics, but a judgment about the technical conception of Being (as *Vorhandenheit, Gegenstand*, or *Bestand*) that still bewitches our age. This conception has its reasons and its successes, but it tends to reduce Being to the order of the producible, thus disguising the more ancient unavailability of Being. If this Being says nothing to us—even post-Heideggerian philosophy, as we saw, understands nothing of it—this is because one can make nothing of it. Precisely, Heidegger replies; but this experience might remind us that not everything belongs to the order of making and calculation.

The catastrophe of this technical intelligence, for Heidegger, is that it cuts off all its connections to a higher order. It is this order, this measure (*Mass*) that is finally indicated by the theme of Being and its oblivion. In a world where everything ultimately depends on man, there is no more place where the divine can be—or it cannot appear except to respond to a human need for reassurance or explanation. It is now nothing more than a manmade idol, deprived of all its divine greatness. To think Being—says Heidegger in the most personal manuscripts that have appeared so far—amounts to thinking the distress of the divinity of the gods (*die Not der Gottschaft der Götter*)[23], that is, thinking of a god that would once again be divine. According to Heidegger, the most vivid symptom of this desolation is that it isn't even experienced as such in a world where everything works, because everything is "under control." He speaks, then, of the distress of the lack of distress, or of an oblivion of oblivion.

One often repeats that our age is one of the disenchantment of the world. Heidegger speaks instead, following Hölderlin, of a *Gottesverlassenheit*, an "abandonment" of the gods, which means not only that the gods are no longer sought by us, but also that they are the ones who have abandoned us, in a sense: that is, they have abandoned us to our own technological idols, they are no longer here to keep our desire for control in check. Here Heidegger's thought is less theophanic than one might think: a common German expression says of a person who seems to have lost his mind that he has been *von allen guten Geistern verlassen*, "abandoned by all the good spirits." In French one would say that he has lost *sa bonne étoile*, his lucky star.

Nevertheless, the idea of an oblivion of Being surely springs from a distress that one could call religious, in the broadest and most indefinite sense of the word. Heidegger's intent is assuredly not to offer solutions or palliatives for this affliction. At the point where we are, "only a god can save us now," Heidegger cries with Cicero.[24] To the contrary, he hopes to fan the flames of our affliction, by crying out, in the desert of the absence of distress, that the human condition lies prey to a dereliction that technical responses, the only ones that have been accepted in this day and age, can never remedy. One feels it in this heartfelt cry:

> Question Be-ing! And in its silence, as the inception of the word, the god answers.
> You may scour all that is, but nowhere does the trace of the god appear.

The formula is so daring that one asks if one has read it correctly. The reign of entities would be the reign of the absence of the god, so that only by way of the silence of Being could a god once again address us? And this is where language would originate? Far from being an isolated statement, this formula is one that Heidegger ritually reiterates in all his manuscripts of the late thirties.[25] Its meaning is clear: in a world where the will to master entities has ended by driving out every experience of the imponderable, only another thinking (*Andenken*) of Being may be able to safeguard the hope of the divinity of the divine. This vigil, perhaps, has everything to do with the reawakening of the question of Being.

—translated by Richard Polt in consultation with the author

Notes

1. SZ refers to *Being and Time*, trans. John Macquarrie and Edward Robinson (New York: Harper & Row, 1962), which will be cited by the pagination of the later German editions, provided in the margins of the translation.

2. "And yet, are not the thought of the *meaning* or *truth* of Being, the determination of *différance* as the ontico-ontological difference, difference thought within the horizon of the question of *Being*, still intrametaphysical effects of *différance*?" Jacques Derrida, "Différance," in *Margins of Philosophy*, trans. Alan Bass (Chicago: University of Chicago Press, 1982), 22.

3. Georg Misch, *Lebensphilosophie und Phänomenologie* (Bonn: Cohen, 1930); 3rd ed. (Darmstadt: Wissenschaftlichen Buchgesellschaft, 1967); see also his lectures of the same period, published under the title *Der Aufbau der Logik auf dem Boden der Philosophie des Lebens* (Freiburg/Munich: Alber, 1994); Hans-Georg Gadamer, *Truth and Method* (1960), revised trans. by Joel Weinsheimer and Donald G. Marshall (New York: Continuum, 2000); Theodor Adorno, *Negative Dialectics* (1966), trans. E. B. Ashton (New York: Continuum, 1983); Ernst Tugendhat, "Heideggers Seinsfrage," in Tugendhat, *Philosophische Aufsätze* (Frankfurt am Main: Suhrkamp, 1992), 108–35; Klaus Held, "Heidegger und das Prinzip der Phänomenologie," in A. Gethmann-Siefert and O. Pöggeler (eds.), *Heidegger und die praktische Philosophie* (Frankfurt am Main: Suhrkamp, 1989), 111–39.

4. Of course, Sartre speaks of Being and ontology in the title of his masterwork; but in the dichotomy *Being and Nothingness*, "being" primarily means the being that is not man—that is, being in itself, which is totally uninteresting. This being mainly serves as a negative backdrop that brings "nothingness," or the freedom of our existence, into sharp profile. Sartre's existentialism, as is confirmed by his definition of it, is "a doctrine which makes human life possible and, in addition, declares that every truth and every action implies a human setting and a human subjectivity": "The Humanism of Existentialism," in *Essays in Existentialism*, ed. Wade Baskin (New York: Carol Publishing Group, 1990), 32. So one cannot speak of a real priority of the question of Being in Sartre, or of any great interest bestowed upon its historical development.

5. Letter of November 6, 1969, cited in Hermann Mörchen, *Adorno und Heidegger* (Stuttgart: Klett-Cotta, 1981), 637.

6. Heidegger, "The Thinker as Poet," in *Poetry, Language, Thought*, trans. Albert Hofstadter (New York: Harper & Row, 1971), 4.

7. GA 1, *Frühe Schriften*, 437. GA will refer to volumes of Heidegger's *Gesamtausgabe*, published in Frankfurt am Main by Vittorio Klostermann.

8. Hans-Georg Gadamer, "Being Spirit God," in *Heidegger's Ways*, trans. John Stanley (Albany: SUNY, 1994), 182. The reference to the black notebooks is found in the most recent prospectuses for the GA from Klostermann.

9. GA 66, *Besinnung*, 415.

10. SZ 4 (my emphasis).

11. GA 17, *Einführung in die phänomenologische Forschung*, 73. The application to the question of Being will come about in 1925: GA 20, *Prolegomena zur Geschichte des*

Zeitbegriffs, 194f.; the German pagination is also provided in *History of the Concept of Time: Prolegomena*, trans. Theodore Kisiel (Bloomington: Indiana University Press, 1985).

12. Heidegger, "Frage und Urteil," in Martin Heidegger and Heinrich Rickert, *Briefe 1912 bis 1933 und andere Dokumente* (Frankfurt am Main: Klostermann, 2002), 80–90. On this point see p. 88.

13. SZ 8; cf. GA 20, 200.

14. SZ 11. One will notice that in this text, the term "Being" is sometimes found without quotation marks, and sometimes with them. Ernst Tugendhat has protested that in either case the question takes on a completely different meaning in German: *Self-Consciousness and Self-Determination*, trans. Paul Stern (Cambridge, Mass.: MIT Press, 1986), 147. Asking about the meaning of a word in quotation marks simply means inquiring into its *signification* (which a dictionary or a conceptual clarification could provide), but when one asks about the meaning of something without quotation marks, one wishes to know its finality: what is the meaning of monochromatic art, of antiglobalization, and so on? It may not be by chance that Heidegger leaves out the quotation marks (as he often does). When he uses them, it seems fair to say that he is trying to get clear about the meaning of the word "Being." But without quotation marks, the question about the meaning of Being becomes more ambiguous, because it now seems to exceed the limits of a semantic clarification. But what does it mean now? Difficult to say in a footnote, but I think that Heidegger always had in view a meaning of Being that would in a certain way transcend the space of language that we hold over it—but that opens up this very space. One can intimate this in the projected third division of SZ, where he explicitly distinguishes the question of the temporality (*Zeitlichkeit*) of Dasein from the Temporality (*Temporalität*) of Being itself. Is there not, Heidegger now seems to ask himself, a Temporality proper to Being itself (as pure emergence) that precedes all the projects of Dasein? But how can we speak of this Temporality of Being itself without passing through Dasein? This is surely the source of the failure of the third division of SZ: it did not manage to speak of the "time" of Being—of Being "itself," as it were—without resorting to the notions of horizon and schema, which still sprang from an overly subjectivist way of thinking. So it was necessary to speak of Being and *its* Temporality in some other way. Heidegger ventures such a new way in his later philosophy, which pursues the strategy of listening to Being as it gives itself within the history of Being—a bewildering strategy, perhaps, but bewilderment is no disaster in philosophy, says Heidegger! However, we cannot envisage such listening except by virtue of a "leap" (*Sprung*), Heidegger insists, which finally "jumps" into the meaning of Being itself. This is the task he assigns to thinking as *Besinnung* (GA 66), which is also presented in "Science and Reflection," in *The Question Concerning Technology and Other Essays*, trans. William Lovitt (New York: Harper & Row, 1977), 180: "To venture after sense or meaning [*sich auf den Sinn einlassen*] [that is, the meaning of Being] is the essence of reflecting [*Besinnen*]." Here there is no question anymore of using quotation marks to speak of the meaning of Being.

15. SZ 12. Cf. GA 20, 405; GA 21, *Logik: Die Frage nach der Wahrheit*, 220.

16. Heidegger, "Letter on 'Humanism,'" in *Pathmarks*, ed. William McNeill (Cambridge: Cambridge University Press, 1998), 256.

17. GA 20, 437.

18. Jean Grondin, "Le sens du titre *Être et temps*," in Grondin, *L'horizon herméneutique de la pensée contemporaine* (Paris: Vrin, 1993), 17–35.

19. GA 60, *Phänomenologie des religiösen Lebens*. The German pagination is also provided in *The Phenomenology of Religious Life*, trans. Matthias Fritsch and Jennifer Anna Gosetti-Ferencei (Bloomington: Indiana University Press, 2004).

20. "Martin Heidegger in Conversation," in Günter Neske and Emil Kettering (eds.), *Martin Heidegger and National Socialism: Questions and Answers*, trans. Lisa Harries (New York: Paragon House, 1990), 82. The formula is rather striking, but it is not a great revelation, for Heidegger had often emphasized the idea of an essential solidarity between Being and man, who are dedicated to each other (*einander übereignet*). See *Identity and Difference*, trans. Joan Stambaugh (New York: Harper & Row, 1969), 39f.; "Who is Nietzsche's Zarathustra?" in *Nietzsche*, vol. 2, *The Eternal Recurrence of the Same*, trans. D. F. Krell (San Francisco: Harper & Row, 1984), 231; etc.

21. Essential happening (*wesen* in the verbal sense) now becomes the essence (or concept) that is fixed by a gaze, losing some of its character of arising. This duality is clearly marked in the title of Heidegger's essay "On the Essence and Concept of *Physis* in Aristotle's *Physics* B, 1" (in *Pathmarks*).

22. I Thess. 5:2. Cf. Mark 13:33, Matt. 24:42; GA 60, 102, 124, 150.

23. GA 66, 255f.

24. "'Only a God Can Save Us': *Der Spiegel*'s Interview with Martin Heidegger (1966)," in Richard Wolin (ed.), *The Heidegger Controversy: A Critical Reader* (Cambridge, Mass.: MIT Press, 1993). Cf. Cicero, *Ad Familiares* XVI, Epistle 12 (apropos of the civil war): *nisi qui deus ... subvenerit, salvi esse nequeamus*.

25. GA 66, 353: "Frage das Seyn! Und in dessen Stille, als dem Anfang des Wortes, antwortet der Gott. Alles Seiende mögt ihr durchstreifen, nirgends zeigt sich die Spur des Gottes." There are nearly identical formulas in GA 69, *Die Geschichte des Seyns*, 31, 105, 211, 214, 221. See also "Building Dwelling Thinking," in *Poetry, Language, Thought*, 150: "Mortals dwell in that they await the divinities as divinities. In hope they hold up to the divinities what is unhoped for. They wait for intimations of their coming and do not mistake the signs of their absence. . . . In the very depth of misfortune they wait for the weal that has been withdrawn."

2

The Temporality of Thinking: Heidegger's Method, from *Thinking in the Light of Time: Heidegger's Encounter with Hegel*

Karin de Boer

Inauthentic and Authentic Thinking

AT THE END OF GA 24[1] Heidegger argues that metaphysics has always based itself, albeit unknowingly, on the same horizon that has guided the usual ontic involvement, that is to say, Praesens. This is evidenced by the meaning of *ousia* as *Anwesenheit*, but equally by Kant's concept of being (449). With this Heidegger has arrived at (that is to say, returned to) his own starting point.

> Reference to the fact that the Greeks understood being on the basis of Present, that is, of Praesens, is a confirmation not to be overestimated of our interpretation of time as that which makes possible the understanding of being, yet it is not its foundation. At the same time, however, it bears witness to the fact that in our own interpretation of being we are attempting nothing other than to repeat the problems of ancient philosophy, so as to let them radicalize themselves in this repeating movement. (449)

It is striking that Heidegger here tones down his great inspiration of 1923, which motivated the entire interpretation, into a *confirmation* of the same interpretation. However, he does not make clear what he means by the "radicalization" of philosophy. Only near the end of the text does he indicate the essential difference between the thematization of beings that occurs in the positive sciences and the thematization of beings in ontology, although both possibilities are grounded in temporality.

> Thus, with the factic existence of Dasein two essential and fundamental ways of
> thematization (*Vergegenständlichung*) are given, both of which are ... despite their
> fundamental difference, apparently interrelated (456).... Our question aims at the
> thematization of being as such, that is, at the second essential way of thematization,
> in which philosophy is to constitute itself as science (458).

We see that Heidegger here still takes the term "thematization" in a neutral, formal sense: it is a thematization of the being of beings that may or may not be objectifying.[2] Insofar as the positive sciences explicitly thematize beings, they share a common ground with the straightforward direction of everyday apprehension (456) and hence (although Heidegger does not say this here) their understanding is as much guided by Praesens as is the everyday involvement with beings. However, the *being* of beings, which the positive sciences must always implicitly intend, can *not* be encountered from this prevailing perspective (457). How, then, can the being of beings itself be thematized? On this Heidegger remarks only that the perspective from which "being" can be thematized is *opposite* to the prevailing direction.

> [T]he projective preconception of being onto the horizon of its understandability ... is
> delivered up to uncertainty and stands continually in danger of being reversed. For
> this thematization of being must necessarily move in the direction of a projective
> preconception that runs counter to the everyday comportment to beings. (459)

If Dasein is guided by Praesens both in its involvement with beings and in the positive sciences, and if ontology unknowingly takes on this perspective, the projective preconception that enacts a countering movement should consist in drawing back from this narrow, one-sided perspective. This would allow it to do justice to the proper character of ecstatic Future and Past.[3]

Heidegger does not consider this further in GA 24—the movement stops, and only the temporal significance of the a priori for the phenomenological method is briefly mentioned again (461f). On the basis of the above, I would like to present Heidegger's line of thought as follows.

Only when Praesens has been disclosed can anything appear as meaningful within that openness. Beings can only be encountered once the being of beings has been understood, but itself remains in the background. To allow beings to be encountered, ecstatic Present opens up a realm within which being can be understood as presence. This is also the case when thinking, from within the given horizon of Praesens, turns explicitly to the being of beings. In the way philosophy understands being, Praesens becomes so predominant that being— the essential as such—can merely be understood as final cause, ultimate ground, or in any case as that which cannot be affected by accidental and concomitant changes.[4] This means that being not only shows forth, but also withdraws from the way in which it presents itself. Heidegger considers this withdrawing movement to first enact the history of thinking.

If thinking is to modify itself so as to accord with its authentic possibilities, it should attempt to turn from beings to their being in a more radical way than metaphysics ever could. This thinking will have to modify the horizon of Praesens in such a way that the primordial threefoldness of Future, Past, and Present is given its due. This occurs at the *existentiell* level in Dasein's authentic modification of its primordial openness, in which Dasein outstretches itself toward its thrownness (opened up by Past) and proper possibilities (opened up by Future). This means at the level of ontology that Past and Future open up a realm within which the absential as such is allowed to occur. In the light of this threefold Temporality, being itself will no longer appear as constant presence but as a presence which is pervaded to the core by absence—just as Dasein may permit the imminent possibility of death in its life.

To put it more concretely, Heidegger will no longer answer the question of "what something is" in terms of a prior ground or essence that also constitutes the ideal of all actual realizations. Heidegger tries to allow the "what" or the essential to show forth as the whole of the counter-striving ways in which a certain formal structure or possibility usually enacts itself and possibly might enact itself. Thus, for instance, the movement of human life can be understood against the background of a prior *archē* and a future *telos* that withdraw from life as it enacts itself, but, as absent, still play a part in it. The *telos* will then no longer appear as a possibility that is given at the outset and increasingly realizes itself. The very idea of a possible complete realization of the essential rests in a predominance of Present, which Heidegger sees as the ground for every fallenness.

The fact that thinking is finite and situated thus ultimately means not so much (or not only) that it is actually part of a concrete history, but primarily that it is guided by a temporal horizon that it has not itself brought about. Only on the ground of "forgetting" this horizon can something like the history of Western philosophy occur. Insofar as Temporality has in itself the tendency to increasingly confine itself to Present, philosophy has no power over the course of its own history. On the other hand, Heidegger will always emphasize that thinking has the possibility of freeing itself from the confined temporal perspective of the tradition. This does not, however, deny the finitude of that thinking. Freedom, whether it concerns the thematization of beings or of being, is always a thrown freedom.[5]

Now that we have clarified how the threefold ecstatic-horizonal time constitutes the final condition of possibility of the understanding of being, the answer to the question concerning the meaning of being has in fact also been given. After all, meaning means nothing other than the toward-which or upon-which

(*Woraufhin*) of the projective preconception (BT 151)—that is, the horizon from within which something is understandable. The unity of the horizonal schemes of time constitutes the meaning of being. This meaning turns out to consist not only of Praesens: if ecstatic Future and Past can extend themselves in such a way that they open up the absential that essentially belongs to being, they shed a different light on being.

Heidegger's remark that the idea of being is not simple or unifold (*einfach*) (196) refers to the primordial temporal horizon within which the being of beings can be understood and explicated in a variable manner. The primordial temporal meaning of being, which constantly threatens to confine itself to mere presence, grounds distinctions such as those between essence and existence or a priori and a posteriori. Hence, the different meanings of being thematized by Aristotle can only arise from within a projective preconception in which Present already decisively dominates the temporal horizon.

On the basis of what has been said up to now about temporality, I will now attempt to elucidate how all Heidegger's analyses are guided by a mode of temporality in which Present does not gain dominance over the other temporal ecstases.

The Temporal Threefoldness of Heidegger's Method

The relation between the different moments of the being of Dasein and the formal concepts which bring that being to light must now be further specified.

In order to thematize the being of Dasein, formal indications are required. To this end, Heidegger takes a concept from everyday experience and deprives it of its ontic content in such a way that only a formal structure remains. This formal structure is then no longer only taken as the condition of possibility of the everyday phenomenon from which it was derived, but rather serves as the starting point for revealing the different possible modifications of that essential structure. After this step has been taken, the analysis relates exclusively to the being of beings.

The concepts are thus made suitable for ontological interpretation by a formalization of the ontic meaning and a deformalization of the obtained formal meaning at the ontological level. Within this deformalization Heidegger always (though not always explicitly) distinguishes an indifferent-inauthentic and an authentic modification, which indicate the essential possibilities of Dasein. A distinction must therefore be made between the ontic or "common" phenomenon from which the analysis starts out and the inauthentic modification of a formal structure that belongs to the *being* of Dasein. Thus, for example, there is a difference between the usual meaning of the concept "guilt" and the turning away from the always already being-guilty, which is an essential moment of the being of Dasein.[6]

Once a formal-indicative concept has been obtained, the being of beings can be further delimited. Such a concept refers to a primordial or formal structure in such a way that the inauthentic and the authentic modification of that structure can also be brought forth. The entire concept of a phenomenon thus comprises (1) the formal or primordial structure, (2) its indifferent-inauthentic modification (the "initially and mostly"), and (3) its authentic modification (the "possibly"). The being of beings, that is to say, the "essential," *is* nothing but the possible modifications in which that formal structure deformalizes itself. Although the order in which Heidegger thematizes the different moments can vary, this threefold structure gives the core of all his analyses.

We still have to answer the question as to how Heidegger understands the difference between this methodical threefoldness and the threefold that grounds the traditional concept of development. We have seen how Heidegger tries to understand the facticity of human life by means of a formal structure that grounds this facticity. Once this structure has been "seen," its most authentic modification can also be delimited. This is a possibility that belongs to facticity only *as* possibility, but as such nevertheless constitutes one of its essential directions. What essentially belongs to facticity is thus understood by conjoining it with a preceding condition of possibility and an authentic modification thereof.

Because Heidegger attempts to show how the indifferent-inauthentic modification of what Dasein essentially and possibly is always threatens to become the only tendency that determines facticity, both the formal structure and its authentic modification must lie *beyond* the realm of presence: what "precedes" is always already past and the "future" is only given as a *possibility* to come. The only, but decisive difference between Heidegger's methodical principle and, for example, that of Hegel, consists in the fact that Heidegger tries to reveal the formal structure and its authentic modification *as* that which retreats from the domain dominated by presence. From the metaphysical perspective, by contrast, the preceding origin (*archē*, ground, essence, idea) will always appear as that which is most present and real, and thus—sooner or later—also guarantees its own adequate actualization.

While the authentic mode of care pertains to the way in which factically existing Dasein bends itself back to the facticity of its own being, philosophy should bend itself back to the origin of everything that is or appears. If this preceding origin is understood as an origin which has never taken place and is always already past, then this is made possible by ecstatic Past. Heidegger tries to let his method be guided by Temporality in such a way that this Past delimits a realm within which being appears as an origin that itself does not belong to the realm of beings.[7] We could say that philosophy has always done this, but has never been sufficiently able to distinguish the proper character of the "preceding" from that which appears from within a horizon of Praesens. Past is then overshadowed by Present.

Just as Past opens up the preceding formal structure that constitutes one of the moments of being, ecstatic Future opens up the realm of the possible. The modification in which the preceding formal structure is possibly given its full due equally does not belong to the realm of presence.

Ecstatic Present appears to play a twofold role. As we know, it opens up the horizon of Praesens that allows beings to appear at all. Present sheds light on beings as they initially and mostly appear. The phenomenologist is able to understand this mode of appearance *as* the indifferent-inauthentic mode of a structure that itself does not appear from within Present alone. From Heidegger's perspective this temporal ecstasis remains embedded between the other two ecstases. Thus, Past and Future may delimit a horizon that allows being or the essential to appear as a presence that is radically pervaded by absence. Against this background the dynamic of human life may appear as itself.

It is difficult to give actual meaning to these abstract remarks. Temporality (*Temporalität*), as the purest mode of temporality itself, can hardly be thematized. This "time" may be said to primordially outstretch itself in a threefold way, such that the being of beings can be understood as (1) formal, preceding structure that (2) initially and mostly deformalizes itself by turning away from itself, but (3) has the possibility of coming into its own. It is important to emphasize, however, that this primordial threefold perspective has always already—that is to say, as soon as Dasein occurs—begun to confine itself. Hence, philosophy has never been able to do justice to the radical absence that constitutes the core of being itself.

The temporal horizon of the preontological understanding of being modifies itself in both everyday ontic involvement and metaphysics—that is, initially and mostly—into Praesens. Heidegger tries to resist this predominance of Present by going along with a primordial temporal projective preconception of being. This three-fold projective preconception never actually occurred in history, and even for Heidegger himself it is a possibility that in a certain sense is impossible. Nonetheless, it is this possibility that guides his attempt to overcome the metaphysical projective preconception of being.

Everything that Heidegger tries to say about temporality, both concerning Dasein and concerning the deconstruction of metaphysics, in my view only gains full significance when it becomes clear how his own analyses are guided by a threefold Temporality. We know that this Temporality is a mode of the temporality that is revealed in *Being and Time* as the fundamental structure of the being of Dasein. In phenomenological ontology as a possible mode of existence, this temporality ultimately enacts itself as a projective, opening movement that allows the being of beings to occur in accordance with its essential threefoldness. Only from within such a temporal horizon might justice be done to the radical difference between beings and being.

Now that Heidegger's method has been interpreted against the background of his concept of temporality, his suggestion that the character of the a priori must be modified becomes more meaningful. Hints about the character of this modification are to be found, for instance, at the end of GA 24 and in GA 20. Here he remarks that the a priori has traditionally been understood as that which was always already there (GA 20: 190). The concept refers to the "preceding," yet it has nothing to do with the time within which all events succeed one another. According to Heidegger, however, the fact that the a priori is not related to this time does not mean that it is above or beyond time. On the contrary; when the temporal meaning of the a priori is taken seriously, the concept pertains to what is "earlier" and thus makes beings possible with respect to their "what" and "how" (GA 24: 461–62). Heidegger, then, takes the a priori to no longer pertain to essence, but rather to the whole of the formal structure and its different modifications. These constitute the being of, for instance, Dasein, and are "earlier" than the concrete individual.[8] Heidegger thus modifies the a priori in such a way that the "preceding" origin is no longer understood as that which was always already there and persists amidst all change, but rather as a condition of possibility, divided within and against itself, that withdraws from the reach of presence. Insofar as every essential structure can only be revealed from within Temporality, this primordial time must therefore itself precede even every a priori.

> Time is *earlier than any possible "earlier"* of whatever sort, because it is the basic precondition for an "earlier" as such. And because time as the source of all enablings (*Ermöglichungen*) is the earliest, all possibilities have, with regard to their enabling function, as such the character of the "earlier," that is to say, they are a priori. (GA 24: 463, cf. BT 419)

In 1925/1926, Heidegger calls the mode of ontology that attempts to enact itself in accordance with this earliest Temporality "phenomenological chronology" (GA 21: 199). Precisely because he traces back the apriorical structure of Dasein to temporality, his philosophy differs from what is usually understood by transcendental philosophy.

Deconstruction, Reduction, and Construction

What has been said up to now about the temporal character of Heidegger's method was, in my view, to have been elaborated in *Time and Being* and the third part of GA 24. In the introduction of GA 24 Heidegger gives a brief sketch of the themes of this part.

First, when the question concerning the possibility of ontology is at stake, it is necessary to thematize Dasein; this being constitutes the ontic (and not the only or final) condition of possibility of ontology.[9] The outcome of the analytic of Dasein would subsequently have constituted the starting point for Heidegger's reflection on the method of ontology. In the second chapter this would have taken shape as a "development of the methodical structures of ontological-transcendental differentiation."[10] Much of what I have said up to now about Heidegger's method would probably have been elaborated in this chapter. Third, the three basic aspects of the phenomenological method—reduction, construction, and deconstruction—would have been thematized (GA 24: 28f). In the fourth chapter Heidegger would finally have been able to delimit more concretely the concept of philosophy. Here he would also have been able to come back to the confinement of the temporal perspective of metaphysics, with which the first part of GA 24 begins (cf. 32).

Heidegger remarks in the introduction of GA 24 that deconstruction, reduction, and construction constitute a unity and must be grounded as a unity, but he does not indicate the character of that ground (31). On the basis of what has been said up to now, these three moments of the method can be understood as grounded in primordial Temporality. This places Heidegger's method in a rather broader perspective. From that perspective it will also be possible to summarize the aspects of Heidegger's method discussed hitherto.

In the introduction of GA 24 Heidegger characterizes philosophy as the mode of knowing that thematizes being (28, cf. 458). Since initially only beings appear, the investigation must start out from beings, in order to then change the perspective in such a way that the being of beings can be thematized. This "leading back of the investigative vision" from beings to their being Heidegger calls phenomenological reduction. Thus, he here explicitly adopts Husserl's terminology, while at the same time distancing himself from Husserl's conception of the meaning of that reduction (28–29). I would like to add here that the "reduction" of beings to their being is, like every mode of thematization, made possible by ecstatic Present.

According to Heidegger, the movement that leads thinking away from beings, which occurs in reduction, cannot be accomplished without a projective, opening movement that leads thinking to being in a positive way. Being must "each time be brought to view in a free, projective preconception." This is the phenomenological construction.[11] The phenomenologist can both explicitly assume and modify the temporal horizon that makes it possible to understand being. This projecting or constructing movement can be conceived as a mode of being-ahead-of-oneself. Thus, the phenomenological construction is itself grounded in ecstatic Future, although again Heidegger does not yet say that in the introduction of GA 24.

The projective preconception of being can only become a free projective preconception when thinking critically reflects on the metaphysical presuppositions that thwart the disclosure of the things themselves. Heidegger constantly traces these presuppositions back to an inadequate concept of being. This moment of the analysis is called deconstruction.[12] This dismantling entails a retrieval of the positive possibilities inhering in traditional philosophy. We recognize here the moment of retrieving repetition; being the authentic relation to Dasein's situated facticity, this moment is grounded in Past.

We can see how Heidegger as it were allows the thematization of being to arise out of a deconstruction of the traditional temporal horizon on the one hand and a constructing modification of this horizon on the other. This deconstructing-constructing dynamic ensures that the turn from beings to their being is enacted appropriately. In an authentic thematization of being, reduction will thus remain conjoined with the moments of deconstruction and construction, which are made possible by Past and Future. Heidegger clearly understands Husserl's phenomenology as a mode of philosophy in which the moment of reduction prevails to such an extent that the traditional understanding of being cannot be modified in an authentic way. In such a reduction Present has gained the upper hand. Heidegger argues that this has been the case throughout the entire history of philosophy.

If we now consider more closely the moment of reduction, we again encounter the temporal threefoldness within that reduction—namely, as the distinction between the formal structure of a phenomenon on the one hand and its different modifications on the other. I have shown how the threefold distinction between the formal structure, its indifferent-inauthentic mode and its authentic mode, is grounded in temporality as Temporality. If reduction enacts itself in an appropriate way, these moments of being will not appear as constantly present. In *Being and Time* and GA 24 Heidegger gives no direct indications about this. As far as I know, he only thematizes the temporal meaning of this methodical threefold in his interpretation of Hegel's *Phenomenology of Spirit*.[13]

This is not yet the end of the story, however. The formal structure that shows forth in reduction as one of the moments of being, is itself structured in a threefold way, at least insofar as the being of Dasein is concerned. Care as formal structure has the moments ahead-of-itself, being-already-in, and being-with. These moments are distinguished with regard to the temporality (*Zeitlichkeit*) that constitutes the final a priori of human existence. This threefold temporal structure of care can modify itself in an inauthentic and an authentic way. A distinction therefore has to be made between the temporal threefoldness of care as such and the way in which this structure enacts or deformalizes itself. This deformalization pertains to the threefoldness which consists in (1) the formal structure itself, (2) its inauthentic modification, and (3) its authentic modification. This threefoldness constitutes the core of Heidegger's method and is grounded in time as Temporality.

I will try to summarize the above. As far as I can see, temporality plays a central part in Heidegger's analysis in three respects. First, with regard to the analytic of Dasein, this time constitutes the a priori of care as such. This structure modifies itself in human life in an inauthentic or an authentic way, depending on the extent to which Present has become predominant.

Second, the being of Dasein can be thematized in an inauthentic or an authentic way in *philosophy*, according to the modification of temporality that grounds philosophy itself. In a phronetic thinking[14] this reduction will remain embedded within the deconstructive and the constructive movement.

Third, it is temporality as Temporality that allows being to be understood and thematized at all. An authentic modification of Temporality permits the formal structure of care and its different modifications to show forth respectively as (1) the preceding origin that recedes from the realm of presence, (2) the tendency that initially and mostly gains the upper hand, and (3) the tendency in which that preceding structure is possibly given its due.

It is quite understandable that these different modes of temporality are difficult to distinguish. After all, the Temporality that grounds every understanding of being is itself a specific modification of temporality. One could say that care as fundamental structure of Dasein modifies itself in authentic ontology in such a way that Past and Future are allowed to reach further into the absential than in all other modifications of temporality. Philosophy is itself a mode of life; it is the mode in which life explicitly comprehends itself. Thus, when Heidegger in turn tries to comprehend the character and the different possibilities of that self-conception, thinking takes on a vertiginous reflexivity. It does indeed seem hardly possible to explain these matters.

Yet the principle is simple. What Heidegger calls temporality is ultimately nothing more than a kind of construction that makes it possible to gain insight into the proper dynamic—divided in and against itself—of life, thinking, and the history of thinking. It is therefore meaningless to ask whether there is such a thing as primordial time. The character of the temproality that concerns Heidegger is in itself such that Present constantly threatens to break away from its juncture with the other temporal ecstases. This temporality is not brought about by human beings. It can, however, be modified in such a way that ecstatic Present no longer overshadows the other ecstases. It is not up to the thinker to let that happen. At most he can try not to thwart the primordial unfolding of threefold temporality. This compliance does, however, demand an active and constant resistance against Present, which inevitably prevails whenever anything is spoken or written.

The detours that Heidegger takes in order to reveal this dynamic can be understood as *indications* of something which is seldom if ever directly thematized. The detour in GA 24 is no more successful in reaching its aim than the analytic of Dasein in *Being and Time*. At the end of GA 24 it seems that Heidegger wishes to testify to this failure. He suggests here that his method has begun to thwart the course of his thinking.

> Precisely when a method is genuine and provides access to the matters at issue, the progress and the increasing originality of the disclosure which is due to this very method will themselves be the cause of its obsolescence. (GA 24: 467)

This remark might relate to the phenomenological request that any interpretation should be in line with concrete experiences of Dasein. I have pointed out that this perspective almost inevitably takes the movement of life to be one of increasing actualization. Must Heidegger, in order to avoid that, also radicalize his own methodical principle? Can Dasein still be the starting point for a deconstruction of metaphysics? It may be that the whole idea of a method has to be relinquished, because the distinction between method and subject matter is based on the practice of the positive sciences. After all, the understanding of being and being as it is understood can never occur without one another. They even seem to be indistinguishable, as Heidegger suggests in 1930.

> Is, then, the relation between being and the understanding of being so elementary that what is true of being is true of the understanding of being as well, that being is identical with its disclosure? (GA 31: 124)

Notes

1. This chapter refers to the following volumes of Heidegger's *Gesamtausgabe* (GA), published in Frankfurt am Main by Vittorio Klostermann: GA 20, *Prolegomena zur Geschichte des Zeitbegriffs*, composed 1925 (published 1979), translated by Theodore Kisiel as *History of the Concept of Time: Prolegomena* (Bloomington: Indiana University Press, 1985); GA 21, *Logik: Die Frage nach der Wahrheit*, 1925–1926 (1976); GA 24, *Die Grundprobleme der Phänomenologie*, 1927 (1975), translated by Albert Hofstadter as *The Basic Problems of Phenomenology* (Bloomington: Indiana University Press, 1982); GA 31, *Vom Wesen der menschlichen Freiheit: Einleitung in die Philosophie*, 1930 (1982), translated by Ted Sadler as *The Essence of Human Freedom: An Introduction to Philosophy* (London: Continuum, 2002). BT refers to *Being and Time*, trans. Joan Stambaugh (Albany: SUNY, 1996). All of these texts are cited by their German pagination, which is also provided in the translations. Translations in this chapter from GA 24 are based on the Hofstadter translation, but have been modified.

2. It is therefore misleading of A. Hofstadter to translate *Vergegenständlichung* as "objectification" (see 398, 456 of the German pagination), when it is crucial for Heidegger to distinguish between an objectifying and a nonobjectifying mode of explicit elucidation or thematization.

3. See F. Dastur, *Heidegger et la question du temps* (Paris: PUF, 1990): "Therefore, temporal ontology is not a 'theory' in the traditional sense . . . for the objectification of being that it requires does not have the meaning of a making present" (108).

4. Thus, projective preconception "takes the direction toward thought, comprehension, soul, mind, spirit, subject, without understanding the necessity of a primordial and preliminary ontological preparation of especially these areas—that is, the necessity of being serious about this work" (GA 24: 459).

5. In *Being and Time* Heidegger indicates the character of this freedom as follows: "Temporality (*Zeitlichkeit*) already holds itself ecstatically in the horizons of its ecstases and, accomplishing itself, comes back to the beings encountered in the 'there' (*das Da*). With the factical existence of Dasein, innerworldly beings are also already encountered. That such beings are discovered along with the 'there' of Dasein's own existence is not something that Dasein can choose. Only *what* it discovers and discloses at times, in *which* direction, *to what extent*, and *in what way*, is a matter of its freedom, although always within the limits of its thrownness" (BT 366, tr. m.). That certainly does not apply to the involvement with innerworldly beings alone.

6. Heidegger formalizes the usual meaning of "guilt" in such a way that only the determination "being-the-ground of a nothingness" remains (BT 283, tr. m.). This formal indication can then be given another, second meaning and come to pertain to the being of Dasein as such: being thrown and radically finite, Dasein essentially falls short, and must take upon itself the responsibility for what it has not itself brought forth. This existential being-guilty then has an inauthentic and an authentic mode, insofar as Dasein itself initially and mostly turns away from the "not" which pervades its being, yet has the possibility of facing up to its essential finitude. The first interpretive movement (the formalization) serves as preparation for gaining access to the being of Dasein, that is to say, to an existential structure. The existential analysis proper subsequently understands this structure in relation to its inauthentic and its authentic modification.

7. In *Being and Time* Heidegger calls the formal, preceding structure an "a priori perfect" (BT 85). In a later note he adds to this: "It is not something ontically past, but rather what is always earlier, what we are referred *back* to in the question of beings as such."

8. Since there is a further distinction *within* the apriorical structure of Dasein between the formal "what" and its possible modifications, this formal structure is again, in comparison with those modifications, the "earlier," and as such disclosed by Past. Heidegger does not thematize this here. Cf. however: "The primordial structural whole of care (*Sorge*) is an existential a priori which as such lies 'before,' and therefore always already *in* every factic 'relation' and 'position' of Dasein" (BT 193, tr. m.). In the existential analysis these factic possibilities can be delimited on the basis of the

inauthentic and authentic modifications of that formal structure. See for the a priori also BT 41, 65.

9. GA 24: 26; cf. BT 11–13 and: "The *concept of philosophy*, as well as that of the *nonphilosophical sciences*, can be expounded only on the basis of a properly understood concept of Dasein" (GA 24: 455).

10. GA 24: 27. The outline of the course indicates that this elaboration corresponds to the thematization of "the apriority of being and the possibility and structure of a priori knowledge" (33).

11. GA 24: 29–30. See for the term "phenomenological construction": BT 375, 376. Cf. Heidegger, *Kant and the Problem of Metaphysics*, trans. Richard Taft, 5th ed. (Bloomington: Indiana University Press, 1997), 163. This construction is distinguished from arbitrary constructions (BT 303).

12. "It is for this reason that all philosophical explanation, even when it is most radical and beginning all over again, is pervaded by traditional concepts and thus by traditional horizons and perspectives. . . . It is for this reason that a *deconstruction*, that is, a critical dismantling of the traditional concepts—which initially must necessarily be employed—with regard to the sources from which they were drawn, necessarily belongs to the conceptual interpretation of being and its structures" (GA 24: 31).

13. See Karin de Boer, *Thinking in the Light of Time: Heidegger's Encounter with Hegel* (Albany: SUNY Press, 2000), 273–77.

14. "Heidegger suggests . . . that, in contrast to the prevailing theoretical philosophy, it should be possible for thinking to accord with the *phronesis* that guides acting and yet, unlike *phronesis* but like the prevailing philosophy, to explicitly focus on the *archai* of being as such. This thinking, which withdraws itself from metaphysics, will be guided from within its factic situation by an ultimate possibility that is not to be actualized, but rather to be kept open. It will be concerned with principles and ends on which causality and chronology have no hold, but which nevertheless, as 'already' and 'not yet,' underlie everything that happens within this domain": de Boer, *Thinking in the Light of Time*, 22.

3

The Constitution of Our Being

Graeme Nicholson

*B*EING AND TIME (*SZ*)[1] did not have the limited aim of a philosophical anthropology—it was written as the introduction to a universal ontological inquiry, a study of "the question of being," *die Frage nach dem Sein*. But the study was to be opened up through a study of human existence, *das Sein des Da-seins*. A study of our own particular way of being was to constitute a "fundamental ontology": examining being initially in our own case, grasping it from the inside, so to speak, we would gain an insight into being itself, an insight that would then permit a broadening of scope, a subsequent treatment of being quite universally. Ontology begins at home.

There were plenty of precedents for the route Heidegger established for his inquiry, and he himself mentions a number of them. On page 12 he mentions Aristotle's *De Anima*, a study of the soul that had great impact upon general ontology, with roots as far back as Parmenides and with influence extending to Thomas Aquinas and beyond. Another example is the Aristotelian *Rhetoric* treated in Sections 29 and 30. As Heidegger says, "the ontic-ontological priority of Da-sein was already seen early on" (p. 12). But the greatest prototype for such a self-broadening inquiry, taking its start from the human being, is one that Heidegger never mentions himself, the combined thought of Socrates and Plato. It is clear from the *Apology* and the *Phaedo* that Socrates had turned away from inquiries into nature such as those of Empedocles and Anaxagoras, turning his attention to himself and his fellow citizens.[2] As Cicero said, "Socrates was the first to call philosophy down from the sky and establish her in the towns and introduce her into homes and force her to investigate life, ethics, good and evil."[3] It was then from this human self-examination, Socrates' "care for the soul," that Plato proceeded toward a universal philosophy, and what marked his philosophy off from that of the pre-Socratics was just that it got this particular start. So I think we can invoke Socrates and Plato together as the prototype for a route that begins by examining *das Sein des Da-seins* and then proceeds to a general ontological interrogation—in Plato's case, that became the theory of ideas; in Heidegger's case it was the question of being as introduced through the ontology of Da-sein. And the precedents in the modern period of philosophy are even more obvious and more numerous, from Descartes on, whose "First Philosophy" started with the *cogito*. What is of course essential for such a pathway is that the initial turn toward the human being, toward Da-sein, be made in the right way.

It seems that the pathway followed by Socrates, Plato and Heidegger is exactly the opposite from that which is followed in today's philosophy of mind. Today's philosophy of mind (or some of it, anyway) seems to just apply the sciences of nature and the sciences of life to our mental life, bringing in data from physiology, psychology and other sciences.[4] Such philosophers appear to think that the human mind will only yield up its secrets to one who has made this long detour through so many sciences, accumulating all their immense detail. Without much exaggeration, we could say that this modern philosophy of mind is the heir of pre-Socratic philosophy, Democritus and Empedocles, for instance, who undertook to study the causes of all the events in the cosmos, and then determined the specific nature and function of the human soul as a special case. But, as I have said, Socrates turned away from that program so as to "know himself," and Plato took his start from Socrates. Now let us see how Heidegger begins.

Section 2 lays out the agenda of *SZ* (p. 7): it is to be "the explication of a being (Da-sein) with regard to its being." That the topic of the book is *das Sein des Da-seins* is reiterated in the introductory chapters (pp. 13, 14, 17, 38, 41 and 42), and at the beginning of almost every later chapter (pp. 53, 114, 130, 180–81, 231, 236, 267, 301, 334, 372, 404.) The present paper will not come close to exhausting the many subtle nuances of the term "Da-sein." Here at the start, I shall just mention one point: that the term has a double value. There are passages in which the term coincides so closely with the term *Mensch*, "human being," that the two words can alternate in Heidegger's prose (pp. 11, 14 and 57). This is the usage that Heidegger is assuming when he writes that Da-sein is "the entity that we ourselves are" (p. 7). On the other hand, Da-sein is not a normal predicate term or a name for our human species. It is never marked as a plural: a common mistake in English-language Heidegger-commentary is the impossible expression "several Da-seins." Heidegger tells us that "the term Da-sein [is] a pure expression of being" (p. 12). The second component of the word is not a normal German noun but a gerund, the nominalized form of the infinitive *sein* (= "to be"). Even when the word is used by Heidegger "ontically," then, to designate a being, *Seiendes*, the one we ourselves are, it has an ontological value as well. Thus it is impossible to substitute the term *Mensch* for it in most passages of *SZ*. For a thorough treatment, which offers by far the best orientation to the problems raised by this term, one should consult the recent book by Raffoul.[5] He refutes both the "humanistic" reading of the text, that would simply identify Da-sein as a human being, and the more recent exaggerated anti-humanistic reading, which alleged that Da-sein had simply nothing to do with the self, the subject or the human being.

Instead of the topic of Da-sein, it is a closely related topic that I shall be discussing here, the *being* of Da-sein. Of course, I'll need to use the term "Da-sein" when I am quoting Heidegger or referring to his text, but when I am writing on my own behalf instead, I'll use personal pronouns such as "I," "you" and "we," not nouns like *Mensch* or *Da-sein*. I feel justified in my preference by the way in which Heidegger himself introduced the term "Da-sein" for the very first time in the book in Section 2; "The entity [*Seiendes*] that each one of us is and that has among its possibilities the raising of the question of being we shall fix terminologically as Da-sein" (p. 7). Heidegger's theme in the book, strictly stated, is not Da-sein but the *being* of Da-sein, i.e., our being.[6] Given this thematic focus, it is inevitable that a certain circularity enters into the argument, modifying its foundational character. The "fundamental ontology" of Da-sein must already incorporate part of the study of being for which it was to serve as a preparation. But according to Heidegger, that is a benign and a welcome circularity.[7]

SZ lays before us the being of Da-sein through several distinct movements of thought, and here I shall retrace three of them. We shall see that existence is the "essence" of Da-sein, that being-in-the-world is the constitution of Da-sein, and that care is the being of Da-sein. In following each of the movements, my intent is not at all to separate them from one another, but rather to bring to the fore the diversity and differentiation that belongs to our being, demonstrating in the case of our own being why philosophy has always returned to the theme of the manifoldness of being. After a study of each of the three, we shall see the way in which they are intertwined with one another to constitute a tapestry that is inwardly complex. And indeed, each one of the three elements is already complex in itself. Here let me point in a preliminary way to the complexity of the first of these themes, existence.

In the course of an important chapter on *SZ*,[8] Pöggeler calls attention to a double meaning of the term "existence," narrow and wide. "Heidegger characterizes existence in the wider sense as the *totality* of factical existence" (*Path*, p. 41; *Denkweg*, p. 56). In many passages of the book, accordingly, Heidegger will speak of existential structures, aspects of our being that he interprets in the light of existence. He employs the term "existentials" or "existentialia" for these

structures: *Existenzialien*, differentiated from categories, which are the determinations of the being of whatever is not Da-sein (*SZ*, pp. 44–45). For example,
we see from the titles of Sections 49, 50, 52 and 53, that they are treating "existential" phenomena, and that their analyses and concepts are "existential"—the
existential analysis of conscience, the existential concept of science, and so on.
But Pöggeler points out that there is also a narrower sense of "existence," or
rather a narrower scope of the term: "[Da-sein] is characterized equiprimordially by 'existentiality' as well as facticity. It is existence in the narrower sense
of the word, the self-projecting potentiality-for-being" (ibid.). Here existence
is limited by facticity, polarized against it, whereas, according to the broader
sense of existence, facticity would be one more existential structure. Heidegger
himself, in fact, called attention to this double scope of the term "existence."[9]
One of the points I'll want to make, however, is that this duality of existence,
narrow and broad, is no mere equivocation on a word. This will concern us in
the next two sections of the paper.

My aim overall will be to show the great success of Heidegger in treating
the constitution of our being. Thanks to the publication of some of his lecture courses from the early 1920s, and thanks to the appearance of Kisiel's
genetic study,[10] we can now study the successive drafts in which Heidegger
sought to find "words to articulate the peculiarly inchoate and purportedly
'ineffable' immediacy of the human situation, Heidegger's lifelong topic."[11]
For his concerns during all those years were being adumbrated under different
names, "Life," the "Primal Something," "factical life" or "facticity."[12] It was
only in the final drafting of *SZ* that Heidegger resolved his terminology in
designating the subject of his study as existence.[13] This enabled him now to
express the theme of the being of Da-sein in relation to the question of being as
such.

In the continuing cycle of the assimilation of, and resistance to, Heidegger's
philosophy, the last ten or fifteen years have brought a new and powerful resistance to the fore. Now we see the frank rejection of the entire topic of being.
Caputo has come to regard "Being" as a mere myth;[14] from the theological
side, Marion claims that "Being" is an idol from which Christians should free
themselves;[15] for both critics, Being (N. B. spelled by both of them with a
capital "B") is a remote, antihuman metaphysical postulate. It is, then, encour-
aging that at the same time we find books such as that by Joanna Hodge,[16]
which grasps the human and ethical character of Heidegger's thinking of being
(which, of course, she always spells with a small "b").

Through Heidegger's reflections, we can come to understand that we are
not just a self-possessed ego with its career to sustain. We acquire access to
something deeper, and a language for expressing it—the promptings of our
pre-personality, not just our self, but our *being*.

I. Existence: The "Essence" of Da-sein

Sections 4 and 9 of *SZ* lay down the determination of the being of Da-sein as *existence*, a point that remains in force throughout the whole of the work that follows. Sections 1 to 3 offer many preliminary remarks on being, but Section 4 is concerned to show existence as the constitution of *our* being (p. 13): it is that form of being to which we, as Da-sein, always stand in relation (p. 12); we always understand ourselves in terms of our existence (p. 12); a concern about existence is woven into our existence itself (p. 12). Much of my exposition will focus on the double point, (a) that we have a concern *about* our existence, (b) one that is already woven *into* our existence. "We come to terms with the question of existence only through existence itself" (p. 12). Heidegger calls a deeply motivated concern of this sort, and the kind of understanding it includes, *existenziell*, which we can translate in today's English as an existential concern and an existential understanding. What then is meant by this term "existence"? The central pointer that is offered in Section 4 is a *link with possibility*. "Da-sein always understands itself in terms of its existence, in terms of its possibility to be itself or not to be itself" (p. 12). That will be at the heart of the following exposition, but first we must take a look at Section 9.

In Section 9 we read "The 'essence' of Da-sein lies in its existence" (p. 42). Thus we can expect that whatever is most characteristic of Da-sein will be marked by existence, e.g., experiences such as death, conscience and language. On the other hand, the quotation marks over the term "essence" are enough to warn us that Heidegger is not employing this term in a traditional scholastic sense or in any standard modern sense. And if we remember that in authors like Aquinas there was a definite polar relationship between *essentia* and *existentia*, that means—given the quotation marks—that Heidegger is not speaking of either existence or essence in a neo-scholastic way. He is also taking his distance from other modern uses of "essence," thus by-passing any statements as to the "whatness" or quiddity of Da-sein, as he stresses on this page (p. 42): "the term Da-sein which we use to designate this being does not express its 'what' as in the case of 'table,' 'house,' 'tree.'" Heidegger is certainly stretching the word "essence" here in a manner that would be worth pursuing, but now it is a different question that I shall pursue: given that existence is *in some sense or other* the essence of Da-sein, how are we to understand existence?

Heidegger guides the reader by way of a lexical orientation on page 42. He will discuss the being of Da-sein under the heading of existence, he says, i.e., under the heading of what he calls in German *Existenz*. But this title "does not and cannot have the ontological meaning of the traditional expression of *existentia*." With this Latin word, Heidegger intends an ontological notion that comes down to us from the scholastic period and the early modern period of philosophy, and it signifies "a kind of being [*Sein*] which is essentially inappropriate to characterize the being [*Seiendes*] which has the character of Da-sein." From this point on in the text of *SZ*, the Latin word is almost entirely avoided.[17] "We can avoid confusion by always using the interpretive expression *objective presence* [*Vorhandenheit*] for the term *existentia*, and by attributing existence [*Existenz*] as a determination of being only to Da-sein."

Although this point is fairly well-known to Heidegger's readers, I do not think everyone has grasped all of its linguistic and logical consequences. *Existenz* is the basic element in the ontology of Da-sein with no application to any other subject. But what was called *existentia* in Scholasticism, and what was called "existence" in the different languages of post-medieval philosophy, is to be interpreted in the sense of *Vorhandenheit*, "objective presence," a notion that has nothing in common with *Existenz* and that should not be applied to Da-sein at all. To do so is to bring about an ontological distortion (*SZ*, p. 55). In Heidegger's view, our modern ordinary language use is quite continuous with traditional metaphysics, and the common usage of modern English and German is continuous in this respect as well with the usage of scholastic and post-scholastic philosophy. Our supposed "intuitive" ideas about existence, and being in general, are by no means "natural" or "immediate" or "unhistorical." They are actually the deposits of traditional ontology and traditional logic, and it is for that reason that we still tend to think that "existence" means being objectively present, *vorhanden*. But the usage of ordinary language is by no means authoritative for philosophy, in Heidegger's view.

Moreover, Heidegger's critical examination of *Vorhandenheit* is not confined to traditional metaphysics and logic, but applies as well to modern philosophy and to modern logic too, with its quantificational calculus. For what is called logic is in fact an offshoot of metaphysics, a point well expressed in the title of Heidegger's 1928 lecture course *The Metaphysical Foundations of Logic*. The sense of the existential quantifier in modern logic is still determined by traditional logic and traditional metaphysics—"existence" is still our way of asserting that something or other, no matter what, just happens to be around or available rather than not being around or not being available. That is *Vorhandenheit*.

So Heidegger has not taken his own term "existence" from ordinary language. In its everyday use, the term "exist" is applied to subjects of great variety (and this is also true of the German noun *Existenz* and verb *existieren*)—to animal species if they are not extinct, and to letters and documents if they haven't been destroyed. The existence of heavenly bodies and tiny particles can be established with certain methods, and we continue to debate the existence of God. In Heidegger's view, our modern ordinary-language use is quite continuous with traditional metaphysics. But, in his work, this is all subjected to an ontological critique.

I began by calling attention to the link Heidegger is establishing between existence (*our* existence, that is) and possibility. Now is the time to follow that up.

In *SZ*, Sections 4 and 9 both underline the key status of possibility within existence. "Da-sein always understands itself in terms of its existence, in terms of its possibility to be itself or not to be itself" (Sec. 4, p. 12). "The characteristics to be found in this being are thus not objectively present 'attributes' of an objectively present being which has such and such an 'outward appearance,' but rather possible ways for it to be and only this" (Sec. 9, p. 42). That is the reason why the term "Da-sein" does not express a "What" as in the cases of table, house and tree—the term expresses only being. And now we see that this *being* is in fact *possibility*. The possibility in question resolves itself into one great alternative— to be myself or not to be myself—which is expressed philosophically as the alternative between authenticity and inauthenticity (p. 43). "And because Da-sein is always essentially its possibility, it *can* 'choose' itself in its being, it can win itself, it can lose itself..." (p. 42). "As a being, Da-sein always defines itself in terms of a possibility which it *is* and somehow understands in its being. That is the formal meaning of the constitution of the existence of Da-sein" (p. 43).

While authenticity is closely intertwined with existence in *SZ*, it is by no means the same thing, and neither is what Heidegger calls the "mineness" of Da-sein's being, its *Jemeinigkeit*. This mineness—that being is in every case my own—is the basis of the possibility for our being ourselves or not being ourselves, but it is not the same thing as existence. Heidegger opens Section 9 by identifying two aspects of our being. (1) The "essence" of Da-sein is its existence. (2) This being is in each case my own. The separation of these two points is articulated again in the first paragraph on p. 43, and again at the opening of Section 12. Heidegger's differentiation between *Existenz*, on the one hand, and *Jemeinigkeit* on the other, proved to be of great importance historically. The current of *Existenzphilosophie* was running strongly in the 1920s in Germany, fed by the reception of Kierkegaard and the influence of Jaspers. Undoubtedly Heidegger was seeking to connect *SZ* to that current (a point made very clear in Kisiel's book), but we have to see that Heidegger's account of the constitution of Da-sein's being differs from theirs over just this point. The category of existence in Kierkegaard and Jaspers was tightly linked to the category of individuality, and defined over against the universal.[18] Their existentialism was turning the tables against a philosophy of "the system," primarily Hegel's, but in principle against all metaphysics that saw the individual as the mere instance of a type, an essence, a universal. Asserting that it is only the individual that exists, they imbued this existing individual with a passion and an inwardness that were certainly novel in comparison to traditional metaphysics. While Heidegger does recognize the individuality of Da-sein in his doctrine that being is in

every case my own, his idea of existence does not derive its content from this
Jemeinigkeit. Therefore, it is not determined through opposition to the universal
or the system. Hence, a discussion of mineness, singleness and individuality
can be left to one side in the exposition of existence. The factor of existence
is neither the authenticity that I may choose, nor the mineness of being that
makes possible the alternative of authenticity and inauthenticity, being myself
or not being myself. Rather, it is the very circumstance of having the alternative,
having the possibility.

The doctrine of existential possibility must be understood in connection
with Heidegger's treatment of understanding in *SZ*, Section 31. Understanding is that disclosure whereby we first become open to a possibility. When we
understand a possibility, in Heidegger's view, we are *projecting* it. Existentially,
we do not merely entertain a possibility—when we disclose it by way of understanding, we are *going* for it. We are by no means open to everything, for
"Da-sein has already got itself into definite possibilities" (p. 144), which, of
course also means: got itself excluded from other ones. The possibilities to
which we are open (that we project) are possible ways for us to be. This is
the *Seinkönnen* that Heidegger speaks of throughout Section 31: the published
translations render this term "potentiality for being," but I prefer a simpler
rendering which I think is ontologically less prejudicial: the ability to be. If you
are setting out to become a forester, you are projecting this as your possibility,
and this is your ability to be a forester, your *Försterseinkönnen*. The *ability* to
be is no "free-floating" possibility that hovers before you; existential possibility
is inseparable from the projection of it, from the anticipation of it. It *is* the
anticipation. The ability to be, possibility with its feet on the ground, is the
union of an anticipated possibility with the very anticipation.

Sections 4 and 9 identified existence as the very alternative or the very possibility of being yourself or not being yourself. That is the possibility that is
most of all your own (*eigenstes*, "ownmost," "most of all your own"). Given the
analysis in the preceding paragraph, then, we can say that *this* ability to be *is*
the being of Da-sein. "Da-sein *is* always its possibility. It does not 'have' that
possibility only as a mere attribute of something objectively present" (p. 12).
Therefore, through existing we are always *concerned* about our own ability to
be, even as we continue perpetually to project it. To that extent, our ability to be
(existence) is divided off from us, separated from our current Now. What can I
be? What can I learn? What might I achieve? How shall I die? With whom shall
I live? To what cause shall I commit myself? What can I know? What must I do?
What may I hope? These are the urgent matters disclosed to us all in the kind of
understanding that Heidegger calls *existenziell*—matters of our existence, *das
Sein des Da-seins*. They are developed at length in the two opening chapters of
the Second Division of *SZ*, on our being-toward-death and conscience.

But our projected ability to be is *not* absolutely divided off from our current being. Even my current being is the ability to be. This connection between that which is projected and that which projects will be Heidegger's subject in Chapters 3 to 6 in the Second Division of the book, where he treats existential temporality. Our present being is the ekstatic opening-out-to our futural ability to be that now concerns us. And so it too is an ability to be. That is what Heidegger means in saying that the "essence" of Da-sein lies in its existence. The movement toward a future ability to be constitutes our current ability to be.

This can introduce us to the narrower scope of existence, which is presented normatively in Section 41. Heidegger's analysis of existence in the narrow sense ties it to the projective understanding of possibility. It means that "Da-sein is always already *ahead* of itself [*ihm selbst vorweg*] in its being. Da-sein is always already 'beyond itself' [*'über sich hinaus'*], not as a way of behaving toward beings which it is *not*, but as being toward the ability to be [*Seinkönnen*] which it itself is" (pp. 191–192). We surpass ourselves, and in that way we are always becoming unhooked from that which we are at present.

Here I would like to show one implication that must arise from Heidegger's analysis, though the text does not contain it: our existence must bring with it our self-interpretation. In Section 32, "Understanding and Interpretation," *Verstehen und Auslegung*, Heidegger stresses that understanding must express itself in interpretation: *Verstehen* projects a "fore-structure" by which a possibility arises for some phenomenon, while *Auslegung* completes the understanding by grasping this phenomenon *as* something. The "as-structure" of interpretation is the fulfillment of the "fore-structure" of understanding. Yet Heidegger himself acknowledges at the end of the first paragraph that his study of interpretation in Section 32 is confined to cases of "inauthentic" understanding, with a focus on entities present in the world, especially as interpreted through perception, which grasps *this* implement *as* a hammer. But *Verstehen* in its primordial form is Da-sein's self-understanding—no doubt on that score in Section 31. Since Heidegger has linked our *existence* so tightly to the projective, anticipatory character of *Verstehen*, he must recognize (and I am sure did recognize) that existence itself incorporates the "as-structure" of interpretation. To exist means to exist *as* a woman or *as* a man, *as* a clown or *as* a sage, *as* an American or *as* an Italian, *as* a believer or *as* an unbeliever. Self-interpretation helps to constitute existence, our human way of being. We are impelled to express ourselves outwardly, to appear in the open domain of public interpretations. And this reveals the inadequacy of an ontology of *life* for the interpretation of ourselves, Da-sein. If we are *alive*, that signifies that our organs and tissues are functional rather than dysfunctional. *Life* is a category in which immanence and self-relation are predominant—it signifies a certain reference of the whole organism to the part and of the part to the whole. But when we *exist*, we are not merely alive but, in addition, thrust out upon a stage of action where every one of our possible deeds has significance. It is just as mistaken to comprehend ourselves under the category of Life as under that of *Vorhandenheit*. I am not relying on ordinary language in making these distinctions, for there is a common locution these days in which one says of a person whose life is utterly lacking in prospects or delights, "She isn't really *living*—she's just *existing*." This locution retains the everyday sense of existence as mere *Vorhandenheit*, not the sense of Heidegger's ontology, and it expresses our true and fulfilled ontological mode as "living." Heidegger would have expressed the point by reversing the two words.

One consequence of noting the need for self-interpretation is that we gain insight into the unity of being. If it is true that self-interpretation is a necessary aspect of human existence, if it is true that to exist *means* to exist as a woman, or a man, or a clown, etc., then we are authorized to make an appropriate exegesis of the word "is" when it serves as a copula, i.e., when it is used to predicate. Thus if I say "Frances is a woman" or "Giorgio is an Italian," I must take the trouble to understand these words in accord with the ontology of existence. To *be* a woman or an Italian is, strictly, to *exist as* a woman or *as* an Italian. We can reach some unity in the interpretation of being when we understand in what way being in the sense of *existence* sustains the predicating gerunds such as "being a woman" or "being an Italian."[19] Philosophical interpretation warns us against assuming that the predicating "is" means the same thing no matter what the subject is, that Frances is a woman in the same way that my desk is wooden.

At this point we can confront the question of Heidegger's use of this word, "existence." Heidegger wanted to express a special ontological constitution of Da-sein, by virtue of which Da-sein always projects a possibility, and particularly the two-fold possibility of being authentic or inauthentic. Self-projection—to be "in advance of itself"—is central to Da-sein's being. But why did Heidegger want to give the name of "existence" to this? What is there in this word that makes it the suitable expression for this constitution of being?

The word "exist" stems from the Latin *existo* or *exsisto*, a complex verb formed from the prefix *ex*, "out," and *sisto*, "stand, be placed." *Sisto* itself arose from the verb *sto*, "stand, be placed," by the reduplication system found in certain Greek and Latin verbs. Thus, the original sense of the verb was "stand *out*, stand *forth*," a sense which philologists have called the local sense of the word. This local sense is apparent not through fanciful etymologizing, but through a reading of classical Latin texts. In Cicero and other texts from that period, *exsisto* means "come forth," "come into view," "rise from the dead," "emerge," "come forward."[20] And the verb *exsto*, which in the perfect tense is not different from *exsisto*, could also mean "protrude, project, stand out." Later evidence makes it apparent that the sense "be, exist" arose *after* these senses. The original sense, "stand out, protrude" developed through "emerge, become visible" to "exist," "be," at the end of the process. Heidegger himself refers to this early sense of the Latin word in lectures of 1927. "In this projection, the Da-sein has already *stepped out beyond itself, ex-sistere,* it is *in* a world. Consequently it is never anything like a subjective inner sphere."[21] My reading of Heidegger, then, is that he is resisting the ordinary-language sense of "existence" and the logical sense of "existence" because of their roots in metaphysical *Vorhandenheit,* a structure which is not applicable to us. Likewise, he resists Kierkegaard's and Jaspers's bond of existence to the category of individuality for philosophical reasons. He does not think that self-projection, in the existential sense of self-displacement into the possible, can be expounded by way of the category of singularity or individuality. Singular entities, as such, need not be involved in self-projection. And, the other way around, there is no need to insist on our singularity in connection with our self-projection. Self-projection can occur in the form of being-with, *Mitsein.* Rather than follow Kierkegaard and Jaspers, then, Heidegger is reviving the ancient sense of the word "exist."

II. Care: The Being of Da-sein

But the ontology of Da-sein is not exhausted by the study of existence. Heidegger opens Section 39 by raising the question of the *whole* of our being, indicating clearly that existence does not fulfill that role. Rather, he says, we can grasp that whole by way of the phenomenon of care (*die Sorge*). I shall not expound care at the same length as existence—instead, I offer a few comments in point form.

(i) The term "care," like others in the book, has a double value: subjectively, care is an orientation to ourselves, and to everything that is, whereby we are connected to them: it is a variant of intentionality. But, onto-logically, care has a triadic constitution. "The fundamental ontological characteristics of this being are existentiality, facticity and falling prey" (p. 191), and here Heidegger claims that this triad constitutes the being of Da-sein. This claim is really the pivot of the whole book, because this triad will be reinterpreted in Sections 65 and following as the sub-structure of our temporality, the prototype for the existential future, the existential past, and the existential present.

(ii) It is in connection with care that existence appears in its narrow scope. Existence, or existentiality,[22] is limited here mainly through being brought into a polarization with facticity. In Section 41, Heidegger reviews his treatment of understanding-as-projection and his account of existence-as-possibility. Projective understanding is that disclosure whereby we are open to possibility. Then he reviews a second mode of disclosure, attunement (*Befindlichkeit*), that had been presented in Section 29. Attunement is our already being in a world, that disclosure whereby we are open to what we already are, and indeed to what *all* things are. Ontologically interpreted, it is the structure of *already* being something, which stands as it were over against the *possibility* of our being, and it is what Heidegger calls our facticity. The third element in our being is the "falling-prey," *Verfallen*, whereby we are drawn to beings rather than to being, and whereby we are drawn away from authenticity. It too is expressed in our ways of disclosing that which is. A fuller account of this third structure would take us too far afield, however, so I shall bracket it, just as I bracketed *Jemeinigkeit* earlier on. Existence is our being-ahead-of-self. In the structure of care, it is unified especially with our already-being-in-a-world, an interpenetration which makes it certain that, in my projection of possibility, there are some possibilities that are open to me while others are not. "Existing is always factual. Existentiality is essentially determined by facticity" (p. 192).

(iii) This facticity of Da-sein is the very "That-ness" of its being, something which has often been intended by commonplace, non-Heideggerian expressions of "existence"—to be a fact, to be a datum, to occur. But Heidegger's own philosophy has displaced existence into the futural *Sich-vorweg-sein*. We are leaning forward. In our factical existence, existence itself (our ability to be) is withdrawn from presence, and to that degree alien. The lectures of the early 1920s had not yet established this polarity between existence and facticity. Rather, they tended to use the term "facticity" for the whole problematic of life and being, as in the series entitled "Hermeneutics of Facticity."[23] *SZ* took a key step forward by differentiating the two and establishing a definite relationship between them.

(iv) Facticity should not be confused with *Vorhandenheit*. "[W]e may not attribute to Da-sein its *own* kind of 'objective presence'.... [T]he factuality of the fact of one's own Da-sein is ontologically totally different from the factual occurrence of a kind of stone. The factuality of the fact Da-sein, as the way in which every Da-sein actually is, we call its *facticity*" (pp. 55–56). Nevertheless, there is some ontological coincidence between facticity and *Vorhandenheit*: to be a given, a datum, a fact, the sheer "Thatness" of being. Not only does this express something we commonly think we intuit under the term "exist"—some readings of Heidegger have given undue prominence to it, i.e., to facticity, and to its related structure, thrownness. Perhaps we are seeing here an influence from Sartre, who can at times identify existence with facticity.

> What is meant here by saying that existence precedes essence? It means that, first of all, man exists, turns up, appears on the scene, and only afterwards defines himself. If man as the existentialist conceives him is indefinable, it is because at first he is nothing. Only afterward will he be something, and he himself will have made what he will be.[24]

What is specific to Heidegger's ontology of Da-sein, on the other hand, is just that existence is differentiated from facticity. Moreover, it is not subordinated to it in the structure of being. Indeed, existence has a certain primacy over it, and that is what justifies using the term "existence" in the broad sense to signify our being as a whole. The substantive point is that in our case there is never a facticity without a possibility, without self-projection, i.e., without existence in the narrow sense. Human beings do not just occur or turn up. Since our "essence" is to exist (ex-sist), we always undertake anew our having to be.

(v) Let us pause over the point that is expressed in the very title of Chapter 6 of the First Division, that "care is the being of Da-sein." We certainly have to ask how that fits with the earlier claim that existence is the "essence" of Da-sein. I suspect that Heidegger's readers have not paused sufficiently over the very phrase "the being of Da-sein," which is a far-from-normal phrase, and hard to interpret. In fact, this is Heidegger's most notable innovation with the word "being": to employ it in these genitive phrases, the being *of* Da-sein (*das Sein des Da-seins*), the being *of* beings, *our* being. They are hard to understand because we cannot take the phrases in any customary way. We cannot interpret the being of Da-sein as the essence of Da-sein, for instance, because that phrase was already consigned to quotation marks: Da-sein has no "Whatness" or quiddity. And we have been told that we cannot construe it as the existence of Da-sein in the common sense of *existentia* or *Vorhandenheit*.

Where existence is the "essence" of Da-sein, we have seen that that means that we are concerned about our futural ability to be—it matters to us, and we anticipate it. And the term "being" can at times signify this existence that we care about. But what Heidegger is saying in Chapter 6 is that, in a more complete and total sense, "being" signifies the very concern or care itself. In this connection, though, the being of Da-sein is not the object of an *existenziell* understanding but an *existenzial* one (see pp. 16 and 192); it is a structure that remains undisclosed to Da-sein's own *existenziell* understanding. It is ontological interpretation that asserts that the *being* of Da-sein is care, and this is an ontological or philosophical application of the term "being." In its everyday life, Da-sein does not focus on its own constitutive care, but on its ability to be.

We could also express the present contrast through a reference to intentionality. Heidegger's variant of intentionality is distinct in two ways. First, it is not any exterior objects of cognition or reference which constitute our primary intentional objects; what comes first is our own existence, the ability to be, about which we care primordially. Second, it is not in the first instance mind or consciousness that is intentional (as in Husserl), nor in the first instance phrases of language (as in Chisholm). Rather the very being of Da-sein, as care, is always intentionally opened up to that about which we care. Our mental and linguistic intentionalities are just the consequence of the ontological structure. If we are all imbued with the *existenziell* understanding of our own existence, whereas it is only our *existenzial* ontology that interprets human being as care, nevertheless the latter is certainly motivated by the former. The futural ability to be about which we care is what first establishes care as the being of Da-sein. We can put this point in Socratic terms: it is the care *for* the soul that first establishes care *within* the soul.

III. Being-in-the-World: The Constitution of Da-sein

Chapter II of Division One lays out what Heidegger calls the "fundamental constitution" (*Grundverfassung*) of Da-sein, to be further investigated in Chapters III to V. He identifies it as "being-in-the-world," and he resolves it into three elements: the world in its worldhood, the "Who" that is in the world, and the very relation of being-in. We may think of this as the proper and technical sense of "constitution" in the tradition of phenomenology, though I have been using the term in this paper in a broader sense, as Heidegger himself often does throughout *SZ* (see pp. 12–13 for one example of many). Heidegger often refers to this as Da-sein's *Seinsverfassung*, the constitution of its being, and so for that reason too it is incumbent on us to examine how his point fits with our two preceding studies. My account will be even more brief than II.

Being-in-the-world is introduced through an exegesis of the term "being," approached through an etymological analysis of *bin* as in *ich bin* (akin to our word "be"). *Bin*, he says, is related to *bei*, so that in origin it means "I dwell, I linger over," an idea that he proceeds to fill out as dwelling in or with the *world*. Thus *sein* should be read as the infinitive of *bin* in this sense. Heidegger points out that all the elements of this constitution should be understood existentially: thus "being-in" is not mere containment but an "existential" relationship (p. 54); the world is not just the collection of all things but an existential structure (p. 64). So the constitution is certainly grasped in connection with the *Existenz* that was introduced earlier. And yet there is a reciprocal relation between Da-sein's "essence" (*Existenz*) and its constitution (being-in-the-world);

Heidegger does not just assimilate this structure to existence, or subordinate it to existence. Da-sein's existence "must be seen and understood *a priori* as grounded upon that constitution of being which we call *being-in-the-world*" (p. 53). One ontological question, then, is how existence is connected to being-in-the-world. To put it formally, how is Da-sein's "essence" connected to its "constitution"? Is it because we exist that we are in the world? Or is it because we are in the world that we exist? Could both be true?

IV. Being and Its Variations

Now I propose to pull together these three elements in the constitution of our being, to see how our "essence" (existence) comes together with our "constitution" (being-in-the-world) and our "being" (care). I'll do this by looking at one short paragraph that comes very early in *SZ*, the second paragraph in Section 4. Here Heidegger uses the word *Sein*, "being," repeatedly. All three of our themes are under discussion here, but without being named or differentiated. We shall see all three of them as variations of being. In each locution where Heidegger speaks of being, we shall see that one of them is intended. Thus the paragraph as a whole offers an outline for the constitution of our being.

In introducing Section 4, Heidegger has been saying that the question of being is of *concern* to us, and this will confirm "the ontic primacy of the question of being" (such is the title of Section 4), which means here the import of this question for the life we lead. The paragraph begins, "Da-sein is a being that does not simply occur among other beings."[25] Differentiating Da-sein from other beings or entities, other things that are, Heidegger says that it does not merely "occur among them" (*nicht nur vorkommt*). The negative of the word *vorkommen* is a subtle foretaste of the way Da-sein is different, for it is not merely present, *vorhanden*, among other things. Now we can specify the contrast further in the light of the later pages we have already reviewed. While other entities occur within the world, Da-sein does not "occur" like them because its constitution is being-*in*-the-world in Heidegger's emphatic sense, dwelling, lingering over. This first sentence, then, has set aside any *Vorhandenheit* of Da-sein, thus making room for *Existenz*. Implicitly, it has invoked the constitution of Da-sein, being-in-the-world. This contrast with other entities does not at all hinder Da-sein's being something that is, *Seiendes*; rather, it brings to the fore the point that Da-sein is a different kind of entity, the point clarified in the next sentence.

> Rather it is ontically distinguished by the fact that, in its being, this very being is of concern to it.[26]

To be ontically distinguished is to be a different kind of being, and we see that the distinction lies in the circumstance that its being concerns it, *ihm geht es um dieses Sein.* We are by no means indifferent to our being, it matters to us. In the exposition, I'll refer to the circumstance that our being matters to us as our non-indifference to our being. Now we must take note of another occurrence of the word "being" in this sentence. Heidegger spoke of the ontic distinction of Da-sein, and yet the true import of this distinction is communicated only subtly in the three words of the present sentence that I shall now italicize: "...ontically distinguished by the fact that, *in its being*, this very being is of concern to it." Heidegger has said with this phrase that the concern we have for our being arises *by virtue* of our being. What differentiates us, therefore, is not a characteristic or property that attaches to our species like the relative hairlessness of our bodies, something ontic. It is an *ontological* distinction, one that pertains to our way of being. To be concerned about our being is fated and ordained for anyone whose being is of our kind. We shall see in a moment that the same will hold for our *relationship* to being and our *understanding* of being—they are not implemented merely by ourselves, but by our very being. So while other things just occur, *vorkommen*, by virtue of their way of being, ours by contrast thrusts us into a concern with this being.

Now in this contrast, it cannot be our existence alone which is salient. Our existence is that character of our being whereby we are ahead of ourselves, out in advance of ourselves. This cannot be the ground for any fate or ordination. The salient factor can only be our facticity and our falling-prey, in their unity with our existence. It is this triad which brings it about that our being concerns us, the triad that constitutes the structure of care.

But in this "concern" that we have about our being, what is it, precisely, that we are concerned *about*? Examining the sentence closely, we discover here a demonstrative "this," *dieses Sein*, which the translation rendered "this very being." So at first glance, the antecedent of *dieses* would be that being, *Sein*, that preceded it in the sentence, and which we have tentatively identified, not as existence, but as care, the unity of existence, facticity and falling-prey. The grammar might thus lead us to think that what is of concern to us is care. Is it, then, that we care about care? We shall see that this is not the case. What concerns us in this way, what matters to us, is specifically our *existence*. At work in this sentence, then, are two meanings of "being," first of all care, and then existence.

In the next sentence, Heidegger draws an inference.

> Thus it is constitutive of the being of Da-sein to have, in its very being, a relation of being to this being.[27]

This sentence is drawing a conclusion (*"Thus* it is constitutive..." "...*gehört aber dann...*"), namely, that we have a relationship to our being. It is inferred from our non-indifference to our being. And that is the reason why we can say, as we did just above, that it is our *existence* that concerns us, or to which we are not indifferent; for just a few lines further down on p. 12 Heidegger says that being to which Da-sein is related is existence, the first mention of existence in the book: "We shall call the very being to which Da-sein can relate in one way or another, and somehow always does relate, existence." So we have a relationship to that which matters to us, our existence.[28] Our being-toward-death, for instance, is a relationship to death, one which may take on different forms—expecting it, hiding it from ourselves, anticipating it, and so on—forms that are analyzed in the chapter on death. We are involved in other relationships to existence as well, i.e., relationships to existential possibility, for what matters to us most of all is how we shall exercise our choices, how we shall define our place in the world, how we shall understand our past life. Concern about existence establishes the relationship to existence.

Heidegger adds in the same sentence that the relationship to existence is constitutive of our being, i.e., it belongs to our *Seinsverfassung*. If we interpret this literally, we might suppose that it is by virtue of our being-in-the-world (our "constitution" in the strict sense) that we have the relationship to existence. But a misunderstanding could arise on that basis: to suppose that being-in-the-world puts us in *relation* to any number of things, things outside ourselves, everything that is *zuhanden* and *vorhanden*, also contexts of meaning, also in relation to the world itself, and *also* in relation to being or existence. We must take every precaution against turning being or existence into that kind of relatum, for that would interpret our relationship to existence as some kind of empirical discovery. Thus, it is unlikely that being-in-the-world is what puts us in relation to our existence. Here we can note two further points.

(i) This relationship is called not only a *Verhältnis* but a *Seinsverhältnis*, a "relationship *of* being." So the relationship *to* being into which our very being or constitution has placed us cannot merely be the *result* of our being-in-the-world, the effect of a cause. It itself is one vital expression of our being. That can only mean an expression of our *existence*; it is an existential relationship. The relationship to being (existence) is no mere fact with which we must reckon. It is, instead, a possibility for us, a part of our ability to be, by virtue of which we are ahead of ourselves, *sich vorweg*. Yet, still, we can continue to ask whether it is our constitution in the strict sense, our being-in-the-world, that puts us into this existential relationship to existence.

(ii) If it is the constitution of our being that brings with it our relationship to being, this must be understood as a two-way relationship. For we note that Heidegger has once again added the three little words, *in seinem Sein*, "in its very being." Because of their parallelism with the words of the previous sentence, we should take these three words, not as an exclusive reference to existence, but rather to the unity of existence, facticity and falling-prey. Thus, it is not through our adopting some particular relationship to being or existence that we first enter into a relationship to being; not, for example, by our having made some decisions about death (perhaps evading it, perhaps anticipating it) that we enter into a relationship to death. We were, rather, cast into that relationship just by virtue of our being. Our being has established our existential relationship to being (existence) in advance of any of our attitudes or decisions. This leads us to clarify what the *Seinsverfassung* (constitution) is by virtue of which we have a relationship to being. Heidegger introduced it again with the demonstrative adjective, *zu dieser Seinsverfassung*, implying that this constitution was already indicated either in the preceding sentence or in the two preceding sentences. What we have read is that to care about our existence is given to us as soon as we are—we can never just occur in the world. That is the constitution of our being. I do not think we can identify the present constitution as, strictly and solely, our being-in-the-world. Instead, this constitution is our care; or rather it is the temporality of Da-sein that will ultimately forge the unity and meaning of Da-sein's essential care, i.e., the temporality that is *the constitution of care*. So it is by virtue of our existential temporality that we are cast into the existential relationship to our existence.

Having derived our relationship to being from our non-indifference to it, Heidegger now undertakes a further derivation: of our understanding of being.

> And this in turn means that Da-sein understands itself in its being in some way and with some explicitness. It is proper to this being that it be disclosed to itself with and through its being. *Understanding of being is itself a determination of the being of Da-sein.*[29]

Here and in many other texts Heidegger identifies two elements that are understood together: we understand *ourselves*, and we understand ourselves in our *being*. Here this is inferred from the foregoing account of the relationship to being, which was a component in our constitution. The *Seinsverständnis* is inferred from the *Seinsverhältnis*, a part of the *Seinsverfassung*. Our being concerns us; hence we have a relationship to it; hence we understand it.

Heidegger has already said—with the three little words—that our concern for being derived from our being. So did our relationship to it. The same point applies to our understanding of it: "It is proper to this being that it be disclosed to itself with and through its being"—not only "with," but also "through." And this is further emphasized in the italicized sentence that identifies our

Seinsverständnis as a determination of our being, *eine Seinsbestimmtheit.* It is an aspect of our being that we are ontological, endowed with the understanding (*logos*) of being (*tou ontos*). "The ontic distinction of Dasein lies in the fact that it *is* ontological."[30] The wording of this claim continues to undergird the running emphasis that our concern for being, our relationship to it and understanding of it are to be understood not only as endowments of ourselves or our species, but as expressions of our being. By italicising the last word *ist*, Heidegger is playing on the double possibility of a German word to function both as adjective and adverb. The ontological character, then, attaches not only to us but to our way of being: we are ontological, but it is also true that we *are*, ontologically.

It is especially ourselves in our existence that we understand in this *Seinsverständnis*. And the wording of the last four sentences makes it plain that according to Heidegger our self-understanding is a function of our understanding of being. We are not disclosed to ourselves except "with and through our being." We are disclosed as existing, for this understanding follows from our relationship to being qua existence. Both our self-understanding and our understanding of being are qualified heavily here: ". . . in some way and with some explicitness." That is how the present text recognizes a distinction that surfaces regularly in *SZ* and other texts of the 1920s. There could be an explicit doctrine of the self and an explicit doctrine of being, both developed with accurate reasoning and sharp concepts, and defended against doubt or antagonism. That would be a philosophical understanding, or what Heidegger calls in *SZ* an ontological interpretation. But what is under discussion here is something far less developed than that, something that is shadowy and vague by comparison, but which nevertheless is present universally in human beings, affording the foundation for the ontological doctrines that philosophers develop. This is the *pre*-ontological understanding of being, *vorontologisches Seinsverständnis*.

Two further possibilities are given to us along with the pre-ontological understanding of being. One is that it should become ontological, as in a philosophical analysis such as *SZ* itself or the present paper. This possibility is pointed out in the paragraph that follows the one I have been quoting. The other possibility is the derivation of all knowledge, especially scientific knowledge, from the pre-ontological understanding of being. True, Heidegger has shown up to the present point only that we possess such an understanding of our *own* being, our own way of being, existence. But the next point, so vital for building up our system of scientific knowledge, is that we also possess an understanding of the being of all things in addition to our own being. The understanding of being is not egocentrically confined (*SZ*, p. 13). There is a difference between our own being and that of other things, yet we also have an understanding of the being of things in the world, so there is a differentiation *within* our understanding of being. This is determined by our being-in-the-world. The differentiation within the *Seinsverständnis* is not empirically grounded, as if, by bumping into different kinds of things, we formed an understanding of them and then of their being; rather, it is an a priori division that lies at the ground of the possibility of experience. The disposition to science is inscribed in our constitution.

V. Summary

Let us take a retrospective view of the last four sections. I have been showing that *SZ* offers a plurality of senses of the term "being," *das Sein*, even when we confine our attention to our own way of being, *das Sein das Da-seins*. *Sein* may be existence (ability to be), or being-in-the-world, or care, and each of these has its own distinct constitution. I believe the analysis shows that it would be futile to proceed by abstraction to formulate an overarching sense of "being," *Sinn von Sein*, that would be generic for the variants we identified. In Section 4, nevertheless, I sought to show that the three variants are not isolated from each other, that they are intertwined to form the genuine constitution of our being, one concrete *Sinn von Sein* rather than an abstract one. We could give expression to it by a series of add-ons: (a) our being is being-in-the-world; yet, by the intertwining, we can now add (b) that to be human means to be *able*-to-be-in-the-world, *In-der-Welt-Seinkönnen*; going further, we add (c) that being human means to be *concerned* about your ability-to-be-in-the-world—*uns geht es um das In-der-Welt-Seinkönnen*. Our existing in the form of care puts us in a relationship to our own being, and prompts our understanding of it. But while we focus on our existing ability-to-be in the pre-ontological understanding of being that we all have, this latter does not encompass the being of Da-sein as care. That our own being is care is occluded in pre-ontological awareness, and only a philosophical interpretation will reveal it. That implies that Da-sein's temporality is never fully encompassed in pre-ontological awareness.

Now the ontology of Da-sein was to serve as the fundamental ontology, the guideline for every other ontological inquiry. That does *not* mean that entities of other groups—animal, vegetable and mineral—will have to exhibit care, existence, or being-in-the-world. Quite the contrary! It *does* mean, though, that we should not expect to find simple or generic formulations of being when we turn to these other domains. That there are manifold senses of "being" is one of the deepest truths of all philosophy. But we might hope that, in these domains too, some of the variants will allow themselves to be woven together.

The fundamental character of the ontology of Da-sein also implies that inquiry into the being of other things will always take its start from Da-sein's pre-ontological understanding of being. I'll conclude by developing that point.

VI. Anthropology and Philosophy of Mind

The inquiry into our own being was undertaken with a view to the question of being generally: what *is* it to be? And the inquiry has led to our pre-ontological understanding of being. By virtue of our constitution as being-in-the-world, this understanding is not solipsistically confined to ourselves, but "implies the understanding of something like 'world' and the understanding of the being of beings accessible within the world" (p. 13). The pre-ontological understanding of being becomes the grounding for the ontologies of specific domains of reality which become disclosed by the special sciences. Section 3 mentions a few of the domains: history, nature, space, life, human being,[31] language, and a bit later it mentions a few divisions of science (not quite overlapping): mathematics, physics, biology, the humanities, theology. The fundamental concepts of a science (its *Grundbegriffe*) constitute the ontology appropriate to the domain it researches. Section 4 clarifies the ultimate root of these regional ontologies: "Ontologies which have beings unlike Da-sein as their theme are accordingly founded and motivated in the ontic structure of Da-sein itself. This structure includes in itself the determination of a pre-ontological understanding of being" (p. 13).

Physics is the science most often mentioned by Heidegger. It becomes constituted as a specific domain of inquiry when its objects are delineated in general through fundamental concepts such as matter, energy, motion, space and time. The initial delineation of this domain, with these fundamental structures, occurred, of course, in pre-scientific experience. But different values or interpretations can be assigned to these fundamental structures, and thereby arise the different versions of physics throughout history. Without some understanding of being there could be no science, and here that means: without an understanding of what it is to be a physical thing there could be no physics. The values accorded to those fundamental structures (matter, etc.) determine what it is to be a physical object, and that constitutes the ontology for the domain that is researched by physics, the domain that Heidegger generally calls nature. Section 69 (b) describes how modern mathematical physics came to be constituted around the time of Galileo. Modern physics arose through a revision of the understanding of being that guided research on nature. For instance, Galileo's science depended upon a "mathematical projection of nature" that projected a priori a universal continuum of space whereby any body could in principle occupy any location (pp. 361–64).

Heidegger has pointed to a number of distinct regional ontologies, not just the physicist's mathematical projection of nature, and what is of interest in the present context is that one of these encompasses the domain he calls "human being," Da-sein. An analytic of Da-sein has served us as a "fundamental ontology" for the purpose of raising the general question of being. But afterwards there will need to be a second study of Da-sein, no longer as a laboratory for fundamental ontology, but rather as one specific domain of that which is. It will be an "anthropology" (see Section 5, p. 17, and Sec. 10, pp. 46–50) which will contain, first, an "ontological foundation" (p. 17) that outlines what it is to be human, and then a detailed study of such phenomena as "body, soul and spirit" (p. 48), a human science that will intersect with psychology and biology (pp. 49–50), and, I would add, with physiology and other medical sciences, and the philosophy of mind. In the course of its analytic of Da-sein, the fundamental ontology will have presented already some of the materials for an eventual anthropology—especially its ontological part—but only in fragmentary form and not in the order that would be required for anthropological theory (p. 17). Earlier I pointed out that *SZ* had to contain some parts of the study of being for which it was to serve as the preparation, implying thereby some circularity in Heidegger's overall project. The anthropology that is already contained in *SZ* counts as a further circularity that modifies the official foundationalism of its method. This is the consequence of granting that, in an ontic respect, Da-sein is the human being. It is not some other entity. The same Da-sein is the subject of a fundamental ontology and then of an anthropology.

Let us then look at a few of these details in the text. Could they be re-worked into the format of a psychology or a philosophy of mind? We could pursue Heidegger's treatment of the emotions, e.g., fear and anxiety (Sections 30, 40 and 68, B), which could certainly be brought into connection with other kinds of psychology. But it will be more germane to this paper to pursue topics in the text that are connected with our "understanding" (*Verstehen*) and therefore our existence, ek-sistence, our *Seinkönnen*, being out in advance of self. These topics lend themselves to a treatment in connection with the philosophy of mind. There are many places where the structure of existence is very given concrete interpretations: the existential structure of Da-sein's death is actually being-*toward*-death (Section 50); the authentic response to anxiety is readiness-*for*-anxiety (Section 60); the existential form of conscience is *wanting-to-have-*a-conscience (Section 54). And now the case that I'll look at in detail: to hear is *to-be-able-to*-hear (*Hörenkönnen*, Section 34).

On pages 163–65, Heidegger is treating hearing as one expression of our understanding, and he intends the latter in his technical sense, being-ahead-of-self. Indeed he makes the claim (perhaps too strong) that "hearing even constitutes the primary and authentic openness of Da-sein for its own-most ability to be (*eigenstes Seinkönnen*)" (p. 163). That is expressed when he calls it *Hörenkönnen*, ability to hear. Section 34 introduces hearing in connection with discourse and language, speech and utterance, so his initial interest is how we hear and understand one another in discourse. What he emphasizes especially is that hearing is ex-sistent or self-surpassing, in being the ground for our paying heed to what is said, hearkening to it. This leads him to take issue with other psychological accounts, which we might assign, actually, to the philosophy of mind. He notes that since hearkening (*Horchen*) is rooted in the *ability* to hear (*Hörenkönnen*), it is "more primordial than what the psychologist 'initially' defines as hearing, the sensing of tones and the perception of sounds" (p. 163). A further transcendence achieved by the hearer is to be brought into contact with that with which the discourse was concerned: "we are already together with the other beforehand, with the being which the discourse is about" (p. 164). In this treatment of the hearing of discourse, Heidegger pictures us as being together in a human world (a *Mitwelt*, a shared world), so that Da-sein's ability-to-be-in-the-world can be expressed as the ability-to-*hear*-[each other]-in-the-shared-world. More than that, we are all motivated to understand one another this way; we have the *concern* to be able to hear in the world. Notice that we can substitute "hear" for "be."

Another opportunity for connecting this to the philosophy of mind appears when Heidegger generalizes his treatment of hearing, going beyond the initial context of discourse, and looks at hearing in relation to our being-in-an-environing-world.

> Hearkening, too, has the mode of being of a hearing that understands. "Initially" we never hear noises and complexes of sound, but the creaking wagon, the motorcycle. We hear the column on the march, the north wind, the woodpecker tapping, the crackling fire (p. 163).

And we are *concerned* to be able to hear things, and different situations actually become expressed in different ways. The woodpecker tapping can be *discerned* by the experienced forester, though not the tyro, whose concern is to become capable of this. An enemy column on the march can be *detected* by an experienced sergeant, not by a raw recruit. Whereas the hearing of discourse expressed our being together with others, some of these modes express our circumspective concern with the environment. In all cases, though, hearing has the existential structure expressed by *Hörenkönnen*. It is always the anticipation of a further hearing; the sergeant *listens for* more clues. The character of hearing as the existing ability to hear is also expressed in the connection between what we hear and what we do. If I can hear the wagons, I know that it is time to leave.

There is a similar point to be made about seeing—it too is a *Sehenkönnen* (Heidegger uses this term on p. 346). To begin with a simple example, an optometrist might ask you what letters you see on his chart. Your likely reply: "I can see *A* on the top line." "Can." That does not mean an ocular potentiality on your part, as if we were ascribing it to you before you entered the optometrist's office, so that, if you *were* to enter the office, you *would* see the letter *A*. No, this expresses the act of seeing itself as "can see." Many more examples can illustrate our concern-for-being-able-to-see-in-the-world: "The ships have arrived. Can you see them?" "Yes." I can quote a sort of gallows ballad by the country singer Johnny Cash, "25 Minutes to Go," in which the hero is counting down the minutes remaining to him. With just three more minutes to go, he is taking leave of his world:

> I can see the mountains,
> I can see the sky.

But the moment of death approaches, and with just one minute left to go, he wails

> I can see the buzzards,
> I can hear the crows.

At this point I may observe that an existential treatment does not lead us to resolve perception or sensation into its separate channels, seeing, hearing, etc. If I can hear the car without seeing it, there is a latent or merely signified portion of my understanding, a portion that very definitely belongs to the understanding. Indeed, even a figure that is seen is actually a fusion of the latent and manifest profiles, like the street facade of a house, where the signified or latent depth of the object has not been brought to view. There is certainly more here than we can now explore—but my present point is that what *Sehenkönnen* and *Hörenkönnen* are *capable of* always outruns the measurable stimulations of the moment.

It follows from these observations that, in an existential analysis, there is no place for what are often called "mental events." It is not only that we cannot reduce our hearing of discourse, or our spotting ships in the harbor, to an auditory or visual mental state—more than that, it is that the ontology of existence cannot accommodate such states or events at all. I have no wish to deny the physical events of stimulation that accompany our bodily exposure to the persons and things in the world. But the "mental events, states, processes" that we call seeing, sensing, believing, etc., are extraneous to any account of human experience. To express the matter roughly, philosophers and others have come to believe in such events or states only because they are thought to be the direct effects of the physical stimulation of our organs, so that, in their absence, one might not be able to explain how it is that we hear woodpeckers or people speaking.

But this brings us to an important confrontation between the existential account of seeing, hearing, etc., and the physicalist or materialist tradition in recent English-language philosophy of mind. And I shall make the case that this tradition has been led to its "mental events and states" because of its adopting a different fundamental ontology from the one we have explored here. Let me refer to one of the seminal papers in this tradition, that of Smart.[32] We read that there is a psychic event: seeing a yellowish-orange after-image (p. 169). Smart maintains that this sensation is not merely *caused by* a brain process, or associated with it in some other way, but is the very same thing, identical with it, just as a lightning-bolt is not merely *caused* by a discharge of ions in the atmosphere but is the very same thing. Now Smart's identity-theory is hardly the last word in the modern philosophy of mind, but I pick it out because of its way of speaking about psychic events, a form of discourse that is retained even by Smart's critics. What if, instead of discussing this "after-image" case in Smart's physicalistic lexicon, we spoke of it in Heidegger's existential terms? Here a critical confrontation can be followed between the physicalist philosophy of mind and an anthropology of existential inspiration.

Following the ontology of existence, we would approach the case supposed by Smart, not as a so-called mental event, but as being *able to see* (*Sehenkönnen*). Suppose a psychologist asks a subject "Do you see a yellowish-orange after-image?" The subject will likely reply, "Yes, I can see it." "Can." To see is to be *able* to see. This expresses the seeing itself as the ability to see. It is basically wrong to bring this experience under the category of events. The main physicalist distortion enters in when we identify the experience as a mental event. Seeing, ability to see, *Sehenkönnen,* is not an event at all. Our current seeing is constituted by the projection of a further seeing in the coming moments, constituted therefore by possibility. This is true even of that seeing which focuses on unreal objects such as a yellowish after-image. Even here, to see that object is to fix it, thus to *seek* to fix it, i.e., to anticipate a further seeing which will focus now on the left side of the object, and then on its right side. This exercise can only be understood in terms of the self-surpassing that informs existence.

I believe that this physicalism arose through the influence of a different fundamental ontology. Whereas Heidegger, like Socrates, begins from ourselves and our being, the contemporary philosophers of mind are often like Democritus, beginning from a survey of nature as a whole, from physics, chemistry, biology and psychology. The philosophy of mind proceeds from nature, with all its laws, toward the human being, by way of the human body which expresses all of nature's laws. But this inquiry too has opted for a fundamental ontology: that of physics. Not only do these philosophers take from physics, chemistry and biology an account of light, sound, stimulation, the neuron, and so on; not only do they regard physics as being the fundamental science within the array of natural sciences; they also treat the regional ontology of nature, i.e., the ontology appropriate to physics, as if it could also be the grounding or fundamental ontology for all other inquiries. The ontological notions appropriate to physics, especially causality and the physical interpretations of time and space, are made into a fundamental ontology even within philosophy. The key problem in this philosophy of mind is that, on the one hand, there is the neuron, the stimulus, etc., and on the other hand there is the sensation, the belief, etc. What is the correlation between the bodily states or events and the mental states or events? These philosophers approach the problem against the background of physics, whose *Grundbegriffe* they are content to treat as fundamental for all ontology.

Such philosophy may suppose that it is getting by with no particular understanding of being at all, but it is easy to show that the bodily and mental phenomena treated by this philosophy are described and understood under categories drawn from the physical domain: causality, and a certain interpretation of time that is assumed in the category of "event" and "state" (mental event and bodily event, mental state and bodily state). But nobody has ever shown that the *Grundbegriffe* of physics are able to furnish a fundamental ontology.

Notes

1. Martin Heidegger, *Being and Time*, translated by Joan Stambaugh (Albany: State University of New York Press, 1996). Like Stambaugh, I'll treat "Da-sein" as an English word, not italicized unless I'm quoting a German context, and, like Stambaugh, I'll hyphenate it, in accord with Heidegger's own suggestion (*op. cit.*, p. xiv). Page references will be to the German text of 1927, as in the margins of the translation.

2. The key texts are *Apology* 19b–24a and *Phaedo* 96a–100a.

3. *Tusculanae disputationes*, 5, 4, 10.

4. These philosophers' work has been widely disseminated and repeatedly anthologized. Later, I shall refer to some of the materials in the anthology edited by David M. Rosenthal, *The Nature of Mind* (New York: Oxford University Press, 1991). My comments in the text could not be applied to those philosophers who work from Artificial Intelligence or mathematics.

5. François Raffoul, *Heidegger and the Subject* (Atlantic Highlands, N.J.: Humanities Press, 1998). Raffoul has assembled all the relevant Heideggerian texts, from the 1920s and later, treating them in much more detail than such earlier works, excellent in their way, as Hubert Dreyfus, *Being-in-the-World* (Cambridge, Mass.: MIT Press, 1991) and Frederick Olafson, *Heidegger and the Philosophy of Mind* (New Haven: Yale University Press, 1987). Raffoul's main target, however, is the "continental" current of an "anti-humanistic" reading of Heidegger.

6. On the absolutely crucial difference between an entity and its being (or between *a* being and its being), see my article "The Ontological Difference," *American Philosophical Quarterly 33* (1996): 357–74.

7. *SZ*, pp. 152–53, 314–15.

8. Otto Pöggeler, *Martin Heidegger's Path of Thinking*, trans. Daniel Magurshak and Sigmund Barber (Atlantic Highlands, N.J.: Humanities Press, 1987). Original publication, *Der Denkweg Martin Heideggers* (Pfullingen: Neske, 1963).

9. Author's marginal note to *SZ*, p. 316.

10. Theodore Kisiel, *The Genesis of Heidegger's Being and Time* (Berkeley and Los Angeles: The University of California Press, 1993). See also the essay by Kisiel "Heidegger (1920–21) on Becoming a Christian: A Conceptual Picture-Show" in Kisiel, T. and John Van Buren, *Reading Heidegger From the Start* (Albany: SUNY Press, 1994), pp. 175–92.

11. Kisiel, in Kisiel and Van Buren, *Reading Heidegger From the Start*, p. 178.

12. Kisiel, *Genesis*, pp. 21–25, 32–35, 123–37, 153–56.

13. Kisiel, *Genesis*, pp. 394–97.

14. John D. Caputo, *Demythologizing Heidegger* (Bloomington: Indiana University Press, 1993).

15. Jean-Luc Marion, *God Without Being*, trans. T. A. Carlson (Chicago: Chicago University Press, 1991).

16. Joanna Hodge, *Heidegger and Ethics* (London: Routledge, 1995), Chapters 1 and 6. One must not overlook, however, her stern criticism of Heidegger's *political* thought and practice in the intervening chapters.

17. The exception: Sections 19–21 which offer an exposition of Descartes with many quotations in Latin.

18. S. Kierkegaard: "This paradox, that the single individual is higher than the universal . . . " " . . . to exist as the individual is the most terrifying thing of all . . . " *Fear and Trembling*, trans. A. Hannay (London: Penguin Books, 1985), p. 84 and p. 102. Or: "Existence separates, and holds the various moments of existence discretely apart . . . " "But if he is a human being, then he is also an existing individual," *Concluding Unscientific Postscript*, trans. D. F. Swenson and W. Lowrie (Princeton: Princeton University Press, 1968), p. 107 and p. 109; the entire thesis of pp. 99–103 is that a system of existence is impossible.

K. Jaspers: "*Existenz*, as the possibility of decision derivable from no universal validity, is an origin in time, is the individual as historicity." *Reason and Existenz*, trans. Wm. Earle (New York: Noonday Press, 1955), p. 62.

19. Details on the predicating gerund appear in my paper "The Ontological Difference," alluded to above.

20. I'm indebted to *The Oxford Latin Dictionary* (Oxford: Clarendon Press, 1968) for specific references to texts of Cicero, Caesar and Lucretius, and to the *Thesaurus Linguae Latinae* (Leipzig: Teubner, 1953) for further references to authors of the classical and post-classical periods.

21. *The Basic Problems of Phenomenology*, trans. A. Hofstadter (Bloomington: Indiana University Press, 1988), p. 170 (pp. 241–42 of the original German text).

22. This phenomenological term was first introduced on p. 13, but, beginning in Section 39, it is often used instead of the simpler "existence" when the narrower scope of the term is under discussion.

23. Heidegger refers back to these lectures in *SZ*, footnote 1, p. 72 (the note appears on p. 401 of the Stambaugh translation, as Note 1 of Chapter III). See also Kisiel, *Genesis*, pp. 26–35.

24. "Existentialism is a Humanism," translated by B. Frechtman, in *Existentialism and Human Emotions* (New York: Philosophical Library, 1957), p. 15. This doctrine is not only found in such popular texts. See, e.g., " *Le cogito préréflexif et l'être du percipere*" in *L'être et le néant* (Paris: Gallimard, 1943), pp. 16–23.

25. *Das Dasein ist ein Seiendes, das nicht nur unter anderem Seienden vorkommt (SZ, p. 12).*

26. *Es ist vielmehr dadurch ontisch ausgezeichnet, daß es diesem Seienden in seinem Sein um dieses Sein selbst geht.*

27. *Zu dieser Seinsverfassung des Daseins gehört aber dann, daß es in seinem Sein zu diesem Sein ein Seinsverhältnis hat.*

28. Whether there really are no other beings that are concerned about their being is a biological question that is incidental here, because our present concern is the positive expression of the being of Da-sein, not a negative characterization of whatever is not Da-sein.

29. *Und dies wiederum besagt: Dasein versteht sich in irgendeiner Weise und Ausdrücklichkeit in seinem Sein. Diesem Seienden eignet, daß mit und durch sein Sein dieses ihm selbst erschlossen ist. Seinsverständnis ist selbst eine Seinsbestimmtheit des Daseins.*

30. *Die ontische Auszeichnung des Daseins liegt darin, daß es ontologisch ist.*

31. So Stambaugh translates *Da-sein* in this context, and, as we shall see, it is the right translation.

32. J. J. C. Smart, "Sensations and Brain Processes," in Rosenthal, ed., *The Nature of Mind*, pp. 169–76.

4

Heidegger's Anti-Dualism: Beyond Mind and Matter

Charles Guignon

1

"To think is to confine yourself to a single thought," Heidegger said.[1] In his case, the single thought dominating his life was the question of being, the question that traditionally is understood to ask: What is it for beings of various sorts to be what they are? The question of being can seem hopelessly abstruse until we see its relevance for the dominant ways of thinking in the philosophical tradition. In Heidegger's view, many of the intractable puzzles that run through philosophy first arise because we uncritically buy into a particular conception of what things are. We assume that anything that exists—whether it be a rock, a tool, a human being, an artwork, a number or a text—must be regarded as a *substance* of some sort. On the traditional view, "substance" refers to that which "lies under" the attributes something has, that which endures through changes of properties. In modern times, under the influence of Descartes, we have been inclined to suppose that there are two basic kinds of substance, mind and matter, where these are understood to refer to basic types of stuff (the nonphysical and the physical). Everything that exists, we assume, must be either material, or mental, or some combination of the two.

Substance dualism provides the basis for some of our most fundamental assumptions about what it takes to make sense of human phenomena. It seems to be crucial, for example, in explaining human agency. The standard conception of action holds that we need to make a distinction between "outer" behavior—the movement of a physical substance—and the "inner" intentions, purposes,

beliefs and desires that cause the behavior. The physical event (e.g., the movement of my vocal chords when I speak) is seen as only an external sign of the
inner intention (e.g., conveying information) that animates the behavior and
makes it into an action. This account of human agency leads to a split between
outer and inner, the physical and the mental, which is so deeply ingrained in our
thinking that even strictly physicalist accounts of human phenomena assume
we must be able to identify some physical correlate of the mental—namely,
events in the brain—if we are to account for human agency.

Substance dualism is also reinforced by one of the most basic assumptions
of modern science: the distinction between what is objective, actually "out
there" in the physical universe, and what is merely subjective, existing only in
our minds. Modern science is built on the assumption that we can abstract
out from experience those features of things we project into them given our
interests and dispositions, in order to be able to identify the characteristics
of reality as it is in itself. For the early scientists, the truly objective features
of a thing were those that are quantifiable—properties such as mass, velocity
and space-time position. In contrast, such features of experienced reality as
function, meaningfulness, aesthetic value and moral goodness were seen as
purely subjective, projections of our minds onto things rather than properties
of the things themselves.

The ability to draw a clear distinction between "what is really out there
in the world" and "what is only in here, in the mind" is rightly regarded as
a cornerstone of rationality. But, as is well known, the subjective/objective
distinction also tends to support the idea that all values and meanings are
ultimately subjective, creations of our own minds, with no basis in objective
reality. The distinction between facts "out there" and purely subjective values
leads to some counter-intuitive consequences. It seems to imply, for example,
that if a child is hit by a car, then something bad has happened not out there in the
street, but rather "in here," in our minds. Such counter-intuitive results suggest
that there is a deep gap between our concrete experience of things in actual life
and the theoretical framework we use to make sense of that experience.

Most attempts to show the relevance of Heidegger's thought for contemporary philosophical problems have tended to focus on his critique of mentalism
and, in particular, his attack on representationalist accounts of the mind. Interpretations of this sort are useful in showing how Heidegger's picture of human
existence undercuts specific assumptions about the mental, but they run the
risk of making it look like his views are consistent with a philosophical natural-
ism that tries to account for everything in purely physicalist terms. In order to
appreciate the full impact of Heidegger's thought, then, we need to see that his
conception of our everyday ways of being-in-the-world puts in question not just
the mental, but the very idea of substance itself, including physical substance.

To get a sense of how Heidegger undermines the substance ontology, it will be helpful to see his attempt to answer the question of being as moving toward a picture of the human as an *event* rather than as a substance of any sort.[2] Starting with a phenomenological description of our "average everyday" ways of being as agents in the world, Heidegger tries to lead us to see that the concepts of mental and physical substance generally have no crucial role to play in making sense of what shows up in our lives. His claim is not that the mental and physical do not exist, but that what we encounter "proximally and for the most part" in our ordinary lives need not be thought of in terms of the substance ontology. In Heidegger's view, our ability to encounter anything, including substances of various sorts, is derivative from and dependent upon a way of encountering things in which the idea of substance simply does not arise. Thus, the account of everydayness aims at *deflating* the notion of substance. The idea of substance turns out to be the product of some fairly high-level theorizing with nothing crucial to contribute to making sense of our lives and our world. As I hope to show, when the distinction between inner and outer is undermined, it becomes possible to see the fact/value distinction as having no general significance beyond the rather specialized concerns of the natural sciences. On the view of human existence that emerges from Heidegger's event ontology, we can see that understanding what we *are* has implications for our beliefs about how we *ought* to live.

2

Heidegger holds that the reason why traditional philosophy has tended to conceive of human beings as *things* or *objects* of some sort is that this is the way entities show up when we adopt a stance of pure theoretical reflection. To avoid slipping into the presuppositions of the tradition, then, Heidegger proposes we bracket the conceptions that arise from focusing on what shows up in the theoretical attitude, and start afresh by looking at the way things show up in the midst of everyday activities in familiar contexts. The goal is to see how far we can go in making sense of human phenomena without imposing concepts drawn from traditional theories. The description of human existence (or *Dasein*, the German word Heidegger uses to refer to the human) gives us a picture of a human being not as a thing or object, but rather as an event, the unfolding realization of a life as a whole. Dasein is described as the entity for whom its being—that is, its life as a whole—is *at issue* for it (32). We are beings who *care* about what we are. In living out our lives, Heidegger says, what we are—our identity as humans—is always *in question* or *at stake* for us.

Because we care about our lives, we are always taking some concrete *stand* on who we are. By taking a stand as a teacher, for example, I give a coherent shape and direction to one important dimension of my life. The specific stand I take in turn gives me some general sense of who I am: as Heidegger says, "It is peculiar to this entity that with and through its being, this being is disclosed to it. *Understanding of being is itself a definite characteristic of Dasein's being.*"[3] As agents who have mastered some set of roles and lifestyles in the world, we all have a "vague, average understanding" of what it is to be (25). Given my understanding of myself as a teacher, I understand a great deal about how school systems work, how I should relate to students and other teachers, how classrooms are to be used, and so forth. It is important to see that when Heidegger speaks of "understanding," he is referring not so much to a cognitive state as to the tacit know-how we pick up and embody as we become initiated into the forms of life of our world. This background sense of how things count in everyday life provides the basis for trying to give an explicit account of what things are all about.

In taking a stand on our lives, we exist as a "happening" or "movement" of a particular sort. Human existence is characterized as a "becoming" or "emergence-into-being," the ongoing flow of a life course "between birth and death" (276). When we conceive of a human as an event in this way, we will see that there are two primary aspects or dimensions that define the structure of a life. The first of these is called *situatedness*, and it embraces all that has come before and is currently defining one's situation in the world. The second dimension is called *projection*, and it refers to the *futural* dimension of a life happening, the way Dasein in its actions is constantly pressing forward toward the realization or definition of its identity. Each of these aspects of human existence should be examined in turn.

To say that we find ourselves "situated" is to say that we are always *thrown* into a world, already under way in realizing specific roles and styles of comportment made accessible by the surrounding cultural context. On Heidegger's view, our thrownness or facticity is something that becomes manifest through the various moods that come over us. We always find ourselves in some mood or other—where even the bland grayness of humdrum existence counts as a mood—and these moods reveal our basic way of being situated in the world.

Heidegger's discussion of moods shows how his conception of Dasein can bypass the inner/outer dichotomy. The German word for mood, *Stimmung*, is also the word for "tuning," as in "tuning a piano," and so it conveys a sense of being tuned in to things in a particular way. At any time, we are attuned to the world through our affective orientation—as fearful, blasé, irritable, upbeat, or some other way. Our moods give us a fix on things, and they thereby make it possible for entities in the world to stand out as *mattering* to us in some determinate way. It would be wrong, however, to think of these moods as inner or subjective. "We must dismiss the psychology of feelings, experiences and consciousness," Heidegger says, and instead think of a mood as "like an atmosphere in which we first immerse ourselves in each case and which then attunes us through and through."[4] Speaking of the mood of grief, Heidegger says, "It is not at all 'inside' in some interiority, only to appear in the flash of an eye; but for this reason it is *not at all outside either.* Attunement is not some being that appears in the soul as an experience, but the way of our being there with one another" (FCM 66). Because moods define how things can *count* for us, they provide the mode of access through which we first gain our sense of where we stand and how things are going. "Attunements are the '*how*' [Wie] according to which one is in such and such a way" (FCM 66).

The second structural component of our lives is projection. In our practical involvements, we are constantly driving forward into the future, underway in accomplishing things. We are always "ahead-of-ourselves" in the sense that, in each of our actions, we are taking a step toward realizing particular possibilities that define our identity as agents of a particular sort: as a parent, a teacher, a coward, and so forth. Heidegger says that this notion of projection is familiar to us from such everyday experiences as "planning in the sense of the anticipatory regulating of human comportment" (FCM 362). In his own use of the term "projection," however, he is trying to get at something more fundamental than conscious goal-setting and planning. "'Projection' does not refer to some sequence of actions or to some process we might piece together from individual phases," he writes; "rather it is what refers to the unity of an action, but of an originary and properly unique kind of action" (FCM 363). This originary action is the defining feature of Dasein's being: it's taking a stand in the sense of giving shape to its life as a totality. To say that we exist as projections into the future is to say that we are always composing our life-stories in the things we do, and that we are therefore ultimately responsible for the *Gestalt* or overall shape our lives ultimately have. This movement toward our own completion (*Ergänzung* [FCM 363]) is called "being-toward-death," where "death" refers not to one's demise, but to the fact that we are finite beings and therefore always stand before the possibility of having no more possibilities.

It is because we exist as a forward-directed thrust toward our completion that Heidegger describes the temporality peculiar to human existence as "bringing itself to fruition" (*sich zeitigen*). As an unfolding life story, Dasein is constantly making decisions about which possibilities it will follow through on and which it will let slide. Taking a stand as a teacher and a parent, for example, I find myself faced with a number of decisions about how to develop a personal style, balance roles, and prioritize goals. It may be the case that many of these decisions are made by simply drifting into certain patterns of action or by doing what seems unavoidable. But even when I act without any thought, I am doing things that define my identity—my *being*—as a person of a particular sort, and in this sense I am, in all my actions, choosing what my life amounts to as a whole.

To be human, then, is to be a *thrown projection*. We find ourselves thrown into a particular situation, with a determinate range of public self-interpretations available to us, and we are always taking up this thrownness in our undertakings as we live out our lives. To say that we exist as thrown projections is to say that, for the most part, we just *are* what we *do*. I am what I make of myself in taking a stand on the possibilities made available in my world. On this account, there are no "essences" or fixed "facts" about humans that determine what they must be or how they should act. This is what Heidegger means when he says, "*The 'essence' of Dasein lies in its existence*" (67). Since the traits we are born with are defined and given a specific shape by the ways we take them over in existing, there is nothing that compels us to be one way rather than another. Whether I realize it or not, my identity is something I am creating through my actions. Because we are all "answerable" or "responsible" for what our lives add up to, Heidegger says that Dasein is always "in each case mine."

3

Hubert Dreyfus's commentary on Division I of *Being and Time* has shown in detail how Heidegger portrays human existence as inextricably bound up with a public lifeworld.[5] On the account of being-in-the-world found in *Being and Time*, to be human is to be enmeshed in a familiar lifeworld—the world of theater, for example, or the academic world—in such a way that, under normal conditions, there is no way to draw a clear distinction between a "self" component and a "world" component. We can get an idea of how Heidegger conceives of this "unified phenomenon" of being-in-the-world if we consider what it is like to actually be caught up in a specific situation. Imagine a case where you have done something socially inappropriate—perhaps worn the wrong attire to a formal function. This situation has a particular significance: it is what we all recognize as an embarrassing situation. Realizing that you are improperly dressed, and feeling the critical gaze of others, you feel awkward and uncomfortable. Being in this situation is part of your thrownness at the moment; it determines what you can and cannot do in this context. Yet, at the same time, the significance of the situation is something you shape and determine through your actions. You can worsen the situation by making a big deal out of it, or you can defuse it by treating it lightly.

This example shows that there is such a tight reciprocal interdependence between self and situation in ordinary contexts that what is *given* in such cases is an irreducible whole, not a mere coupling of two distinct items. Heidegger's claim is that, when everything is running its course in familiar situations, the distinction between self and world presupposed by the tradition simply does not show up. To use Heidegger's example, in hammering boards together in a workshop, what presents itself is a unified flow of agency that pours through the hammering into the carpentry project while forming the worker as someone who is building something in this context. On this account, it is only when there has been a *breakdown* in the smooth flow of practical dealings that a hammer can show up as some "thing" out there to be reckoned with.

The everyday practical world we find around us is always a shared, social world. As we are engaged in our everyday activities, we act according to the norms and conventions of the public in such a way that there is no sharp distinction to be made between ourselves and others in these contexts. It is through the medium of the common world that we first find ourselves as agents of a particular sort. Even working alone in a cubicle involves being attuned to the patterns and regularities that make possible the coordination of public life. It follows that for the most part we exist not so much as "centers of experience and action" as instances of the "they" or "anyone." We do what anyone would do in ordinary contexts because we have been socialized into the practices of our historical culture. Growing up into the public world, we come to master a public language, with its inbuilt way of sorting things out, and we become initiated into these standardized ways of responding and acting in our world. Through this enculturation, we become place-holders and representatives of the forms of life laid out by the they.

We are now in a position to understand how Heidegger transforms our view of what is involved in making sense of human action. As we noted earlier, the standard view of action holds that human agency is intelligible only if it is seen as causally grounded in mental intentions. Action is conceived as physical movement prompted or accompanied by a sort of mental commentary. In contrast, Heidegger's description of Dasein as an unfolding event suggests that broad areas of our active lives can be made intelligible without recourse to an ongoing mental accompaniment. When we see what is involved in ordinary being-in-the-world, we can see that our undertakings make sense and are intelligible as actions not because of their relation to mental causes, but because of the way they figure into the shared practices and patterns of intelligible behavior of our culture. I understand the smile of a passing acquaintance, for example, not by trying to divine what is going on in her head, but by understanding the place of such gestures in our world. In such cases, questions about the inner thoughts and intentions of the agent usually have no point. Almost anything, or nothing in particular, might be going through her mind as she walks by.

Heidegger is suspicious of any attempt to drive in a wedge between gestures and the inner mental items that purportedly cause them. He says, for example, that blushing "is a gesture insofar as the blushing person relates to fellow humans."[6] For large parts of our lives, what we do is intelligible as action because of the way it bodies forth a shared understanding of what things are all about, not because of the inner processes that might accompany our movements. The mistake, Heidegger says, is to "misconstrue everything as an expression of inner psychic states—instead of seeing the body-phenomenon in its interhuman relatedness."[7] When someone blushes in response to a situation, we encounter this response as meaningful because we understand its role in our shared social practices. Given our understanding of our familiar cultural world, we see the blushing person as someone who is embarrassed because her action is undignified according to current social standards, not because she has dishonored her clan or sinned before God. In gaining access to the meaning of gestures of this sort, the distinction between inner and outer simply has no role to play.

Even in the case of more complex actions, our ability to understand what people do is rooted not so much in grasping their mental states as in seeing how the action fits into the overall pattern of their lives in their entirety. When a coworker steps forward and takes charge in a crisis, we usually understand this person's action not by trying to guess what she is thinking, but by recognizing how this sort of action flows quite naturally out of the character traits that define her identity as a person of a particular sort. Her actions manifest her being as a confident, take-charge sort of person. And these character traits are themselves not usually encountered as outer expressions of something inner. On the contrary, the beaming self-confidence we encounter in this person is something that is constituted by her concrete ways of acting in this and similar situations over the course of her life.

Seen from this standpoint, the confident person's *being* is something that comes to be defined and realized in what she does: this is what Heidegger means when he says, "being-a-self *is*, in each case, only in its process of realization."[8] This person *exudes* confidence in her actions—she "bodies it forth" in her ways of being present in the world—and this is generally so regardless of what might be going on in her mind at any time. Her ways of acting, we might say, "let-confidence-be" as her mode of presence in the world—they don't just point to some underlying mental state. Of course, there are cases when someone's mode of behavior is deceptive, cases where a person's actions are not at all indicative of what they really are. But Heidegger would say that dissonances of this sort are possible only against a broad background in which, proximally and for the most part, people just *are* what they *do*.

On this conception of our being as agents, it is not just others whom we know by their actions. Even our *own* being as humans of a particular sort is something we discover, in most cases, not by introspection, but by grasping the meanings our actions have in the public world. It should be obvious that many of the traits I regard as most fundamental to my identity are not things I discover through inward-turning. I find out whether I am a warm and loving person or a witty person not by self-reflection, but through seeing how my ways of acting go over in public. Even my own feelings are often accessible only in terms of their place within the public world. For example, I know that what I am feeling in a particular situation is shame by grasping the public imports that define the meaning of the situation. If I were to depend entirely on introspection in such a situation, I might discover a burning, dysphoric sensation. But I could know that this sensation is the experience of shame—rather than, say, spite— only because I grasp the meaning of the situation and my place in it. Thus, Heidegger says that "even one's *own* Dasein becomes something that it can itself proximally 'come across' only when it *looks away* from 'experiences' and the 'center of its actions,' or does not yet 'see' them at all. Dasein finds 'itself' proximally in *what* it does" (155).

In laying out this picture of human existence, Heidegger is not claiming that there are no mental events or that the mental is never important in understanding others or ourselves. Rather, his aim is to deflate the uncritical assumption that any attempt to understand humans must take recourse to the mental. Given the view of being-in-the-world as our most basic way of being, the mental comes to be seen as something that shows up only through the medium of our shared practices and interactions as agents in the world. Instead of being something that is central to any understanding of the human, the mental comes to be seen as something derivative, a phenomenon that may appear on the scene under certain conditions but is not necessarily crucial to making sense of the human.

One risk of developing an anti-mentalist ontology of this sort is that one might conclude from this critique that only physical substance is needed to make sense of what we encounter in the world. But it is important to see that Heidegger's critique of substance ontology cuts against the idea of the physical as well as the mental. According to his description of the everyday, practical lifeworld, what we discover in our ordinary practical dealings is not a collection of material objects occupying positions in a space-time coordinate system, but contexts of equipment whose own way of being is more like an event than a substance. The phenomenological description of activity in a workshop is supposed to show that what we encounter around us in such dealings is ready-to-hand equipment that "comes to hand" in our ways of handling the context and doing things. What is "given" in such cases is an ongoing flux of activity in which the *being* of equipmental entities is defined by the specific ways they flow into our practical dealings within the context. We encounter a hammer, for example, in its function of hammering, and this functionality is not just a property we ascribe to a pre-given material thing, but instead is "*ontologically definitive*" for the being of the hammer (116).

The upshot of this account, as Dreyfus has shown, is a conception of the world as an unfolding field of relations that gains its significance and structure from the undertakings of those who are at home there. Given this picture of the worldhood of the world, the idea that the world consists "at first" of present-at-hand physical things is seen as an "illusion" (421) that arises only when there is a breakdown in our ordinary ways of being-in-the-world. Heidegger's characterization of being-in-the-world undercuts the idea that we need to draw a distinction between the inner and the outer in making sense of either human phenomena or the familiar world in which we live. The twin ideas of a mental and physical substance begin to look like high-level abstractions, the result of imposing ideas derived from detached theorizing onto life rather than ideas that actually arise within the course of life itself.

4

Earlier I suggested that Heidegger's critique of substance dualism might help us resolve some of the puzzles built into the subjective/objective distinction in moral philosophy. As we saw, this distinction provides the basis for thinking that there is a sharp distinction between objective facts, on the one hand, and subjective values, on the other. Of course, the fact/value distinction is usually framed not in terms of the notion of substance, but as a point about the nature of knowledge. But the issue is often described in terms of a distinction between what is "in here," in our minds, and what is "out there" in the world, and this seems to presuppose a distinction very much like that presupposed by substance dualism. It would seem, then, that Heidegger's attempt to describe human existence in a way that undercuts this opposition would carry implications for the traditional way of distinguishing facts and values.

We can start to see how Heidegger would deal with the subjective/objective distinction by looking at his description of the worldhood of the world. In his view, our most basic way of encountering the world is as a field of significance in which entities show up as *counting* or *mattering* in specific ways in our undertakings. What we encounter in hammering in a workshop is not a material object we then invest with a use-value. Instead, when we are fully absorbed in an everyday activity of this sort, what initially shows up for us is an unfolding flow of functional relationships—an equipmental totality—in which the "ontological definition" of the hammer is determined by the way it is ready-to-hand in building something. Heidegger calls this holistic web of interrelations that defines a lifeworld "significance" (120). What is "out there" in the world in our most basic ways of being, on this account, is a field of significance relations organized around the projects we are undertaking as agents in the world.

Heidegger takes great pains to show that this context of equipment should not be regarded as something constructed or constituted by our minds. In terms of his description of being-in-the-world, we ourselves, as agents involved in these contexts, gain our own identity, and so *become* the humans we *are*, through the medium of the world in which we find ourselves. In working in the woodshop, I can understand myself as a home craftsman or an amateur, but not as a priest saying Mass. What this shows is that our own being as agents is something that is defined and realized only through our concrete ways of being involved in specific situations. Moreover, as we have seen, our identities are made possible by the sets of interlocking and contrasting roles that are laid out and sustained within our historical culture. Only because of this web of relations can I *be* a teacher in relation to students or a parent in relation to children and other parents. It follows that my concrete ways of being as an agent are defined by the coordinated practices and forms of life of the public world. This is why Heidegger says that "the they itself articulates the referential context of significance" that makes up worldhood (167).

Given this description of being-in-the-world, it would be wrong to suppose that meanings and values only arise "in here," in our minds. For *we ourselves* are always already "outside" as participants in a shared we-world. Heidegger calls our attention to the etymology of the word "existence"—literally, "standing outside"—in order to drive home the point that being human is never a matter of being "in here," encapsulated in a subjective container, but is "always already outside," caught up in the midst of things in a shared world. What is "bedrock," on this description, is the meaning- and value-laden world we find around us in everyday life. This familiar lifeworld is said to be *more primordial* than the world posited by the natural sciences—where the term "more primordial" means that the objective world is derivative from and parasitic on the lifeworld—whereas the "objective" world lacks the resources for accounting for the possibility of the lifeworld.

Heidegger's description of human existence also has implications for our understanding of what constitutes the most completely realized form of life for humans, a way of life described as "authentic."[9] This conception of an ideal life is best understood by contrasting it with an inauthentic existence. Earlier we saw that, in average everydayness, we generally live as participants in the they, doing what *one* does as *anyone* would do such things. This tendency to fall into step is not something accidental or unfortunate; on the contrary, it first lets us be social beings with some grasp of what is possible in our world. But Heidegger holds that this way of being a "they-self" can have pernicious consequences. When we live as place-holders in the public world, we tend to simply drift into socially defined slots, enacting the different roles we have to play according to socially approved norms, and trusting we are living well so long as we do what one does. The result is that our lives tend to be fragmented and disjointed, a series of disconnected episodes with no underlying unity or continuity. We then forget that the possibilities we are assuming in our lives are just that: possibilities, not necessities or actualities. Living as a they-self, we abrogate all responsibility for our lives and throw ourselves into the busy-ness of rituals and chores, as if doing what "one" does could guarantee that we are living properly.

Such a life, in Heidegger's terms, is "inauthentic." The German word for authentic, *eigentlich*, comes from the stem meaning "own," so an inauthentic life is one that is "unowned," not really one's own. Why such a way of life is unowned becomes clear only through facing up to one's own finitude—one's being-toward-death. When we confront the fact that we are finite beings, that we constantly face the possibility of no more possibilities, we can come to see our own lives in a new way. Instead of drifting into possibilities and doing what one does, we can begin to live in a way that is characterized by a lucid sense that each of our actions is constituting our life stories as a whole, "from birth to death," and that we alone are responsible for what our lives amount to as a totality.

Using a vocabulary Heidegger does not use, we might say that being authentic points to certain character traits or virtues that contribute to achieving the fullest realization of our ability-to-be as humans. These include such traits as steadiness, integrity, clear-sightedness, intensity, and a unifying focus that imparts continuity, cumulativeness and purpose to one's life. The idea that such a life is worth pursuing is not, strictly speaking, *entailed* by Heidegger's description of Dasein. A person might understand Heidegger's overall account of human existence and still continue to be inauthentic without being guilty of an error in logic. But, logical entailment aside, I think one can say that the connection Heidegger makes between what human existence *is* and *what it ought to be* is one that reflects the connections we actually do make in our forms of practical reasoning.[10] Here, insight into facts about human existence does seem to provide rational motivation for accepting evaluative judgments about how we ought to live.

The conception of authentic existence has one further consequence for our understanding of the evaluative dimension of life. In Heidegger's view, when we recognize that all our possibilities of self-interpretation are drawn from the historical culture in which we find ourselves, we will also gain a deeper sense of our belongingness in and indebtedness to that historical context. We experience the shared background into which we are thrown as a *heritage* we need to take up and carry forward in the actions that make up our own lives. A crucial component of authentic existence, then, is seeing one's own life story as implicated in and contributing to the wider story of what Heidegger calls the *sending* or *destiny* of a historical people. And to see this is to recognize that authentic existence involves taking a stand on the concrete situation defined by one's social world in order to realize the goals definitive of one's historical culture. Authentic existence is a way of *acting*, not a way of thinking.

To conclude: I have tried to show how Heidegger's conception of human existence as an event seems to collapse the distinction between subjective and objective. In place of the traditional picture of subjects confronting a world of brute, meaningless objects, we get a picture of life as an unfolding "happening" that is enmeshed in a meaningful lifeworld and woven into a shared history. The ultimate justification for embracing this view depends, I suspect, on Heidegger's ability to make good on his claim that his characterization of the world is "more primordial" than the one we get from science and detached theorizing—a claim I have not addressed here. But even without this justification, we can see how Heidegger's critique of the substance ontology liberates us from the assumption that the only way to answer the question of being is in terms of the substance ontology.[11]

Notes

1. "The Thinker as Poet," in *Poetry, Language, Thought*, trans. A. Hofstadter (New York: Harper & Row, 1971), 4.

2. In his lectures of 1919, Heidegger proposed that we think of the situations characteristic of human life as "events" (*Ereignisse*), where the notion of an event is to be distinguished from that of a process (*Vorgang*). The description of a life situation suggests that events and processes have different structures. A process is an occurrence in the space-time coordinate system in which a cause brings about an outcome (effect). An event, in contrast, has both a meaning for someone and a complex narrative structure in which an undertaking is brought to fruition through a coherent, interconnected flow of events. See "Über das Wesen der Universität und des akademischen Studiums," in *Zur Bestimmung der Philosophie, Gesamtausgabe*, vol. 56/57 (Frankfurt am Main: Vittorio Klostermann, 1987), 205–6, translated as "On the Nature of the University and Academic Study" in *Towards the Definition of Philosophy*, trans. Ted Sadler (London: Continuum, 2000), 173–74.

3. *Being and Time*, trans. J. Macquarrie and E. Robinson (New York: Harper & Row, 1962), 32. Hereafter cited in parentheses. Where Macquarrie and Robinson translate the noun *Sein* as "Being," I use the lower case "b" in all quotations.

4. *The Fundamental Concepts of Metaphysics: World, Finitude, Solitude*, trans. W. McNeill and N. Walker (Bloomington: Indiana University Press, 1995), 67. Henceforth cited parenthetically in the text as FCM.

5. Hubert L. Dreyfus, *Being-in-the-World: A Commentary on Heidegger's "Being and Time," Division I* (Cambridge, Mass.: The MIT Press, 1991).

6. Medard Boss, ed., *Zollikoner Seminare: Protokolle, Gespräche, Briefe* (Frankfurt am Main: Klostermann, 1987), 118, quoted in Fred Dallmayr, *Between Freiburg and Frankfurt: Toward a Critical Ontology* (Amherst: The University of Massachusetts Press, 1991), 235. An English translation of the text Dallmayr cites is found in *Zollikon Seminars: Protocols—Conversations—Letters*, trans. Franz Mayr and Richard Askay (Evanston, Ill.: Northwestern University Press, 2001), 91.

7. Ibid.

8. *The Metaphysical Foundations of Logic*, trans. Michael Heim (Bloomington: Indiana University Press, 1984), 139, my emphasis.

9. Though the discussion of authenticity in *Being and Time* is not limited to working out a conception of an ideal way of life, Heidegger does say that there is "a factical ideal of Dasein" underlying his ontological interpretation of Dasein (358). Presumably, this ideal can be discussed and evaluated on its own terms. See my "Becoming a Self: The Role of Authenticity in *Being and Time*," in *The Existentialists: Critical Essays on Kierkegaard, Nietzsche, Heidegger, and Sartre*, ed. C. Guignon (Lanham, Md: Rowman & Littlefield, 2004): 119-32.

10. Robert Brandom argues against "the dogma of formalism" and in favor of construing practical reasoning as involving "material inferences" in *Making It Explicit: Reasoning, Representing, and Discursive Commitment* (Cambridge, Mass.: Harvard University Press, 1994), 97–105.

11. My thanks to Steve Crowell and Richard Polt for help in formulating some of the ideas found in this chapter.

5

The Genesis of Theory, from *The Glance of the Eye: Heidegger, Aristotle, and the Ends of Theory*

William McNeill

THIS CHAPTER EXAMINES THE PROBLEMATIC origins of the separation between the theoretical comportment of science—but also of philosophy itself, insofar as the latter (from Descartes, through the speculative metaphysics of
German Idealism, to Husserlian phenomenology)[1] itself becomes "scientific,"
severed from the immediacies of human *praxis*—and so-called "practical," circumspective involvement as traced in Heidegger's *Being and Time* (1927). To
this end, we shall attempt to follow two different accounts of the genesis of
theoretical comportment. The first appears to be merely a reworking of the
story of "natural genesis" that we find in Aristotle. The second concerns what
Heidegger himself terms the "existential genesis" of theoretical comportment,
a genesis which, as we shall examine, has its ultimate roots in the ecstatic temporality of Dasein, or, more precisely, in the Temporality of being itself.[2] In
addition to raising hermeneutic concerns about the "scientific" and thematizing aspirations of *Being and Time* itself (aspirations that Heidegger would
subsequently acknowledge as inappropriate), the present chapter also leads us
to examine Heidegger's early understanding of science as a thematizing objectification of beings. Finally, this context provides the opportunity for an initial
orientation regarding the place of *praxis* in *Being and Time*.

The Natural Genesis of Theory

One account of the genesis of the foundation of philosophical and scientific knowledge in the sense of theoretical contemplation is presented in §13 of *Being and Time*, where Heidegger argues that knowledge in the sense of cognition represents a founded mode of being-in-the-world. Heidegger also refers to the cognitive knowledge (*Erkennen*) of world as an "existential 'modality' of being-in" (SZ 59).[3] Cognitive knowledge of world is here to be understood broadly as the cognitive apprehending of intraworldly beings in their being, although the clear distinction between world as constitutive of Dasein's being and "world" in the sense of intraworldly beings will be made only in the following section. Such knowledge, Heidegger goes on to point out, can develop autonomously once it has emerged; it can become the specific undertaking of science, and assume authority over Dasein's being-in-the-world (SZ 62).

Cognitive knowledge, in other words, although it is a form of theoretical comportment, is not yet science; for one thing, it has yet to establish its own procedure in terms of method, which would first grant it the requisite autonomy, distance, and independence from involvement with other beings in the world, that is, from "praxis" in a broad sense. Heidegger's phenomenological account, however, seeks to question the nature of the severing that would take place at that very moment when theoretical comportment in the form of science would establish its autonomy from such involvements. His reflections on cognitive knowledge and its genesis are introduced, he explains, because cognitive knowledge of the world is mostly or even exclusively taken to represent the phenomenon of being-in. This is the case not merely in the epistemological approach of *Erkenntnistheorie*; rather, quite generally for the most part "practical comportment is understood as '*non*theoretical' or 'atheoretical' comportment" (SZ 59). Dasein's understanding of itself as being-in-the-world, Heidegger argues, is misled by its according such priority to cognitive knowledge.

Heidegger's interpretation of the genesis of cognitive knowledge is opposed to those models that seek to understand cognition as arising out of the "transcendence" of an independently existing subject with respect to an object. It aims, in effect, at attaining a more originary, phenomenologically more adequate understanding of transcendence itself. It does so by arguing that Dasein's modes of being, as ways of being-in-the-world, are ontologically prior to any "transcendent" relation toward either a "subject" or an "object." For one thing, the way in which a being manifests itself to us in its phenomenal appearing is determined in part by the manner of our comportment toward it, that is, by a particular mode of our being in each specific case. A being or "object" appears quite differently to us depending on whether we are involved with it in a process of producing something, or merely contemplating it free from any involvement. Different again are the ways in which we encounter and relate to another human being. This indicates that there is no such thing as an object *per se* or an object *in general*, independent of its appearing. And the same goes for the notion of a "subject." We as "subjects" appear very differently to ourselves—we have a very different relation toward ourselves—depending on whether we are actively involved in or given over to some task of making, engaged in a relationship with other human beings, or merely reflecting on ourselves by way of philosophical or scientific contemplation. Dasein in its *metaphysical* "neutrality"[4] is ontologically prior to any subject or object, indeed to any being or entity whatsoever, because it first constitutes the site of our possible relationality toward any entity: the way in which Dasein exists co-determines the way in which an entity is given to and for us; it co-determines the kind of being that an entity has in each particular case. The being of Dasein, that is, being-in-the-world, determines at least in part both what an entity is for us (its whatness or *essentia*) and the way in which it is or appears in any given instance (its *existentia*). Cognitive knowing, as one possible ontic relating toward beings, is ontologically *founded* in being-in-the-world, in which beings are first uncovered. And if there is indeed something like a *transcendence* implied in every relationality toward something, then such transcendence, Heidegger argues, demands to be understood not in terms of a "subject," but in terms of our ontologically prior being-in-the-world, that is, in terms of Dasein as a "clearing" (*Lichtung*) or site of disclosure. Furthermore, these reflections suggest that the *world* is not simply "nature" in the Kantian sense of the totality of beings existing before us, as though they were independent objects given for our cognition (SZ 60). Rather world must belong to transcendence itself; indeed, Heidegger will later interpret it as the "horizon" of transcendence.

The analysis of cognitive knowing as a founded mode of being-in-the-world is thus intended to point toward the unitary phenomenon of *world* and of Dasein's *transcendence* as ontologically prior to any distinction between "theory" and "praxis"—understanding the latter now in the broad sense of doing and making, as opposed to theoretical contemplation. How does Heidegger's initial, extremely condensed account of the genesis of cognitive knowledge unfold?

Knowledge in its cognitive mode is said to have its prior grounding in our already being alongside or in the presence of (*bei*) the world, which does not simply mean a "fixed staring" at something purely present-at-hand. Being-in-the-world is initially a kind of concern, where concern (*Besorgen*) does not refer to the economic or "practical" activities of Dasein, but is employed as an ontological term to designate a particular way of being-in-the-world (SZ 57). Broadly speaking, *Besorgen* refers to any mode of comportment concerned primarily with "things." In its concernful existence, Dasein, according to Heidegger, is *"captivated* by the world of its concern" (SZ 61). And this kind of captivation belongs intrinsically to our involvement. In order for cognitive knowledge to be possible as a "contemplative determining of what is present-at-hand," there must first be what Heidegger refers to as a "deficiency" of our concernful involvement. In our holding back from our involvement in producing and manipulating things, concern transposes itself into the sole remaining mode of being-in, a mere tarrying alongside (*Verweilen bei*). It is *on the basis* of this kind of ontological relation to world, Heidegger explains, that we can then encounter intraworldly beings simply in their pure look (*Aussehen*) or *eidos*, and explicitly view or look at them as such. Such mere looking at beings (*Hinsehen*) is a mode of being-in-the-world; indeed, it remains a mode of concern, albeit a "deficient" one. Moreover, as a looking *at*, it always entails a particular way of taking up an orientation toward something, a "setting our sights upon" whatever is present-at-hand. This directionality or orientation of vision occurs prior to our encountering beings as this or that; it takes over a "viewpoint" (*Gesichtspunkt*) *in advance* from the beings it encounters (SZ 61). We see beings always already in this or that respect.

Dasein's vision must thus be oriented in advance in terms of the particular "viewpoint" it looks at and the perspective it adopts toward things. In the case of merely looking at things, our seeing must have a prior directive to contemplate those beings solely in terms of their outward appearance or *eidos*, and not, for example, in terms of the end that these beings are to serve in a process of making. In "merely looking" at a hammer with respect to its form or shape, its purpose remains irrelevant. The way in which we see particular beings is in general dependent upon the end at which our seeing aims in advance. In the specific case of making or producing something, the end or perspective in terms of which we see things is the final product or work itself, the *ergon* as *telos* of the productive process. Yet as *telos*, our vision of the work to be produced is also *archē*, in the sense that such vision orients and regulates the entire activity of production in advance. In *technē*, that is, in the specific knowledge that guides the involved process of making or producing something, this end or purpose must also be taken up into, or taken account of in, our prior "seeing." For Plato and Aristotle, this antecedent seeing, this prior "vision," is of course the nonsensible *eidos* or *idea* sighted in the soul of the craftsman, the idea contemplated by the "eye of the soul." The thrust of Heidegger's argument in §13 seems to be that because that activity which appears to be a nonproductive, disinvolved contemplation of things nevertheless still contemplates objects in terms of their *eidos*, such contemplation remains derivative, dependent upon the kind of knowing pertaining to productive comportment. It appears to take as its model a key moment of productive knowledge or *technē*: the antecedent sighting (*theōrein*) of the *eidos*. Furthermore, the question arises as to whether this allegedly "disinvolved" contemplation is really as disinvolved as it tends to claim. Is it not also guided in advance by a specific end, a certain purpose and ideal? Its end is precisely that prescribed and made possible by the kind of seeing intrinsic to *technē*: the releasing or freeing (*Freigabe*) of an entity into an independent self-subsistence, a lying present-at-hand before us. The pure contemplation of things would thus be merely a mode of concern, the extraction of the theoretical moment within *technē*, and in its essence no different from the latter. What we think of as "theoretical" contemplation, cognitive knowledge, would *in essence* be no different from productive comportment.

Heidegger proceeds to outline, very concisely, how such pure contemplation of something can in turn establish itself as an independent or autonomous way of being-in-the-world. Looking at things can become an independent way of dwelling alongside beings in the world. In such *dwelling*, which is a holding back from manipulation or utilization, there occurs an *apprehending* of what is present-at-hand. Such apprehending occurs by way of addressing and discussing something *as* something. It is a way of *interpreting* things that allows us to determine them as this or that, and the resulting interpretations can be retained and preserved in sets of assertions. In short, science becomes possible as one particular development of theoretical apprehending.

It seems clear that Heidegger is here presenting us with a concise account of the genesis of theoretical comportment. It is not so easy, however, to assess what status this account is intended to have; in particular, what its implications are for the Aristotelian distinctions between *theōria*, *praxis*, and *poiēsis*. One temptation would be to read the passage as an attempt to reverse the prioritizing of "theory" over "praxis." Theory would merely be a founded mode of praxis. Such a reading might indeed seem to be suggested by the closing paragraph of §12, where Heidegger indicates that the traditional "priority" of the cognitive mode of knowledge has led to practical comportment being understood as *non*theoretical, that is, still in terms of theory as primary. Heidegger's account might thus be seen as undermining such primacy by instituting a reversal. However, this reading would not only leave intact the same oppositional structure; it would also overlook Heidegger's insistence that concern (*Besorgen*) is not equivalent to "practical" activity, even if we take the term "practical" in a broad sense that encompasses both doing and making. Theoretical contemplation is also a mode of concern. Furthermore, the exemplary mode of concern discussed here is certainly not *praxis* in the narrow (ethico-political) sense understood by Aristotle, namely, that of doing as opposed to making, but *Herstellen*, "producing," *Hantieren*, "manipulating" or "handling" things, "and so on" (SZ 61). In Aristotle's terms, the know-how pertaining to such modes of comportment is *technē*, not the *phronēsis* of *praxis*. What seems clear from these considerations is that Heidegger, while emphasizing the way in which theoretical contemplation emerges within the context of a worldly involvement with things, and specifically with producing or making, is not indicating any ontological order of founding with respect to these two modes. The initial goal is to make both forms of comportment visible as modes of worldly concern.

Given these preliminary considerations, what does Heidegger's account of cognitive knowledge as a founded mode ultimately tell us? It tells us nothing. Nothing, that is, concerning the *ontological* genesis of cognition or theoretical comportment. What it provides is merely an account of the *ontic* genesis of cognitive knowledge. If cognitive knowledge is grounded in concern in the broad sense of a worldly comportment with things, then such concern must, as prior to any differentiation into particular modes, first be understood by the analytic in terms of being-in-the-world as the a priori, existential-ontological constitution of Dasein. It demands to be understood in terms of Dasein's being as a transcendence that first makes possible all such comportment. Thus Heidegger, pointing to what is implicit in even the most provisional thematizing of the phenomenon of cognition, reminds us that "Cognitive knowledge is a mode of being of Dasein as being-in-the-world, it has its *ontic founding* in this ontological constitution" (SZ 61, emphasis added).

If, therefore, cognitive knowledge of world is announced in the title of §13 as a "founded mode," then the founding at issue is *ontic*, and, as the title indicates, merely intended to "exemplify" or provide an illustration of Dasein's being-in. Indeed, so little does this account clarify the ontological genesis of cognitive or theoretical knowledge that it seems to accord entirely with Aristotle's account of the genesis of knowledge as presented in Book I of the *Metaphysics*—to accord, in other words, with that account of the genesis of theoretical comportment which Heidegger in the 1924/1925 *Sophist* course described as arising from the "natural" or everyday understanding and interpretive tendency inherent in Greek existence (GA 19, 65ff.): theoretical contemplation began when human beings had leisure (*scholazein, diagōgē*), when the necessities of life had been fulfilled (*Met.*, 981 b21f., 982 b24f.). Just as Heidegger in the *Sophist* course translates *diagōgē* as (among other things) *Verweilen*, "tarrying" (GA 19, 68), so too in §13 of *Being and Time* the word *Verweilen* characterizes freedom from involvement in producing and manipulating things.

Ontologically, Heidegger's account here clarifies nothing. At most, it serves to point toward the ontological dimension of being-in-the-world or originary transcendence in terms of which the ontological problematic of the genesis of *theōria* can first be raised in a phenomenologically appropriate manner. In particular, we should note that the account has given no indication as to why precisely contemplation of the *eidos* came to serve as the exemplary model for a thinking associated with leisure or tarrying alongside things. Heidegger points more explicitly to this question in a later note added to his text, precisely where the account might seem to offer an explanation of how a contemplative looking at something in terms of its *eidos* can arise. This marginal note reads:

> Looking away from . . . does not in itself give rise to looking at. . . . Looking at . . . has its own origin and has such looking away as its consequence; contemplation [*Betrachten*] has its own origination. The look at the *eidos* demands something else. (SZ 61 n. a)[5]

What this "something else" is whereby contemplation originates is an existential-ontological question that cannot yet be raised in this preliminary context of the analytic of Dasein. Yet our remarks on the genesis of theoretical knowledge in the *Sophist* course already suggest that the answer has to do not only with the fact that the primacy of vision in Greek thought is indicative of a desire for enduring presence, but—and perhaps more importantly—that it has just as much to do with the possibility of independence (*Eigenständigkeit*) and self-subsistence, in particular, with the possibility of establishing a freedom and independence from immediate involvement and from all the absorption and captivation that such involvement entails.

Dispersions of Vision: Theory, Praxis, Technē

Our account thus far suggests that both theoretical contemplation and making or producing are to be understood as modes of a particular comportment of Dasein which Heidegger names *Besorgen*. *Besorgen*, or "concern," does not therefore refer to "praxis" in the loose sense (doing and/or making), as opposed to "theory." Nor does it refer exclusively to making or *poiēsis*.[6] It does, however, as we noted, refer to a broad sense of comportment that is primarily concerned with "things." But what exactly does the term "things" include? The possible objects of *Besorgen* are not just any entities regarded in whatever way.

Heidegger addresses this issue in a provisional manner in §15 of *Being and Time* when discussing which beings we should consider in attempting to make visible Dasein's everyday being-in-the-world. The beings we encounter within the world are generally "things." Yet Heidegger warns that if we understand things to be defined by their substantiality, materiality, or the extrinsic value they have, we may be led astray ontologically. Such ontological determinations only conceal our preontological understanding of these seemingly most proximate beings of our everyday concern. At this point Heidegger notes that the Greeks indeed had an appropriate term for "things":

> The Greeks had an appropriate term for "things": *pragmata*, that is to say, that which one has to do with in one's concernful dealings (*praxis*). But ontologically, the specifically "pragmatic" character of the *pragmata* is precisely what the Greeks left in obscurity; they thought of them "proximally" as "mere things." We shall call those beings which we encounter in concern *equipment* [Zeug]. (SZ 68)

Praxis is here translated as *besorgender Umgang*, "concernful dealings." But does this mean that we should equate *Besorgen* with *praxis* in the narrow Aristotelian sense? Clearly not, for Aristotle's more narrow conception of *praxis* belongs to the realm of ethico-political affairs, concerned primarily with human beings and not with "things." Yet perhaps it does indeed fall under the more general, less "technical" sense of *praxis* that was prevalent in Greek thought, and which is also found in Aristotle. *Praxis* in this more general sense could include doing (in the ethico-political sense), making, or even contemplating: in this sense, any human activity is a *praxis*. "Things" or *pragmata*, Heidegger would later note in another context, can indeed refer to this more encompassing sense of "*praxis* taken in a truly wide sense, neither in the narrow meaning of practical use (cf. *chrēsthai*), nor in the sense of *praxis* as moral action: *praxis* is all doing, undertaking, and sustaining, which also includes *poiēsis*."[7]

Yet why does Heidegger say that *pragmata*, referring to the "objects" of *praxis*, is an "appropriate term" for "things"? The reason is presumably that such beings demand to be understood ontologically *from out of praxis* itself (and this means in terms of their properly *worldly* character), and not as independently subsisting entities, initially devoid of any worldly character. However this, it seems, is precisely what the Greeks did not accomplish.[8] They left the "pragmatic" or *praxis*-like character of these things *ontologically* obscure. And this, by implication, because they failed to achieve a sufficiently originary, ontological understanding of *praxis* in all its moments. As is now well-known in the light of the publication of the Marburg lecture courses from the period of *Being and Time*, this inadequate interpretation of the ontological character of "things," and by implication of *praxis* itself, occurred, on Heidegger's reading, due to the ascendancy of a "technical" way of thinking about things, one that, deriving from the experience of craftsmanship, came to understand "things" in terms of the *theōria* deriving from *technē*, while (most rigorously in Aristotle) reserving *praxis* and its specific kind of knowledge (*phronēsis*) for the realm of human ethico-political affairs.[9] This derivation is corroborated by a marginal note that Heidegger subsequently added to the expression "mere things":

> Why? *eidos*—*morphē*—*hulē!* coming from *technē*, thus an "artisan" [*künstlerische*] interpretation! if *morphē* not [interpreted] as *eidos*, [then as] *idea*!

If the objects of *praxis* or concernful activity were understood as "mere things," this occurred, on Heidegger's account, because they were viewed essentially as though they were material (*hulē*) to be worked upon by a craftsman. Material, as a natural resource of *technē*, came to be regarded as *mere* material, yet to be given shape and form (*morphē*) by the craftsman who in advance sights the *eidos* or visible look of the thing to be produced. Things thus come to be seen as "mere" things: the thing is only fully a thing when it has achieved its *telos* (the stamp of its *eidos*) as the completion of its form. Taken in itself, the thing is deficient with regard to its proper form, yet to be bestowed by human intervention.

But of course, this *telos* or end is not, properly speaking, the ultimate end of the material product or "thing." Once produced, the product is there to be acted upon again; it once more becomes subservient to human *praxis*. As Aristotle notes, the end of *poiēsis* is *praxis* (*Nic. Eth.* 1139 b1). Subservient to the end of human *praxis*, the product is ontologically incomplete or underdetermined when considered independently of such *praxis*. For every human product is made *for* something; it finds its end in the realm of human affairs. In its very being, a product of human making is something that exists for some further human activity. Its way of being is constituted by an "in order to ... " Taken *in itself*, however, it can be viewed as a mere thing to be acted upon. This view of the object of *praxis*, the *pragma*, as a "mere" thing results from a technical interpretation or way of thinking that views things in respect of their self-subsistence as something present-at-hand.[10] Yet this also implies that the *praxis/poiēsis* distinction itself, when applied in too absolute a manner, lies at the root of a reductive understanding of "things." It is only because the *praxis*-like dimension of the making or producing, and indeed also of the *theōria* inherent in *technē*, is overlooked or eclipsed that the "thing" can be seen as having in itself no worldly or *praxis*-like character, and that this very seeing or *theōrein* can likewise disregard its own embeddedness in human *praxis*, become "unworldly."

A more originary interpretation of *praxis*—but also, presumably, of *theōria* and *technē*—is thus called for, one that remains attentive to the properly worldly character of all involvements. And this entails an interpretation of what, in general, being-in-the-world (or "Dasein") means. The phenomenon of concern, or *Besorgen*, will thus have to be understood in terms of its ontological rootedness in being-in-the-world, in transcendence, in Dasein's originary being as care and as temporality. In *Being and Time*, Heidegger initially seeks to resist a merely technical-theoretical interpretation of things by focusing on things as equipment, in their readiness-to-hand, intrinsically constituted by an "in order to" or purpose and thus, in their being, referred to the ontological realm of Dasein, of the being that we ourselves in each case are. Such readiness-to-hand (*Zuhandenheit*), as the analysis clarifies, and not presence-at-hand (*Vorhandenheit*), constitutes the manner of being that such "things" properly have in themselves (SZ 71, 75). This of course might be taken as a merely "subjective" interpretation of the being of independent entities, whose proper independence science would respect more carefully via the supposed neutrality of its theoretical vision that observes and contemplates things as self-subsistent in their "objective" presence-at-hand. Yet such an objection presupposes human *praxis* to be a realm of merely subjective activity, belonging to and under the control of individual human beings as subjects, and subsequently extended ontologically to include other things within it. In this perspective readiness-to-hand appears as a mere "aspect" ascribed by human "cognition" to things that already exist independently of any relation to us (SZ 71). *Being and Time*, by contrast, opens itself to the possibility that "human activity" or *praxis*, properly understood, is not merely human at all in the modern subjectivist sense, but a kind of activity that demands to be understood more originarily in terms of the worldly disclosure of being that occurs in each case as a mode of being-in-the-world, or Dasein. The primacy of this disclosive relation to world is indicated in §16 when Heidegger shows that the being of things in their readiness-to-hand presupposes a certain "nonthematic" presence of world, a presence which, from the perspective of the supposedly pure presence-at-hand disclosed by the theoretical gaze, is rather an absence or withdrawal of world. The proper being of equipment, its readiness-to-hand, is graspable "only on the basis of the phenomenon of world" (SZ 75–76).

This nonthematic presence of world in its absence belongs intrinsically to our "circumspective" concern with and absorption in our worldly involvements with things. It occurs in and amid the circumspection (*Umsicht*) that guides our understanding of our involvement with things. For all understanding, Heidegger will emphasize, is intrinsically constituted by "seeing" (*Sicht*) as a primary manner of access to beings in their being. Likewise, all Dasein's seeing or sighting of things in their being is intrinsically an understanding. But not all seeing is theoretical or thematic. We have already noted Heidegger's argument that concern in the sense of equipmental involvement cannot be thought adequately in terms of theoretical or cognitive knowledge. In §15 he underlines the point in the following way:

> Just *looking at* the particular qualities of the "outward appearance" of things, however sharply we look, is incapable of discovering anything ready-to-hand. The gaze of the merely "theoretical" look at things is deprived of any understanding of readiness-to-hand. Yet our dealing with things by manipulating them and using them is not blind; it has its own kind of vision, by which our manipulation is guided and imparted its specific thingly character.[11] Our dealing with equipment subordinates itself to the manifold assignments of the "in order to." The vision [*Sicht*] with which it thus accommodates itself is *circumspection* [Umsicht]. (SZ 69)

Circumspection, the seeing specific to equipmental involvements, should not, therefore, be analysed on the basis of *theōrein,* or starting from a theoretical perspective on things, but must be seen phenomenologically, in its own right. Theoretical and circumspective seeing, although both are ways of seeing as well as modes of concern in the sense indicated, should not be confused with one another. Yet nor, Heidegger continues, may they be understood by imposing the traditional, yet ill-defined opposition of "theory" and "praxis":

> "Practical" comportment is not "atheoretical" in the sense of being sightless, and its difference from theoretical comportment is not simply due to the fact that in theoretical comportment one contemplates, while in practical comportment one *acts,* and that action must apply theoretical cognition [*Erkennen*] if it is not to remain blind; for just as contemplation is originarily a kind of concern, so too action has *its* vision. Theoretical comportment is a noncircumspective merely looking at things. But the fact that this looking is noncircumspective does not mean that it follows no rules: it constructs a canon for itself in the form of *method.* (SZ 69)

As we have noted, the fact that Dasein's theoretical comportment is noncircumspective does not preclude the possibility that it is a (ontically) founded or derivative mode of circumspective concern. Contemplation, as noncircumspective, remains a kind of concern. Heidegger therefore seeks to emphasize that one should not view "theoretical" and "practical" comportment as mutually exclusive ways of being that reciprocally supplement one another. Theoretical comportment is itself a form of acting, of comportment, just as practical comportment (or "action" in a broad sense) is also a seeing, indeed one that does not first need "theory" to inform it. Is not the kind of interpretation that posits "theory" and "practice" as existing independently of one another and then subsequently entering into a relation of hierarchy or supplementarity itself already the result of a theoretical perspective?

Heidegger's point, then, is not that there is no difference between theoretical and circumspective comportment, between "theory" and "practice." Quite to the contrary. His point is simply that this difference must be understood in terms of its unitary ground, as a distinction between different modes of (concernful) being-in-the-world, different ways of uncovering beings within the world. Another way of putting this, in more temporal terms, is to say that the difference between these different modes of comportment is not a difference that simply obtains *within* the horizon of an already existing presence. Rather, such difference occurs as a disclosive, intrinsically differential and finite happening in which the disclosure of world itself is at play. But what exactly is "world"? What is the strange presence-in-absence of world that marks the very difference or differentiation between circumspective and theoretical seeing?

Before approaching the answers to such questions, we must attempt to clarify further what is being asked. Heidegger indicates that the difference between these different modes of concern, namely, theoretical and circumspective comportment, is to be understood phenomenologically in terms of dispersion (*Zerstreuung*):

> With Dasein's facticity, its being-in-the-world has in each case already dispersed or even split itself into particular ways of being-in (SZ 56–57).

> Our dealings have already dispersed themselves into a multiplicity of ways of concern. The kind of dealing that is closest to us is, as we have shown, not a merely cognitive apprehending, but rather that kind of concern which manipulates things and puts them to use; and this has its own kind of "cognition" [*Erkenntnis*]. (SZ 67)

Circumspection and theoretical contemplation are dispersed, already differentiated ways of concern. This dispersion is not only factical, but also historical, that is, it occurs as the concrete enactment of certain interpretations of the being of beings. From the point of view of the analytic, however, the difficulty remains of how to access Dasein's being prior to such dispersion. In terms of what can we recognize such dispersion *as dispersion?* The analytic of Dasein aims to uncover the originary being of Dasein which, far from being reducible to any of these dispersed modes, would constitute the ground on which they could first be understood as such. These dispersed modes of Dasein's being, as ways of concern, of *Besorgen* (but also of "solicitude," *Fürsorge*) that unfold factically as specific ways of relating to beings, will be understood more originarily on the ground of Dasein's being as care (*Sorge*). But in what sense does "care" constitute a "ground" of being-in-the-world? And in what sense is such a ground to be conceived as "unitary"?

It is important to understand that this is not an instance of positing the One as the ground of the Many in a manner which we find throughout the history of philosophy. Ground and its unity here, in the analytic of Dasein, are not opposed to or set over against dispersion; and such dispersion is not posited as something that could or should be overcome. Traditionally, ground is understood philosophically as that which already is, that which is most constantly present, that which already underlies a possible multiplicity of (temporally or contingently dependent) determinations: in Aristotle, it is *to ti ēn einai*, "that which already is (has been) in being"; it is primary *ousia* or "substance"; and the same understanding of being is employed in Aristotle's understanding of the "soul" (*psuchē*)[12]—notwithstanding the fact that the *human* soul is also an *archē* of *praxis*, an *archē* determined as *hou heneka*, an "origin" that can freely relate to and anticipate itself, its own being, as its end. This end of the human soul, of human being as such, itself tends—with the ascendency of theoretical contemplation—to be understood as an already existing, already present ground (*nous*), a ground that "always" already endures and needs only the act of theoretical contemplation to come into its own (authentic) being, into its ownmost *ergon*, its ownmost self-enactment and end (*en-ergeia, entelecheia*), its ownmost self-presence. The *being* of the "self" thus tends to be understood already in Aristotle, and henceforth in the history of philosophy, as an already present ground. The understanding of the soul in Aristotle is of course not at all identical to the determination of the self in modern subjectivity: The Aristotelian "soul" comes into its ownmost being not by a reflective intuiting of itself as the ground of thinking, as in Descartes—a thinking that then relates all worldly beings back to itself as their unitary ground whose temporal self-oblivion and fallibility is made good by the Christian Creator-God—but rather by its contemplation of the divine presence of the world itself. And yet there is a certain sameness and continuity here from Aristotle to modernity in the determination of true being by way of *theōria*.

By contrast to this traditional understanding of ground, the analytic of Dasein does not conceive of the unitary ground of Dasein's being—its being-a-self as being-in-the-world—as an already existing or already present, a priori ground that transcends temporal determination or is attained contemplatively in transcending the temporal and finite. Rather, the unitary ground of Dasein's being, *as transcendence*, is itself shown to be intrinsically temporal, factical, and historical. In other words, transcendence, as the originary ground of Dasein's being, is not a transcendence *of* (in the sense of exceeding or going beyond) dispersion, but a transcendence *already in* dispersion. Transcendence and dispersion, ground and multiplicity, are not mutually exclusive, precisely when Dasein's being is seen as *praxis* and not conceived in a theoretical or speculative manner. But *praxis* in this sense is to be conceived in a broad sense, more originarily than in the narrow Aristotelian sense of ethico-political *praxis* that tends to oppose such *praxis* to *theōria* (as well as to *poiēsis*). Theoretical contemplation, as a mode of dispersion, is already a *praxis*: a kind of concern, grounded in Dasein's own being as care. And here we can already discern the overall thrust of the analytic of Dasein compared to Aristotle's understanding of human existence, namely, to problematize the privileging of *theōria* and of presence in the Greek understanding of existence by giving priority to the finitude of Dasein's existence as *praxis*, yet in a manner that does not simply oppose this level of *praxis* to *theōria*, but interprets its intrinsic temporality in a more radical sense than that allowed by merely contrasting it with the theoretical disclosure of time and presence in terms of the "now" (*nun*) and the "eternal" (*aei*). The authentic disclosure of the presence pertaining to Dasein's existence will be granted by the *Augenblick*, the glance of the eye of a finite temporality, and not of a theoretical transcendence.

How, then, can we access Dasein's being as an originary and unitary ground of all its dispersed modes of comportment, including theoretical and circumspective? It should now be clear that what is entailed in this task is *not* to access Dasein's being *prior* to its dispersion, as we expressed it above. The task, rather, is to access it—to let it be seen beyond, or even in, its self-concealment—in and amid such dispersion, in the finite temporality of this very dispersion. Dasein's transcendence in dispersion is *unitary* in the manner of its temporalizing, and not as a prior, already existing ground. In already being dispersed into (being "alongside" [*bei*] and involved in) one possibility of concern, Dasein is also presented (as already being in-the-world) with other possibilities, which it holds "present," and it maintains itself in an openness (ahead of itself) for other possibilities of its being that have yet to emerge. This already being presented with and holding itself open for other possibilities (other possible modes of comportment and dispersion) is *not closed off* by Dasein's existing in dispersion, but as a primordial or originary way of being, is already maintained as such in and throughout all factical existing.

Yet what manner of access is appropriate to this originary and unitary phenomenon of Dasein's being as care? What kind of phenomenological "seeing" will disclose Dasein's being as such even in its dispersion? What is required, according to Heidegger, is a "*unitary* phenomenological look" at Dasein's being as a whole, a "complete look through" the whole of Dasein's being in all its structural (ultimately temporal) moments. And this can be neither the kind of theoretical or circumspective looking that remain directed toward beings (as present-at-hand or in their readiness-to-hand) but not toward being; nor can it be an "immanent perceiving of experiences," which likewise remains oriented toward that which is merely present. It must, rather, be a seeing intrinsic to "one of the *most far-reaching* and *most originary* possibilities of disclosure," a mode of disclosure lying in Dasein itself (albeit for the most part dormant), namely, the fundamental attunement of *Angst* which discloses being-in-the-world as such (SZ 180–82). The seeing intrinsic to this manner of disclosure will subsequently be interpreted as the phenomenon of the *Augenblick*. Yet is not the disclosure granted by the *Augenblick*, which grounds and informs the entire analytic of Dasein, itself in a certain tension with the proposed phenomenological nature of the investigation? For phenomenology, Heidegger has indicated, is "primarily a *concept of method*" (SZ 27). And as such it is science (*Wissenschaft*): "science of the being of beings—ontology" (SZ 37). Its task is to make being as such, and initially the being of Dasein, explicit or thematic. Yet are the scientific and thematizing aspirations of such phenomenology ultimately appropriate to disclosing the being of Dasein? Are they not remnants of the theoretical desire, itself already in dispersion, and requiring the construction of method in order to guide it?

For the moment, we shall merely leave these as questions. The present section has served to indicate the centrality of the unitary problem of transcendence and world for understanding the status of theoretical comportment in *Being and Time*. The issue of the temporal finitude of Dasein's being, as a being-in-dispersion, will prove crucial to the problem of accounting thematically for the *ontological* genesis of theoretical comportment.

Notes

1. Kierkegaard and Nietzsche represent the most notable rebellions against this scientific-speculative aspiration of philosophy, although in ways that, from a Heideggerian perspective, do not adequately fathom the historical determination of metaphysics. On Heidegger's reading of Nietzsche, see William McNeill, *The Glance of the Eye: Heidegger, Aristotle, and the Ends of Theory* (Albany: SUNY, 1999), part 3.

2. The existential genesis of theory is not discussed in this selection. See McNeill, *The Glance of the Eye*, 72–80.

3. SZ will refer to *Sein und Zeit* (Halle: Niemeyer, 1927). Where reference is made to marginalia, I have used *Sein und Zeit*, 15th ed. (Tübingen: Niemeyer, 1979). Translations from *Sein und Zeit* are my own.

4. On the metaphysical neutrality of Dasein, see Heidegger, *The Metaphysical Foundations of Logic*, trans. Michael Heim (Bloomington: Indiana University Press, 1984), 136ff. For a discussion of this neutrality, see Jacques Derrida, "Geschlecht: Sexual Difference, Ontological Difference," trans. R. Berezdivin, in *A Derrida Reader*, ed. Peggy Kamuf (New York: Columbia University Press, 1991). See also our remarks in "Care for the Self: Originary Ethics in Heidegger and Foucault," *Philosophy Today* 42, no. 1/4 (1998): 53–64.

5. The German *Betrachten* may be translated as either "contemplation" or "observation." For our purposes here, the two may be taken as equivalent, and as referring to "theoretical" seeing. In part 2 of *The Glance of the Eye*, we show that such "theory" is still understood in too general a sense that has yet to be more historically specified.

6. Jacques Taminiaux is overly restrictive in aligning Dasein's everyday comportment and understanding with *poiēsis* as opposed to *praxis*, and in suggesting that Dasein's circumspective seeing "has no eye for *Dasein* itself" (*n'a pas d'yeux pour le* Dasein *lui-même*). See Jacques Taminiaux, *Lectures de l'ontologie fondamentale* (Grenoble: Millon, 1989), 157. Cf. Taminiaux, *Heidegger and the Project of Fundamental Ontology*, trans. Michael Gendre (Albany: SUNY, 1991), 118. A complete blindness to one's own being would be just as phenomenologically incomprehensible as a complete severing of *poiēsis* from *praxis*.

7. *What Is a Thing?* trans. W. B. Barton Jr. and Vera Deutsch (Chicago: Henry Regnery, 1968), 70. This point is noted by Robert Bernasconi in "The Fate of the Distinction between *Praxis* and *Poiesis*," in *Heidegger in Question* (Atlantic Highlands, N.J.: Humanities Press, 1993), 7. The same point is made by Heidegger in *Introduction to*

Metaphysics, trans. Gregory Fried and Richard Polt (New Haven: Yale University Press, 2000), 61. Cf. also *Einführung in die phänomenologische Forschung, Gesamtausgabe*, vol. 17 (Frankfurt am Main: Vittorio Klostermann, 1994), 45.

8. Heidegger does not clarify precisely who these "Greeks" are, but it should be evident—as we shall explain in a moment—that Plato and Aristotle are intended primarily.

9. On the derivation of this "technical" understanding of things, see in particular *The Basic Problems of Phenomenology*, trans. Albert Hofstadter (Bloomington: Indiana University Press, 1982), 106ff. See also Taminiaux's commentary in *Heidegger and the Project of Fundamental Ontology*, 83ff.

10. The nature of this reduction of the thing would later be considered in greater detail by Heidegger, and specifically in the context of *technē*, in "The Origin of the Work of Art" (1936), in *Off the Beaten Track*, ed. Julian Young and Kenneth Haynes (Cambridge: Cambridge University Press, 2002). See part 1 of the essay, "The Thing and the Work."

11. Here we follow the first edition. Later editions have *Sicherheit*, "security," in place of *Dinghaftigkeit*, "thingly character."

12. See *De Anima*, 412aff.

6

Being-with, Dasein-with, and the "They" as the Basic Concept of Unfreedom, from *Martin Heidegger: Phänomenologie der Freiheit*

Günter Figal

Being-with and Dasein-with

Given that Heidegger is initially concerned with the inexplicitness of being-with-one-another, it should come as no surprise that he begins his analysis with the question of how others are "also encountered" in Dasein's everyday association with useful things.

> The "description" of the surrounding world nearest to us, for example, the work-world of the handworker, showed that together with the useful things found in work, others are "also encountered" for whom the "work" is to be done. In the kind of being of these things at hand, that is, in their relevance, there lies an essential reference to possible wearers for whom they should be "cut to the figure." Similarly, the producer or "supplier" is encountered in the material used as one who "serves" well or badly. The field, for example, along which we walk "outside" shows itself as belonging to such and such a person who keeps it in good order, the book which we use is bought at such and such a place, given by such and such a person, and so on.[1]

Here it first seems as though others are simply "appresented" through useful things, which are what is primarily discovered, and thus as though the fundamental difference between beings that do not have Dasein's way of being and being-with is becoming blurred.[2] Heidegger himself anticipates this and states the following objection:

> But our characterization of encountering the *others* is, then, after all, oriented towards one's *own* Da-sein. Does not it, too, start with the distinction and isolation of the "I," so that a transition from the isolated subject to the others must then be sought? (SZ 118, BT 111, translation modified)

But for Heidegger this supposition is a misunderstanding, and as he continues,

> In order to avoid this misunderstanding, we must observe in what sense we are talking about "the others." "The others" does not mean everybody else but me—those from whom the "I" distinguishes itself. They are, rather, those from whom one mostly does *not* distinguish oneself, those among whom one is, too. This being-there-too with them does not have the ontological character of being objectively present "with" them within a world. The "with" is of the character of Da-sein, the "also" means the sameness of being as circumspect, heedful being-in-the-world. (SZ 118, BT 111)

We can easily understand what Heidegger means here if we avoid the term "relevance" and, in keeping with the examples he cites, simply say that every production of something takes place with a view toward its possible use. As a norm, such use is use by others. It is true that all behavior is "for the sake of" one's own Dasein in the sense that one wants to be one's receptivity for the openness of beings in a definite way; but a series of activities can still only be performed because there are others for whom those activities are meaningful. Others are in turn defined by their activities, so that Dasein as being-with is "essentially for the sake of others" (SZ 123, BT 116). One is oneself an other, insofar as one makes possible through one's own actions the actions of others. Talk of "others" makes sense only from the first-person perspective, and this perspective characterizes everyone with whom one is.

Accordingly, "being-with" means, for one, that each of us in our everyday taking care is referred by others and their taking care to the totality of useful things in which we operate—and when we use the term "reference" here, this implies that others remain "initially and for the most part" inexplicit. For instance, the supplier of materials does not generally call attention to himself per se. Now of course this does not mean that others are altogether disregarded; instead, they remain inexplicit from the standpoint of taking care as long as taking care remains unproblematic. Yet "being-with" does not just mean being referred to one's own work by those who deliver the material for it or who assign the job to get done. It also means that those things that do not belong to one's "workworld" can be grasped as useful things. Heidegger indicates this with another example of how others are "also encountered" with useful things: "The boat anchored at the shore refers in its being-in-itself to an acquaintance who undertakes his voyages with it; but even as a 'boat strange to us,' it points to others" (SZ 118, BT 111, translation modified). The reference here does not consist in how, say, we explicitly occupy ourselves with the owner or user of the boat, but in how others' possible association with it makes the boat intelligible in its handiness; we do not have to deal with something ourselves to know it is a useful thing, for there are always already others who are able to deal with it in this manner.

Although we can say that others are initially and for the most part inexplicit, we must also say that they have been freed:

> The world of Da-sein thus frees beings which are not only completely different from tools and things, but which themselves in accordance with their kind of being as *Da-sein* are themselves "in" the world as being-in-the-world in which they are at the same time encountered. These beings are neither objectively present nor at hand, but they *are like* the very Da-sein which frees them—*they are there, too, and there with it.* So, if one wanted to identify the world in general with innerworldly beings, one would have to say the "world" is also Da-sein. (SZ 118, BT 111)

The freeing of others can initially be understood by analogy to the freeing of useful things, and like this type of freeing, the freeing of others can be interpreted both "ontically" and "ontologically." If we reserve the term "relevance" for beings such as useful things, we cannot say of others that they are "relevant" and leave it at that, if only because freeing is to be thought of here as reciprocal. Yet the matter does admit comparison. For it is only on the basis of the inexplicitness of others that we are capable of concentrating on an activity, and since such inexplicitness does not come about by way of an interpretation that discovers a disposition, it is perhaps best to say that others essentially "hold themselves in reserve" and that we leave them in this reserve. In their holding themselves in reserve, others are "Dasein-with." Contrary to Heidegger's formulation, Dasein-with is never, strictly speaking, "innerworldly" but only "in the world"; being-with-one-another in the world then means primarily to reciprocally let one another behave.

We can again clarify what it means to let one another behave by way of an example. Contexts of action are frequently compared to games or are illustrated in reference to them.[3] For instance, chess players do not act together in the sense that they explicitly occupy themselves with each other by, say, making their moves a topic of conversation and critically or approvingly commenting on them. Naturally, they may do so, but whenever they do they are not actually playing. In the playing of the game itself, in the concentration on their individual moves, they nevertheless behave toward each other, primarily by letting each other have their turn. I do not mean simply that chess players do not normally hinder each other from moving their pieces on the board, but that above all they let each other have their turn by giving each other the chance to develop their own strategy, in that each player's own move itself opens up further moves. Chess players reciprocally refer to the constellation of pieces by drawing the attention of their partner through their own moves toward an ever new constellation, and by holding their own personality in reserve, each invites the other to deal with this new constellation. Seen in this way, what makes the game possible is the opening up and keeping open of possibilities for action. Part of such keeping open is that one restricts oneself in the game to being a player: one acts only within the framework of the current game, and it is only on the basis of this holding in reserve that one can act at all. Of course, a game can be compared to everyday contexts of action only to a certain extent, because a game, unlike such everyday contexts, has standardized rules of play; in other words, it is clearly fixed which type of actions belong to the game and which do not. But even everyday contexts of action are unproblematic only when they have similar restrictions. To be sure, these restrictions are such that they cannot in every case—perhaps only in a few cases—be given as rules that can be formulated unambiguously. But it is true of all everyday contexts of action that we can behave in them only in a particular way, and insofar as we do this we always also hold ourselves in reserve. From this point of view, everyday action can never be grasped only as the explicit coordination of various actions in the service of a common goal, but instead always includes an openness for each other—an openness that consists in the fact that in many ways we do not relate to each other.

Now if the above interpretation is accurate, when Heidegger grasps our behaving toward each other as "concern" (*Fürsorge*), this cannot simply mean "acting on each other's behalf." Like "taking care" (*Besorgen*), the term "concern" includes "deficient modes"[4] such as "being without-one-another, passing-one-another-by, not-mattering-to-one another" (SZ 121, BT 114). It is important to note, however, that the deficient modes of concern have a different status than those of taking care. The former play an essential part in the everydayness of Dasein, for "these modes of being show the characteristics of inconspicuousness and obviousness" (SZ 121, BT 114). Even though "Dasein initially, and for the most part, lives in the deficient modes of concern" (SZ 121, BT 144), it would be a mistake to interpret these modes as complete indifference and then to oppose them to explicit forms of associating with each other in which we are "affected" by or "interested" in each other. Heidegger's point is precisely that he interprets even what might appear superficially to be indifference as a kind of concern; "caring" for each other for the most part does not mean explicitly occupying ourselves with each other.

That this is the case may be seen precisely in the two "extreme possibilities" of concern (SZ 122, BT 115). The first of these possibilities consists in putting oneself in the place of someone else in taking care and so "leaping in" for him; the one who is thereby cast "out of his place" "steps back so that afterwards, when the matter has been attended to, he can take it over as something finished and available or disburden himself of it completely" (SZ 122, BT 114). However, this "concern that leaps in" is not an explicit relation to others, even when the one who is displaced is thereby made "dependent and dominated" (SZ 122, BT 114), for this kind of concern is carried out precisely in dealing with the things that are to be taken care of. Put differently, we can only do something for someone else by letting his holding himself in reserve refer us to the activity in question. Naturally, the one who is displaced can react to the one who does this with distrust and resistance. But such a reaction is always only the articulation of one's own lack of explicitness for him who has taken one's own place. Whoever brings himself explicitly into play lets it be understood that he was not explicitly in play before.

But the concern that "leaps ahead" and is the contrasting possibility to "leaping in" also does not explicitly occupy itself with an other. To be sure, such concern touches on "the existence of the other" (SZ 122, BT 115), but in a way that when one "leaps ahead," the other can "become . . . free" for his existence (SZ 122, BT 115). How in particular this is to be understood can be clarified only through an interpretation of "authentic existence." Without anticipating this interpretation, we can illustrate what Heidegger has in mind with a sentence from the 1925–1926 course *Logic: The Question of Truth*. For instance, the hearers of a lecture are never something one "takes care of": "Communication and directing towards the seeing of a matter is never a taking-care, insofar as the seeing of the matter cannot actually be produced by the lecture, but can instead only be awakened, released."[5] Basically Heidegger is only making a pithy comment here about the art of Socratic dialogue. Even if at first glance this dialogical art consists in adapting oneself to another and taking into account his possibilities for understanding, it is still not explicitly occupied with him. We cannot lead someone else to an insight if we do not always also look away from him, and by concentrating on the matter, open up for him the possibility of achieving his own relationship to it. This type of "concern" is essentially "considerateness" and "tolerance" (SZ 123, BT 115), that is, it consists in letting others behave.

Nonetheless, the foregoing interpretation of the freeing of Dasein-with still remains "ontic." Although this freeing can be understood by analogy to the freeing of useful things, it does not depend on someone's factically being left to his reservedness. Instead, others must also be freed precisely when we explicitly occupy ourselves with them; that such occupation is at all possible implies that we must have already been involved with them as possible partners in action, or more accurately, that we must have always already been involved. We are "with them" insofar as we are opened up for them, and they are "there with" us insofar as they themselves are at all possible partners in action for us. Openness for each other is the presupposition for being able to act with each other or letting oneself be referred to one's own action by others, and thus first of all for explicitly relating oneself to them.

"Self" and the "They"

What it means to relate to others explicitly is admittedly not yet clear. Because our dealings that take care are always characterized by the inexplicitness of others and because every action with each other is impossible without this inexplicitness, we might easily presume that we become explicit for each other only when we speak with or about one another. For only in discourse do we possess the possibility of determining how others behave and of comparing that to our own behavior, so that the question of how the context of "I"-statements is to be thought can also be adequately addressed only by taking into consideration discourse about each other, whether such discourse is outwardly articulated or remains unspoken. If we interpret "I"-statements as articulations of attentiveness toward something, then these statements, on the one hand, stand in connection with dealings that are initially not articulated linguistically, and insofar as such dealing is made possible in part by others, these statements also stand in connection with others. On the other hand, because others are also able to form "I"-statements, these statements always also stand in the context of other "I"-statements, and only when we take this context into account can we understand why Heidegger claims that the "who" of everyday Dasein is not "I myself." "Self" is a term that does not express self-reference, but rather the context of "I"-statements. It belongs to the self-evident intelligibility of the self to be in this context.

This thesis, which may right away strike us as surprising, can be clarified initially by a brief observation about the everyday use of the word "self." "Self," in grammatical terms, is a "demonstrative pronoun." However, this is misleading, because the term is in fact used not in a deictic sense but contrastively. In the sentence "Peter himself broke the vase," we are made to understand that it was *no one other* than Peter—like, for example, the dog, as Peter had claimed. Along with "I," the word "self" also has this function, so that the statement

"I myself am of the conviction that p" means something different than "I am of the conviction that p." Whoever says "I myself" not only expresses his attentiveness toward something, he sets himself off against others and their way of behaving. Moreover, he sometimes also makes it clear that he is explicitly laying claim to certain attributes or ways of behaving as his own; from this perspective we can explain why the capacity to develop such attributes and ways of behaving, as well as how they then constitute a person, is designated as "the self."[6] In any case, the point I want to emphasize is that it is only in the context of saying "I myself" that talk of "the others" receives its full sense. However, to claim that saying "I myself" always sets me off against others is certainly not to imply that an unmistakable difference exists between "me myself" and others. If such a difference existed, saying "I myself" would not at all be necessary. The utterance of the sentence, "I myself broke the vase," is meaningful only if it is not clear who it was. The same is true when someone says "he himself" is of the conviction that p; he is not merely contrasting his position with someone who asserted that q, instead he means that he is not simply repeating the assertion that p.

Accordingly, the presupposition operative in "I myself"-statements is that there is fundamentally no way of behaving that can be accomplished by only *one* alone. Furthermore, ways of behaving do not become explicit as long as they are accomplished undisturbed, and with any such disturbance, what first draws attention is not how we are behaving, but what is making the disturbance—thus what is lacking or faulty about the useful thing. Ways of behaving are first encountered as the ways of behaving of others, for the others "*are* what they do" (SZ 126, BT 118); that is, with their definite ways of behaving, others also come into view as "these definite ones." They are always "these definite ones" insofar as what they do admits comparison with our own doing, and this comparability also allows us to distinguish ourselves from each other. The common pursuit of the same or similar things is, as Heidegger says, characterized by "distantiality":

> In taking care of the things which one has taken hold of, for, and against others, there is constant care as to the way one differs from them, whether this difference is to be equalized, whether one's own Da-sein has lagged behind others and wants to catch up in relation to them, whether Da-sein in its priority over others is intent on suppressing them. Being-with-one-another is, unknown to itself, disquieted by the care about this distance. Existentially expressed, being-with-one-another has the character of distantiality. The more inconspicuous this kind of being is to everyday Da-sein itself, all the more stubbornly and primordially does it work itself out. (SZ 126, BT 118)

The relations to others Heidegger has in mind here are what we ordinarily know as "competitiveness," "ambition," "oppression" and the like. So it seems strange when he claims that disquiet about the distance from others is "concealed" in Dasein. He cannot mean that we know nothing in an everyday way about competition, ambition, and oppression. In addition, Heidegger mentions in a different context that we can do or want to do something "purely out of ambition."[7] What he must mean, then, is that being-with-one-another is characterized by "distantiality" even when one is supposedly concerned about unity or agreement with others. For then one is trying to eliminate one's differences from the others, so that even here in being-with-one-another a "being-against-one-another" is at play (SZ 175, BT 163). Insofar as all behavior that is explicitly accomplished by "oneself" is marked by others, Heidegger can speak of the "domination of others" (SZ 126, BT 119). This domination does not consist in the fact that we are always subjected to the influence or enforcing of a decision by others; it can be manifest even in our own dominion over others. Instead the critical point here is that all behavior explicitly accomplished by "oneself" is a behavior in otherness. Otherness in this sense does not mean becoming other, or "alter-ation."[8] For the concept of becoming other implies that one does not primarily experience *oneself* in being-with-one-another—and that it is not primarily in *being-with-one-another* that one experiences oneself—but that instead one can also be the "pure Ego of my pure cogitations,"[9] and one becomes an empirical "I" only when one comes into community with others. Aside from the fact that it is difficult to think such a "becoming" at all, otherness and the way it comes to expression in saying "I myself" is possible only under the presupposition of being-with and Dasein-with. "Otherness" designates solely the way in which one's own behavior is explicitly determined as one's own.

As the colloquial use of the phrase "I myself" attests, this explicitness is not tied to definite others. Whoever says "he himself" has done such and such does not necessarily set himself apart from definite others; possibly he does not even know who might otherwise be responsible for the deed in question. The same holds true when someone wants to be better than others; he does not have to think about definite persons, and if he should ever happen to do so, what takes priority for him is what they do and how they do it. The others retain a certain inexplicitness in coming into view only in accordance with what they do. Because saying "I myself" is never determined only by definite others but is determined by an otherness that is ultimately uncontrollable in its singular possibilities, the openness of Dasein-with comes to appear in explicit being-with-one-another. Now being-with-one-another, as the medium in which one achieves one's own explicit definiteness, is what Heidegger calls the "they." The "they" is characterized by "inconspicuousness" and "unascertainability" (SZ 126, BT 119), and in this it unfolds "its genuine dictatorship" (SZ 126, BT 119). This dictatorship consists in how "they" give the answer beforehand—or 'dictate'—which activities are deemed worthwhile and how the performance of these activities is to be evaluated. Seen in this way, "they" articulate meaningfulness, which, as Heidegger expressly makes clear, is tied to discourse (GA 20, 275). Once again, the "they" as obvious or self-evident has somehow always already been pronounced and as such is the "obvious intelligibility of me myself."

Whoever "himself" wants to be better than others because of that already oriented toward what "they" in a certain respect do and say. What "they" do and say is "average": "The they maintains itself factically in the averageness of what is proper, what is allowed, and what is not. Of what is granted success and what is not" (SZ 127, BT 119). The "care of averageness" (SZ 127, BT 119) can be understood in terms of the fact that one's own behavior becomes explicit in relation to others' behavior; it is ultimately care for this explicitness, for no one can set himself apart from others, and by so doing explicitly be "he himself," if others' behavior does not thereby remain *comparable* with his own behavior. Whoever wants to be better than others—or at least as good as them—must in principle also see what they do as achievable. The presupposition that the everyday being of others only comes into view as doing enables Heidegger to also speak of the "*leveling down* of all possibilities of being" in relation to averageness (SZ 127, BT 119). The differing possibilities of behavior must be leveled out according to the measure of comparability.

In view of the misunderstandings that have repeatedly sprung up around Heidegger's conception of "they," I first want to emphasize that his analysis is not intended as "cultural criticism." Heidegger does not enter into a critique of the anonymity of mass society. The references to public transportation and the news media are solely illustrations of the comparability of behavior that characterizes the "they": "every one is like the next" (SZ 126, BT 127) as a user of trains, cars and planes, as a television viewer and newspaper reader. But this is not because of modern means of transportation or modern information technology. The comparability of behavior is also the precondition for public appearance or standing, and what Aristotle describes as the *politikos bios* can, at least in part, be reformulated in terms of Heidegger's conception of the "they," to the extent that the "political life" is concerned only with honor (*timē*). One could also see Hegel's conception of a self-consciousness that is dependent on others as an attempt to bring into view the structure that is at issue for Heidegger. It should be noted that what is *not* being asserted by these references is that Hegel's conception of self-consciousness and Aristotle's analysis of honor are the same as Heidegger's conception of the "they." The working out of a structure in a philosophical theory is so bound to the fundamental concepts of that theory that an attempt to bring Heidegger and Hegel into dialogue would first require developing Hegel's fundamental concepts. That is not my intention here. Suffice it to say that it makes a vast difference whether the talk is of self-consciousness, as in Hegel, or whether, as in Heidegger, it concerns how one's own behavior becomes explicit in relation to others' behavior. Like Hegel's conception of self-consciousness, Heidegger's conception of "everyday being a self" is certainly a philosophical conception, and as such it is to be distinguished from critical diagnoses of culture or society in that it lays claim to being plausible in itself and not only with respect to particular historical conditions.

But even when the philosophical import—or more accurately, the "daseins-analytical" import—of Heidegger's elucidation of the "they" is taken seriously, this elucidation has often been misunderstood. One such misunderstanding consists in interpreting the "they" as a mode of determination by outside forces and opposing this mode to the mode of self-determination. That the "who" of everyday Dasein is the "they" then means: "I allow what I respectively do and intend and how I understand myself to be determined by what *one* (the they) regards as good, and I do not determine it myself."[10] To be sure, this interpretation takes up a distinction that is fundamental for further developments in *Being and Time*, namely the distinction between the "self of everyday Dasein," the "they-self," and the "*authentic self,* the self that has explicitly grasped itself" (SZ 129, BT 121). But what this interpretation leaves out of consideration is the point of this distinction. This consists in the fact that there is talk of a "self" of everyday Dasein at all. If this "self" is nothing other than what is expressed in saying "I myself," as has been shown, then being in the "they" is precisely not a "letting oneself be determined," but rather the everyday way of self-determination. From this it admittedly follows that even the "authentic self" can now no longer consist in acting deliberately, that is, from a reasoned choice.[11] Indeed, for Heidegger the "they" renders in advance "every judgment and decision" and thereby takes "the responsibility of Dasein away from it" (SZ 127, BT 119); it is by letting oneself be "disburdened" in this way (SZ 127, BT 120) that one is characterized by "dependency" (SZ 128, BT 120). However, this means that all decisions and judgments are made everyday in the way of saying "I myself" and in this are determined by the structure designated as the "they"; to the extent that saying "I myself" is a comparing oneself to others and thus a setting oneself apart from them, it expresses a reliance on others that we can call "not standing on one's own" or "dependency" (*Unselbständigkeit*). This dependency is disburdening in that in everydayness, it always provides possibilities for comparison as one makes judgments and decisions. Besides, it is not enough to refer to the deliberateness of action, for deliberation alone is still not a criterion for "independence" over and against the "they." Actions motivated by envy or ambition can also be highly deliberate. Furthermore, every process of deliberation that guides action is in one way or another related to others. Insofar as actions are justified by the grounds given for them, these grounds—in order to be accepted at all—must take into account what "they" say, that is, they must abide by the comparability of actions. If we determine the independence of those acting in terms of the process of deliberation that informed their actions, then we have at best succeeded in arriving at a pragmatically conceived concept of independence and must disregard the structural dependency through which one is bound to an other in saying "I myself." "Independence" can then only mean that someone does not primarily do what he does from an orientation toward others, and in this sense someone, even if he acts out of ambition, would be called "independent," just as long as he is not totally obsessed by his ambition. In such an obsession, the determination by outside forces consists in the fact that "something is happening in me,"[12] and is, seen in this way, the same thing as the Platonic-Aristotelian *kata to pathos zēn* (living according to passion). Yet the *pathē* occupy a completely different place for Heidegger than they do for Aristotle, and besides, Heidegger's concept of independence is not intended pragmatically.

Until this point it has admittedly remained unclear why Heidegger's conception of the "they" is to be conceived as the basic concept of unfreedom. In order to answer this question, it may seem obvious to return to the interpretation of the "they" as determination by outside forces. But in the framework of this interpretation, one could not even define "unfreedom" in the Aristotelian sense, for Aristotle does not hesitate to call behavior "free" even if it is strongly determined by affect. If we designate the conception of the "they" as the basic concept of unfreedom, we are not in addition saying that the "they" is as such identical with "unfreedom." If we suppose that "authentic being a self" is "being free," then if we were to identify the "they" with "unfreedom," "authentic being a self" and the "they" would be cast as rigid alternatives. That Heidegger is not asserting this is made clear when he says: "*Authentic being one's self* is not based on an exceptional state of the subject, a state detached from the they, *but is an existentiell modification of the they as an essential existential*" (SZ 130, BT 122). Accordingly, even in authentic being a self one is determined by the structure of the "they," and if that were not the case, as "authentic self" one would have had to stop being this definite one among others. Moreover, if the "they" were identical with unfreedom, then as this definite one among others, one would always be unfree. However, we are unfree only if we are exclusively oriented by the structure of the "they" and want to be nothing but a definite one among others. What is foreclosed through this is how one "authentically" is, and "authentically" one is characterized by disclosedness. The closing off of disclosedness presupposes disclosedness; it is the dominance of the appearance of disclosedness rather than disclosedness itself. Yet the appearance of disclosedness is behavior, and if we want to grasp how the dominance of appearance can at all come about, we must first investigate the relation between disclosedness and behavior. This relation is the difference of freedom. The "they" is an appearance of this freedom insofar as ways of behaving are made familiar within it. Without the "they" there is no behavior.

—translated by Julia Davis and Richard Polt

Notes

1. *Being and Time*, trans. Joan Stambaugh (Albany, New York: SUNY Press, 1996), 111 (German page 117). Henceforth cited as "SZ" followed by the German pagination, and "BT" followed by the English pagination.

2. Thus Michael Theunissen writes, "Encounter in *Being and Time* hardly means: *We* encounter *each other*, but almost entirely: Inner-worldly beings encounter a *Dasein* that lets itself be encountered": *The Other: Studies in the Social Ontology of Husserl, Heidegger, Sartre, and Buber*, trans. Christopher Macann (Cambridge, Mass.: MIT Press, 1984), 181.

3. As a classic text on this point, see Wittgenstein's *Philosophical Investigations.*

4. On this term cf. Klaus Hartmann, "The Logic of Deficient and Eminent Modes in Heidegger," *Journal of the British Society for Phenomenology* 5 (May 1974): 118–34.

5. *Logik: Die Frage nach der Wahrheit, Gesamtausgabe*, vol. 21 (Frankfurt am Main: Vittorio Klostermann, 1976), 222.

6. On this use of the expression see esp. G. H. Mead, *Mind, Self and Society from the Standpoint of a Social Behaviorist* (Chicago: University of Chicago Press, 1934).

7. *History of the Concept of Time: Prolegomena*, trans. Theodore Kisiel (Bloomington: Indiana University Press, 1985), 245.

8. On this concept cf. Theunissen, *The Other*, 89.

9. Edmund Husserl, *Phenomenology and the Foundations of the Sciences, Collected Works*, vol. 1, trans. Ted E. Klein and William E. Pohl (The Hague: Martinus Nijhoff, 1980), 100.

10. Ernst Tugendhat, *Self-Consciousness and Self-Determination*, trans. Paul Stern (Cambridge, Mass.: MIT Press, 1986), 206.

11. Cf. Tugendhat, *Self-Consciousness and Self-Determination*, 215–17, 265.

12. Cf. Tugendhat, *Self-Consciousness and Self-Determination*, 250.

7

Subjectivity: Locating the First-Person in *Being and Time*

Steven Crowell

> This must be constantly borne in mind, namely, that the subjective problem
> is not something about an objective issue, but is the subjectivity itself.
>
> —Kierkegaard

IT IS THE CHIEF TASK of philosophy of mind to provide an account of intentionality. What this amounts to can be variously formulated: How is it possible that consciousness is consciousness 'of' something? How can our mental states have 'content'? What accounts for the 'as-structure' of our experience? And so on. How one formulates the question is already the outline of an answer, and so debates in philosophy of mind are inseparable from decisions about broader questions of philosophy. One such decision concerns the ontology of, as Heidegger puts it, "the entity which is intentional."[1] John Haugeland has usefully distinguished between 'right-wing' (or individualist) and 'left-wing' (or socialist) theories of this entity.[2] Individualist positions, broadly Cartesian in orientation, tend to link the question of intentionality quite closely to aspects of the first-person stance. For such theories, content is either 'in the head,' and then some plausible account of how such content can deliver the world as it purports to do must be given; or else 'meaning just ain't in the head,' in which case the task is to explain the relation between so-called 'wide' and 'narrow' content, or why I sometimes seem authoritatively to know what I am thinking about (first-person authority).[3] Socialist positions, in contrast, emphasize the activities of the entity who is intentional, arguing that the 'as-structure' of experience is tied to the normativity inherent in social practices and has little or nothing to do with the 'mental' in the Cartesian (and broadly psychological) sense stressed by the individualists. For these theorists, first-person authority is either denied outright (Wittgensteinian behaviorism), or else relegated to a non-explanatory role.[4]

If I am allowed an unconscionably gross simplification, I would say that the fundamental issue separating positions in philosophy of mind concerns the place of the first-person in an account of intentionality. In any case, this simplification guides this chapter, for the issue has played an important role in assessing the phenomenological accounts of intentionality given by Husserl and Heidegger. It is often held that the first-person perspective, so crucial for Husserl, occupies no significant place in *Being and Time*.[5] I shall argue the contrary, that first-person authority plays a decisive role in Heidegger's account of intentionality. This will prove to be a somewhat peculiar notion of 'first-person authority,' but I will defend it by offering a 'phenomenological interpretation' (in Heidegger's sense) of *Being and Time* in which I show, first, that there is an account of first-person authority in that text and, second, that it is not a mere afterthought but is indispensable for clarifying the 'ontic transcendence' whereby we grasp something as something. More specifically, I will argue that Heidegger's phenomenology of conscience (*Gewissen*) is an account of first-person self-awareness—or the 'subjectivity of the subject'[6]—and that the sort of first-person authority embedded in this account constitutes the origin of reason. By reason here I mean, minimally, the ability to think and act not merely in accord with norms, but *in light* of them. The thesis is that for Heidegger, first-person authority is what transforms (factic) 'grounds' into (normative) 'reasons' (*Gründe*) *and* explains how it is that Dasein dwells in a world and does not merely function in an environment.[7]

Two Conceptions of First-Person Authority

Let us begin by noting why it is commonly held that there is no significant treatment of the first-person (or 'subjectivity') in *Being and Time*. One reason is that Heidegger's text is frequently understood as a complete rejection of all things Husserlian. As Heidegger wrote to Jaspers in 1926, "If the treatise has been written 'against' anyone, then it has been written against Husserl."[8] Now consider David Carr's claim that Husserl's "phenomenology is not just about experiences, or even about experiences and their objects, but about the first-person standpoint itself. . . . It is about what it means to be conscious or to be a conscious being, to be a subject, a self, or an ego."[9] If this is essentially correct (as I take it to be), it might seem that in rejecting Husserl Heidegger must lose all interest in "the first-person standpoint itself." Such an impression can only be enhanced if one considers why Husserl is interested in the first-person stance in the first place—namely, because it apparently possesses authority with regard to its *contents* (intentional experiences), on the one hand, and with regard to its *self-awareness* (as transcendental ego), on the other. Neither conception of first-person authority seems present in Heidegger's text.

On the matter of Husserl's interest in *Erlebnisse,* for instance, Hubert Dreyfus has argued that Heidegger's account of Dasein as a kind of 'comportment'— skillful coping in the world—renders any appeal to 'conscious experiences' otiose in an explanation of intentionality. The mental—in the traditional sense of consciousness as psychological subjectivity—becomes a rather minor modification of 'mindless coping' according to explicit or tacit norms of social or 'background' practices. These practices suffice to explain how things can show up 'as' the things they are. Hence, "we are not to think of Dasein as a conscious subject" since any such traditional conception must, according to Dreyfus, reintroduce what Heidegger specifically rejects: the Cartesian 'cabinet of consciousness' with its 'mental representations' that are supposed to be foundational for our access to the world.[10]

Similarly, on the question of the authority of first-person self-awareness, Heidegger is apparently quite clear that little is to be gained ontologically from such self-awareness. First, though it is true that the "question of the 'who' [of Dasein] answers itself in terms of the 'I' itself, the 'subject,' the 'Self'" (BT 150/114), Heidegger is quick to point out that this gives us nothing more than a mere "formal reflective awareness of the 'I'" (BT 151/115). And it seems obvious, as Dreyfus argues, that "such self-referential consciousness is not the subject-matter of *Being and Time,*" since "according to Heidegger such consciousness is a special mode of revealing and a derivative one at that."[11] As Heidegger puts it in *Basic Problems of Phenomenology,* a deliberate, reflective "I-awareness" is "only a mode of self-*apprehension,* but not the mode of primary self-disclosure." This latter is a self-awareness mediated by social practices: Dasein "never finds itself otherwise than in the things themselves"; it does not "need a special kind of observation" because when "Dasein gives itself over immediately and passionately to the world, its own self is reflected back to it from things."[12] Even if formal-reflective I-awareness has some sort of authority, it is hard to see how it could be of much philosophical interest.

These arguments are compelling, but to say that the first-person stance does not have its traditional significance in Heidegger's text is not to say that it has *no* significance at all. It is not impossible that explicit criticism of the Cartesian tradition coexists with an implicit *existential reinterpretation* of aspects of that tradition, such that there is a recognizable role for first-person authority, but one that is identified neither with privileged access to the content of my mental states as foundational for intentionality nor with a formal-reflective I-awareness supposedly definitive of who I am as 'transcendental' ego. This, at any rate, is what I hope to show in what follows.

In presenting Heidegger's existential reinterpretation I shall not focus on the first sense of first-person authority, concerning a special warrant regarding the content of my mental states, but on the second sense, concerning the peculiar character of first-person self-awareness. A reinterpretation of the first would indeed be possible. It would start by demonstrating that Husserl's concept of first-person warrant does not commit him to representationalism or 'internalism,' and that Heidegger was aware of this. The latter's remarks about the 'cabinet of consciousness' are directed specifically at Nicolai Hartmann and not at the phenomenologists.[13] Thus, if it turned out that there were a philosophically interesting sense in which reference to consciousness *had* to figure in an account of intentionality,[14] this would not by itself be an argument against Heidegger's position, since he is not committed to the view that any appeal to first-person consciousness must involve one in the dead-end of a 'worldless' subject. Nevertheless, because Heidegger is practically silent on any role that first-person warrant might play in the account of intentionality,[15] the whole argument would require lengthy reconstructions. It is quite different with respect to the second sense of 'first-person authority,' however. For *Being and Time* is explicit about what an existential reinterpretation of first-person self-*awareness* should look like, and it also suggests (though not nearly as explicitly) just why such a reinterpretation is crucial to the account of intentionality. So to this I now turn.

A Gap in the Account of Self-Awareness in *Being and Time* Division I

For all its usefulness, Heidegger's account of ontologically primordial self-awareness as a reflection back from the things with which I am practically absorbed cannot be considered an adequate account of self-awareness. Nor did Heidegger intend it as such. This is because the 'I' who is reflected back in this way is "the 'who' of *everyday* Dasein," and this, as Heidegger says, "just is *not* the 'I myself'" (BT 150/114). Thus Dasein, as "I myself," must be capable of another—and ontologically no less authoritative—mode of self-awareness, one not subject to Heidegger's objections against the merely formal character of reflective I-consciousness. The trick is to say what such a form of self-awareness can be.

An approach can be made by recognizing that the everyday mode of self-awareness in which "Dasein understands itself proximally and for the most part in terms of its world" (BT 156/120) is not a genuine *first-person* mode of self-awareness. As Heidegger argues, "the self of everyday Dasein is the *one-self*" (BT 167/129), and it becomes evident from his description of the one-self that it understands (is aware of) itself wholly in third-person terms—a fact that has implications for his account of intentionality.

Central to that account is Heidegger's claim that things show up 'as' something originally within the context of our practical *dealings* with them. It is because everyday Dasein engages in goal-directed actions that things show up 'as' fit for the task, useful 'in order to' drive nails, and so on; only so can they be assigned some non-arbitrary 'significance.' About this 'assignment,' Heidegger emphasizes two things. First, it is holistic: "Taken strictly, there 'is' no such thing as *a* tool. To any tool there always belongs a totality of equipment" (BT 97/68), since to be a hammer or a pen is to be defined in instrumental relation to other things such as nails or paper. Second, the structure (intelligibility) of this equipmental totality derives from Dasein's own 'practical identity,' which Heidegger terms the *Worumwillen*: an "ability to be for the sake of which" I myself am (BT 119/86). This concept is meant to account for the non-arbitrary attribution of goal-directedness to my activity—that is, it is to serve the role of establishing an *intention*, without which no *specific* 'assignment' of functions to things could be made. Heidegger's innovation here is to locate this intention not 'in the head' but in practices themselves, as 'ways for me to be' in the world. One cannot simply identify this practical identity or 'for the sake of' with social role (mother, professor, mail carrier), since not all goal-directed actions belong to socially and institutionally *defined* practices. Nevertheless, it can serve its function in the account of intentionality only because it, like social role, is necessarily *typical*. Only because my behavior is understood (not only by the other but by I myself) as a type does it have the relation to specific norms *of* the type that render it 'intentional' behavior—that is, assessable in terms of success or failure.[16] Heidegger expresses this fact with the claim that everyday Dasein is governed by "publicness," that it "concerns itself as such with *averageness*," and that it is "diffident" (*abständig*), careful that it *not* distinguish itself from others (BT 126–27, 164–65). For this reason Heidegger designates the self of everyday Dasein the 'one-self.'

Heidegger's account of the one-self, then, describes my practical identity as a specific form of anonymity: engaged in the world, I am aware of myself only as 'another' or as 'anyone'—that is, in third-person terms. As typical, my practices belong within what Heidegger calls a 'totality of involvements,' and because it is in terms of such practices that I am "reflected back to [myself] from things," *I myself* make sense only within that same totality. I am a *persona* (mask). To the extent that my practical identity is typical—and there can be no other kind—there is essentially no difference between the way things come by their 'as-structure' and the way I come by mine. It is true that Heidegger *signals* a difference between our awareness of things, of others, and of myself—namely, as *besorgen*, *fürsorgen*, and *selbst-sorgen*—but Division I does not account for these different phenomenological features of our experience, and because it does not, a gap opens up in its account of intentionality.

The gap appears because Heidegger holds that in order for something to be assigned a *definite* significance (an 'in order to') in the totality of involvements the latter must "itself [go] back ultimately to a 'towards which' in which there is *no* further involvement" (BT 116/84)—that is it must be anchored in something 'autotelic,' something that does not receive its 'assignment' of significance from something else but "has assigned *itself* to an 'in order to'" (BT 119/86). Without such a being it would be impossible to say whether something was functioning well as a heater or poorly as an air conditioner; it takes on a definite meaning in light of that 'for the sake of which' *I* am using it. But what or who am 'I' here? If I, in turn, am assigned 'my' significance instrumentally, then the totality of involvements is once again underdetermined and the intentionality of experience has not been explained. For this reason, Heidegger identifies "Dasein's very being" as "the sole authentic 'for the sake of which'" (BT 117/84)—that is as "a 'towards which' in which there is *no* further involvement." And yet, nothing in his account of the *Umwillen* or significance of the one-self allows us to see *why* it has no further involvement, why it is *not* just another instrumentality. For as typical, any 'for the sake of' can also be understood instrumentally: I can be a professor in order to make a living, be a college student in order to avoid the draft, be a father in order to carry on the family line, and so on.

Heidegger is right that the totality of involvements must be anchored in a being "in which there is *no* further involvement"—that is in a being for whom things *matter*, a being "for which, in its being, that very being is essentially an *issue*" (BT 117/84). But such a being must be capable of a mode of self-awareness other than the one that characterizes its practical identity. In addition to its everyday (third-person) mode of self-awareness, Heidegger owes us an account of Dasein's first-person awareness of 'I myself,' an account of the subjectivity that belongs to, but remains invisible in, the one-self. Without it, his account of intentionality remains incomplete. And if third-person self-awareness is necessarily typical, it is not unreasonable to expect that first-person self-awareness will be radically indexical.

Is there such an account to be found in *Being and Time?* In approaching this question I will begin by considering certain peculiarities of first-person self-reference (saying 'I') that any theory must account for. The idea is to take these features of first-person self-reference as indicators of the nature of first-person self-awareness and then see whether anything in *Being and Time* addresses what is distinctive about that nature.[17]

First, the proper use of 'I' infallibly picks out the entity it purports to refer to—both in the sense that it cannot fail to refer, and in the sense that it cannot fail to pick out exactly what it purports to pick out. By contrast, in using a proper name or definite description to refer to the same thing, I could always fail in either way. But since the one-self is aware of itself precisely in so far as "it does *not* distinguish itself from others," when *it* says 'I' both the definiteness and infallibility of its self-reference remain unaccounted for. It is always prone to a 'failure of reference' or an 'error of misidentification.'

Second, if we distinguish a subjective from an objective use of 'I,' we note a crucial aspect of first-person self-reference. An objective use of 'I' (as in "I am bleeding" or "I am six feet tall") presupposes that I have established certain properties as true of an object in the world and that I have identified myself with that object. Thus I could be in error if the object in question turns out in fact not to be me. The subjective use of 'I' (as in "I believe that Heidegger wrote *Being and Time*" or "I feel anxious") involves no such presupposition.[18] The possession of identificatory knowledge is neither a necessary nor sufficient condition for successful use of 'I' in these cases. As Castañeda observes, "there is no third-person special characteristic that one has to think that one possesses in order to think of oneself as I."[19] In short, such self-identification is immediate, non-criterial, and non-inferential.

This point will prove crucial for establishing the place of first-person self-awareness in *Being and Time*, since it shows that even though self-identification of the one-self is neither immediate nor non-criterial—that is, the awareness of myself "reflected back from things" is always *as* something (father, professor, etc.) and thus mediated by criteria belonging to these types or roles—this does not mean that, should such criteria be unavailable, I could not intelligibly refer to, or identify, myself.

Finally, use of 'I' to designate 'I myself' *requires* that I "dispense with every type of third-person reference."[20] That is, I have not mastered the use of 'I' unless I understand that it does not, as Zahavi puts it, merely "single a specific person out in a given context"—the person who is speaking—but demands also that I be "aware that it is [I myself] who is referred to." And this sort of self-awareness cannot be captured in any third-person terms, since "no matter how detailed a third-person description I give of a person, this description cannot entail that *I* am that person."[21] Hence, the way 'I' refers cannot be reduced to any form of the way third-person terms pick out entities in the world. If it could be so reduced it would be impossible to understand the *surprise* exhibited (to use Nozick's example) by Oedipus when he discovers that he is the very entity to whom he was (*successfully*) referring all along in third-person terms.

Before showing that Heidegger provides an account of first-person self-awareness that does justice to these peculiarities of self-reference, it may be useful to identify two solutions to the problem which he rejects. The first is Husserl's theory that saying 'I' ultimately refers to a unique transcendental *ego* that eludes all type-concepts, including natural kind concepts. Because the 'I' is identifiable prior to all 'worldly' predicates, Husserl takes it to pick out an unworldly entity in a sense that supposedly avoids the paradox of a 'piece of the world' constituting the world as a whole. Though the situation is complicated,[22] it is clear that Heidegger wants to avoid positing anything like an ego as the referent of 'I.' Whatever tensions there may be between first- and third-person self-reference will be explained, instead, as existential modalities of *Jemeinigkeit.*

The second rejected approach is that of Wittgenstein in the *Tractatus.* There the peculiarities of immediate, non-criteriological, non-inferential self-reference do not reflect an entity in or beyond the world, but the 'limit' of the world itself. On this view, there *is* nothing of which I am aware when I am aware of myself in first-person perspective, and the whole issue of 'subjectivity' becomes a philosophical non-starter. Some have held that this is precisely *Heidegger's* approach to the issue.[23] Rather than argue against this interpretation, however, I will try to establish that there *is* an account of first-person self-awareness in *Being and Time* by considering the relation between Division I and Division II of that text.

About this strategy the following should be emphasized straightaway: First, though Division II offers an account of 'authentic' being-a-self to complete Division I's exploration of the everyday one-self, it would be a mistake to equate first-person self-awareness with authenticity. As Heidegger tells us, "authentic existence" is "only a modified way in which such everydayness is seized upon" (BT 224/179). The authentic self's awareness of itself is thus not free of the machinery of third-person description that supports the one-self, as is required by our analysis of first-person self-reference; it too is "reflected back to itself from things." Second, since "the 'one' itself articulates the referential context of significance" (BT 167/129)—and so, as Dreyfus argues, all intelligibility is *everyday* intelligibility because the one ultimately "makes . . . significance and intelligibility possible"[24]—it must be the case that Dasein's first-person self-awareness, like Wittgenstein's 'I,' is not a mode of *intelligibility* at all. Does this not reduce the very notion to incoherence? If being-in-the-world were equivalent to acting in the world this conclusion would follow, but Heidegger's position is more complicated. While both the one-self and the authentic self are 'actors,' there is a condition in which Dasein no longer acts, the condition of the *collapse* of the one-self. Here we find both the place and the importance of first-person self-awareness in *Being and Time.* In this putatively negative phenomenon, where the care-structure is not yet the resolute committed authentic self engaged in the world, there lies a positive phenomenological content—not some further content descriptive of myself that more richly answers the question of who I am, but my very subjectivity.

The Collapse of the One-Self as First-Person Self-Awareness

I shall pursue the familiar details of the care-structure—existentiality, facticity, and discourse—only so far as is necessary to see how the breakdown of the one-self can yield a positive grasp of subjectivity. Heidegger associates facticity with *Befindlichkeit* and argues that the "primary discovery of the world" is a function "of 'bare mood,'" thanks to which the world is there as mattering to us in some way or another (BT 137–38, 176–77). Existentiality, in turn, is associated with *Verstehen*—not the thematic understanding of this or that item in the world, but the *self*-understanding Dasein exhibits as it "presses ahead" into that "ability to be for the sake of which it itself is" (BT 119/86). Finally, 'discourse' (*Rede*) is "the articulation of intelligibility" (BT 161, 203–4), that is the ontological ground of communication. Now the salient point here is that since the 'one' articulates "the referential context of significance"—the world—as such, the one-self cannot be identified with some limited set of possibilities. All possible ways in which the world can matter, all possible self-understandings or 'for-the-sake-ofs,' and all possible discursive communications belong to the one-self—as public, conforming, normalized third-person Selfhood. A genuine first-person self-awareness would thus seem to be strictly impossible.

And so it would be, if self-awareness were necessarily linked to 'possibility' in Heidegger's sense. But this is not the case, as can be seen from Heidegger's account of the *breakdown* of the one-self. This modification of the care-structure has special methodological significance, as Heidegger says, because it is "what Dasein, *from its own standpoint*, demands as the only ontico-ontological way of access to itself" (BT 226/182). And this, I shall argue, is equivalent to providing phenomenological access to 'subjectivity' as the condition of possibility for authentic selfhood—a condition that has more in common with what Kierkegaard identified as 'inwardness' than it does the Cartesian stream of *Erlebnisse* that we share with higher animals.

First, if everyday Dasein's moods are that whereby the world matters to it, it is in *Angst* that the world is given in such a way that it *no longer* matters at all. Entities in the world no longer speak to me (the pure 'that it is' is all that remains); the world is uncanny (*unheimlich*); my involvements with others 'recede' until I grasp myself as the *solus ipse* (BT 186–89, 231–33). This does not mean that I find myself alone; rather, I discover my subjectivity, a dimension of my being that is extrinsic to every 'totality of involvements.' Only now does it become ontologically apparent (though still only negatively) how I can be a 'toward which' that 'has *no* further involvement.' Second, if all mood has its self-understanding, then the understanding belonging to *Angst* must stand in stark contrast to all those 'for-the-sake-ofs' in which the world matters to me in some way. If things in the world lose all significance, this is because the practical self-understandings that support them have all collapsed. In anxiety I can no longer "press forward into possibilities," can no longer cope in terms of some ability to be. But if that is so, how can I be aware of myself, since I am no longer "reflected back to myself from things"? Such a state Heidegger calls 'death'—in which I exist as "the possibility of the impossibility of being there" (BT 294/250). The "impossibility of being there" does not refer to demise, to my absence from the realm of the living; rather, it indicates that my self-awareness, or self-understanding, is not dependent on any one of my abilities to be or on all of them taken together. There is a way that I am which is not an ability to be. Since 'understanding' my 'finitude' in this sense contrasts with all *possible* concrete 'for-the-sake-ofs,' it is a form of inwardness, altogether invisible ('unintelligible') from the standpoint of the one-self. In Heidegger's terms, death is unrepresentable, my 'ownmost' possibility.

Finally, Heidegger identifies the third moment of the care-structure in breakdown—discourse—with conscience (*Gewissen*), emphasizing its break with the one-self by noting that conscience discourses exclusively in the mode of "keeping silent." However, where the analyses of *Angst* and death yield insights mainly into what the first-person is not, Heidegger's analysis of the two sides of conscience—"what is talked about" and "what is said" (BT 317/272)— elucidates the *positive* role of first-person self-awareness. By "what is talked about" Heidegger means that "to which the appeal is made"; by "what is said" he means what conscience "gives to understand" about that to which the appeal is made. Analyzing the first, Heidegger provides an existential ontological account of the peculiarities of first-person self-reference; analyzing the second, he shows the philosophical significance of subjectivity. I shall examine each in turn.

First-Person Self-Awareness in the Call of Conscience: Radical Indexicality

That to which the call of conscience is addressed is 'Dasein itself.' Now, since Dasein is not an entity with properties, the 'itself' (Dasein's *Jemeinigkeit*) must be understood as involving modalized *possibilities* for being itself. To mark this modalization Heidegger distinguishes between the one-self and the 'Self.' The phenomenon of conscience belongs to the breakdown of the one-self: "And because only the *Self* of the one-self gets appealed to and brought to hear, the 'one' collapses" (BT 317/272). What Heidegger here misleadingly calls the 'Self' is, I believe, more properly thought as the subjectivity, or first-person self-awareness, of Dasein.[25]

In the language Heidegger uses to describe this Self or subject, it is easy to recognize the peculiarities of first-person self-reference we identified above. First, according to Heidegger, my awareness of myself as the one addressed in the call dispenses with all third-person identifying descriptions: "Not to what Dasein counts for, can do, or concerns itself with in being with one another publicly, nor to what it has taken hold of, set about, or let itself be carried along with," but only the "Self of the one-self gets appealed to" (BT 317/272). Thus, in grasping my Self (as 'subject'), I do so in an immediate, non-criterial, and non-inferential way. I am not, in other words, aware of myself *as* anything; nevertheless, I can 'identify' myself. Dasein therefore 'knows' itself to be irreducible to any definite description, no matter how detailed—including the comprehensive narrative of its own life. The first-person cannot be absorbed into its own history.[26]

Second, the lack of such identifying descriptions does not make the identification less, but rather more, certain. Conscience, as a kind of first-person self-reference, infallibly picks out its referent. As Heidegger writes, even though "the call passes over *what* Dasein, proximally and for the most part, understands itself *as*," nevertheless "the Self has been reached, *unequivocally and unmistakably*" (BT 319/274). The call is 'unequivocal'—it always picks out just the thing it aims at—because it is non-criterial: first-person self-reference is a pure indexical, not based on any potentially misfiring definite description or ostention. And it is 'unmistakable'—cannot fail to refer—because the call is immediate and non-inferential. In hearing the call I am addressed in such a way that the question of whether there *is* anyone to whom the call is addressed makes no sense.

This 'unmistakability' is the key to the analysis of conscience and shows the existential origin of Wittgenstein's idea that the subject is the limit of the world. Heidegger notes that "when the caller reaches him to whom the appeal is made, it does so with a cold assurance which is uncanny but by no means obvious" (BT 322/277). *Why* is it futile to argue with this 'cold assurance' of conscience, to appeal to mitigating circumstances, to try to hide? If we had only Division I to go on the answer would by no means be 'obvious,' since from the public point of view I am exclusively what I do, and those public descriptions can always be misapplied, even by myself. I can always 'fail to recognize' myself in them or be in error about whether they apply to me. In Division II, however, the reason for this 'cold assurance' with which I am identified in the call becomes clear: "when Dasein has been individualized down to itself in its uncanniness, it is for itself something that simply cannot be mistaken for anything else"

(BT 322/277). *For itself*—that is, from the first-person point of view—Dasein is "radically" deprived "of the possibility of misunderstanding itself" because it is not "reflected back from things" but rather directly confronts the mineness of *Existenz* as such.

Thus when Heidegger writes that "the call is precisely something which *we ourselves* have neither planned nor prepared for nor voluntarily performed, nor have we ever done so," "we ourselves" is used in the sense of the one-self. The call is neither an intentional act of expectation, desire, or belief, nor a 'performance' by the 'agent' in the world; rather, 'It' calls, "against our expectations and even against our will" (BT 320/275). Yet it "does not come from someone else who is with me in the world" either. The 'It' who calls is "from me and yet from beyond me and over me" (BT 320/275). Heidegger resolves this paradox by appealing to the modalized structure of *Existenz*: it is "Dasein, which finds itself [*sich befindet*] in the very depths of its uncanniness," who is "the caller of the call of conscience" (BT 321/276). By worldly criteria, such a caller is "nothing at all" (BT 321/276), and yet "the call comes from that entity which in each case I myself am" (BT 323/278). In conscience we learn what it *means* to say 'I myself.'

Here we locate the place of the first-person in *Being and Time*. It is neither the one-self (who says 'I' but not as 'I myself'), nor the authentic Self (a 'modification' of the one-self), but the hidden condition of both. The uncanny "nothing at all" revealed in breakdown and voiced as conscience is Dasein's "*basic kind of being in the world*, even though in an everyday way it has been covered up" (BT 322/277). Thus even though the call "to the Self in the one-self does not force it inwards upon itself, so that it can close itself off from the 'exterior world'" (BT 318/273), this is not because subjectivity is always somehow 'part' of that world or totality of significance. Rather, it is because this image of subjectivity—an 'interior' space of representations cut off from the 'external' world—is *not subjective enough*. Such an interior psychological space *is* merely a peculiar part of the world in Heidegger's sense, whereas subjectivity, conscience as Kierkegaardian inwardness, is the hidden condition of the world as a space of meaning. Admittedly, we have not yet discovered what it is about conscience that makes it such a condition, but the second aspect of Heidegger's analysis—his account of "what is said" in the call—provides just that, and with it the philosophical significance of first-person authority in *Being and Time* becomes apparent.

Conscience: the Origin of Reason

Heidegger's great achievement in *Being and Time* is to have demonstrated that care is prior to reason—that *homo cura* is more fundamental than the *animal rationale*. But the account of intentionality offered in Division I contains, as we saw, a gap: the analysis of practical, goal-oriented action supplies a necessary but not a sufficient condition for the intelligibility (world) upon which intentionality depends. A further condition on intentionality is provided by Division II's account of subjectivity as inwardness, conscience as first-person self-awareness. But why is conscience a necessary condition of intelligibility? The thesis I would like to explore is that it is because intelligibility involves something like the *capacity* for 'reason' in the sense of an ability to act in light of norms, and that conscience is the origin of this capacity.[27]

Support for this identification can be gleaned from the word—*Gewissen*—itself, for it invites the sort of analysis Heidegger offered when he introduced the notion of *Gestell* in "The Question Concerning Technology." There Heidegger explained that the *Ge-* prefix signifies a kind of "gathering" that "primordially unfolds"—not a mere collection but that which delimits the "essence" or being of what is gathered, that which makes it what it is, "enables" it.[28] Accordingly, *Ge-wissen* would signify a gathering of 'knowing'; conscience would be what enables the various (practical and theoretical) modes of knowing in the broadest sense, that from which *episteme, phronesis,* and so forth, 'primordially unfold.' It is instructive to note that this is just the role Heidegger attributes to *nous* (reason) in his *Sophist* lectures.[29] A second consideration ties the notion of conscience to that of reason. As a call, conscience is something that is heard (*gehört*). Though the call is "silent," Heidegger insists that it thereby "loses nothing of its perceptibility" (BT 318/273). The word he uses here is *Vernehmlichkeit.* To perceive in this way—*vernehmen*—is indeed to hear, but it is a hearing whose acoustic dimension is subordinated to a responsiveness to meaning, just as the *Sicht* (sight) of *Umsicht* is similarly subordinated.[30] Now this very term—*vernehmen*—is the root of the German word for reason (*Vernunft*). This might suggest that conscience (*Gewissen*) is the gathering-enabling of knowing and deliberating precisely as the hearing-perceiving (*vernehmen*) of a call, or meaningful claim, the response to which (*ver-antworten*) is a unique 'possibility' for being: *Vernunft.*

Primary support for the thesis, however, is found in Heidegger's description of "what is said" in the call, namely, the accusation "Guilty!" As he did with the concept of death, Heidegger formalizes the everyday notion of guilt in such a way that "those ordinary phenomena of 'guilt' which are related to our concernful being with others will *drop out*"—phenomena related to everyday "reckoning" as well as to "any law or 'ought'" (BT 328/ 283). Artificial though it seems, this formalization simply reflects the character of the call as that mode of discourse which articulates the *un*intelligibility of Dasein when, as *Angst*/death, its ordinary ties to the world break down. From this point of view, "being-guilty" is not a "predicate for the 'I am'" (BT 326/281), contingent upon some worldly relation; it is the fundamental *condition* of subjectivity, the first-person,

as such. The call 'articulates' an understanding of one's own being prior to any
sense of 'owing' or indebtedness—any sense of having, through one's actions
in the world, incurred debts or obligations—because, as Heidegger states, such
a mode of being is the *condition of possibility* for indebtedness and obligation
(BT 329/284). "What is said in the call" articulates the self-understanding
(self-awareness) of that being who is the ground of obligation. But in what
sense?

When am I indebted to someone? When do I owe someone something? It
cannot be simply when I take something that someone has in her possession,
or when I receive something from someone. Rather, there must be a norm of
appropriate exchange in place. Now this norm cannot simply be something that
is imposed on me from the outside—a behavior that is enforced, say, by social
(herd) conditioning in such a way that typical and normal behavior of the herd
results. This could never establish that 'I' *owe* someone something, but only
that there has been a failure to conform to what is typical or expected. *Being-
indebted* is not simply a state but something that I, from a first-person point
of view, must be 'able to be'; and this means that I must be able to *recognize* the
norm as normative, that is, as a claim *addressed* to me and not merely a pattern
descriptive of 'our' normal behavior. The fact that I can be characterized from a
third-person point of view as 'owing' something is ontologically parasitical on
being capable of first-person self-awareness in Heidegger's sense.[31] If one says
that this ability is made possible by 'internalization' of the social sanctions that
normalize the behavior of the herd, this can be accepted only if one also accepts
that this internalization changes everything.[32] For it signifies a being who no
longer merely conforms to norms, but who can act 'in light of' them. To act
in light of norms is to recognize them as claims to validity and so, potentially,
to *measure* them against an altogether different sort of standard—a 'meta-
norm' that Heidegger, following Plato, occasionally names 'the good.'[33] This is
the sort of first-person authority that derives from first-person self-awareness
as conscience. In Heidegger's terms, first-person authority is responsibility
(*Verantwortlichkeit*). Responsibility transforms a creature who is 'grounded'
by social norms into a ground of obligation—one who 'grounds' norms by
giving grounds, that is, reasons.[34]

The claim that first-person authority consists in the possibility of grounding
as reason-giving is, I believe, entailed by Heidegger's (alas, obscure) description of 'being-guilty.' Heidegger begins with Dasein's thrownness—the fact
that Dasein "has been brought into its 'there,' but *not* of its own accord" (BT
329/284)—and identifies this as the "ground" (*Grund*) of Dasein's "potentiality-
for-being" (BT 330/284). What sort of ground is that? Against the traditional notion of a self-grounding transcendental subject, Heidegger emphasizes
Dasein's lack of "power" over this ground: Dasein is "never existent *before* its

ground, but only *from* it"; and this means "*never* to have power over one's being from the ground up" (BT 330/284). Many readings of thrownness—and so of the nature of this ground—have been offered. For instance, it has been read as Nature, as the particular social practices into which I am born, as historical situatedness, and so on. Without taking a stand on the correctness of any particular reading,[35] they all take such a ground of Dasein to be something that determines, conditions, or explains significant aspects of behavior (for instance, the *range* of possible choices). Because they lie by definition beyond Dasein's power, such grounds belong essentially to third-person accounts; that is, they provide reasons for Dasein's behavior that are not (and cannot be) *Dasein's reasons.* In McDowell's Sellarsian terms, the grounds espied in Dasein's thrownness locate Dasein within the 'realm of law' (whether natural or bio-social), not the 'space of reasons.'[36] That is, whatever it is that provides the ground of Dasein's "possibility for being" and brings Dasein "into its 'there'" may indeed normalize behavior, but it is insufficient to generate the sort of obligation analyzed above; it does not provide reasons—grounds—in the sense of justifications.

However, while Dasein, as thrown, is grounded in this sense, this does not exhaust the meaning of 'being-guilty.' Heidegger argues that Dasein *is* this thrown ground only "in that it projects itself upon possibilities into which it has been thrown" (BT 330/284); that is the 'Self' or subject as such "has to lay the ground for itself," as "existing" it "must *take over* being a ground" (BT 330/284).[37] But what can it mean to say that Dasein must "take over being a ground"? Here too there are some usual readings, none of which can be quite right. To say that to take over being a ground is to acknowledge my facticity—to adopt a kind of anti-transcendental philosophical humility in the face of a higher power, as it were—does not do justice to the idea of *being* a ground. More promising is the idea that I "take responsibility" for my facticity, 'own' it, make it my own through the "*choice* of one possibility" (BT 331/285). But while it is true that Dasein can choose itself transparently, in full knowledge that it thereby 'waives' the choice of other possibilities, this cannot be the whole story. We might say that in this way Dasein *commits* itself to something specific in which it finds itself thrown. But it seems that to "take over being a ground" cannot simply be a matter of entering 'seriously' into a game, so to speak, whose rules and norms are already established 'as' rules and norms. If I am right about the kind of grounds that Dasein's thrownness provides, these do not yet suffice to constitute genuine 'games,' since games involve a sort of free-play in which I play not only according to the rules but in light of them. To stop with the concept of commitment (resoluteness) is to allow the first-person no role in the *constitution* of the 'space of reasons,' when in fact—as I believe Heidegger's text suggests—it is essential to it.

On this reading, to "take over being a ground" would be to translate, as it were, grounds as given determinants into grounds as (justifying) *reasons* (*Gründe*). This translation occurs when, in breakdown, I grasp the givens as mere *claims*, that is, as 'possibilities' opened up by Dasein's 'understanding of being' itself. To recognize the character of grounds as possibilities is what Heidegger calls "freedom" (BT 331/285).[38] Freedom is not essentially the ability to choose between possibilities, but the difference between the third-person and the first-person as such. Animals, one might say, can choose whether to run and hide or stay and fight, but freedom consists in the gap that opens up between *any* such goal-directed action in the world and the *breakdown* of all that—in *Angst*/death—which reveals my having to "take over being a ground." Yet we must be clear here: it is not the capacity for breakdown itself that is decisive, since animals, too, can break down. When animals break down, however, they lose themselves entirely, have 'nothing left.' Dasein can break down in this way, as in the extremity of psychosis. But in the face of *Angst*/death Dasein can also discover a hidden resource, its being-guilty, the ability to *take over* being a ground. What conditions one is thus exposed as a mere claim, for whose grounding—in the sense of measuring that claim in light of a meta-norm—I am called to be responsible. In this way conscience is the origin of reason.

Conscience is first-person authority as Kierkegaardian inwardness—invisible (and hence paradoxical) to third-person accounts of identity. And thus one might think of Abraham when Heidegger speaks, in his 1929 inaugural lecture, "What is Metaphysics?" of the "anxiety of those who are daring" as "in secret alliance with the cheerfulness and gentleness of creative longing."[39] What looks like a collapse of everything that matters instead reveals the condition for the possibility that anything can matter at all. In this sense, "subjectivity is the truth"—not because it is the site of an irrefragable evidence, an interior space of certain representations, but because, apart from all practical identity, all *Umwillen*, I am a being through whom obligation—that is, first of all, responsibility for reason—enters the world. This is the *positive* meaning of the claim that Dasein is the "sole authentic for the sake of which," something "in which there is *no* further involvement," an end in itself.[40]

Conclusion: First-Person Authority and the Good

Let me conclude by bringing out one more bit of evidence that suggests that conscience, as "taking over being a ground," is the origin of reason. This comes from the essay "Vom Wesen des Grundes," which Heidegger contributed to Husserl's *Festschrift* in 1929. There the question that *Being and Time* leaves unspoken is made explicit: "To what extent does there lie in transcendence the intrinsic possibility of something like *Grund* [ground, reason] in general?"[41] Dasein's 'transcendence' here means the casting of "something like the 'for the sake of' projectively before it." "Although it exists in the midst of beings and embraced by them," writes Heidegger, "Dasein as existing has always already surpassed nature" (EG 109), and it is by means of such transcendence, or surpassing, that "Dasein for the first time comes toward that being that *it* is, and comes toward it *as* it 'itself'" (EG 108). As we have seen, Dasein can come "toward that being that it is" in two ways: the way of everyday Dasein "reflected back from things," and the way it comes "toward it *as* 'it itself'" in the collapse of the one-self. Though both of these are modes of self-relation or self-awareness, we have seen that only the latter suffices to explain why Dasein is something like an 'end in itself' that can anchor the teleological 'totality of involvements' into the intelligibility of a world. In "Vom Wesen des Grundes" Heidegger explains this fact by interpreting Dasein's surpassing of beings in terms of Plato's *agathon epekeina tes ousias*—the good beyond beings. "Yet may we interpret the *agathon* as the transcendence of Dasein?" he asks; and answers: "the essence of the *agathon* lies in its sovereignty over itself [*Mächtigkeit seiner selbst*] as *hou heneka*—as the 'for the sake of' it is the source of possibility as such" (EG 124). Only as *sovereignty* is self-awareness the anchor of intelligibility, and only the first-person of Division II is sovereign in the sense of "taking over being a ground." To say that the essence of the good lies in sovereignty is to say that the meta-norm of 'the good' itself emerges, as such, only with conscience. Sovereignty over myself is not a matter of self-creation or 'self-fashioning'; nor is it the essence of the good in the sense that whatever I choose is *eo ipso* right. Rather, thanks to sovereignty—the ability to take over being a ground—I am able to judge and act 'in light of' the good, in light of 'what is best'; that is, in terms of (justificatory) *reasons*. This does not mean that I must 'know the good'; it signifies only the emergence of what can be called a *critical practice* in the existing of an entity that is sovereign over itself, an entity for whom the question of what *ought* to be makes sense.

The essence of this critical practice is responsibility (*Verantwortlichkeit*). Heideggerian 'freedom' means that "there occurs the Dasein in human beings, such that in the essence of their existence they can be obligated to themselves," thereby in turn "making possible something binding, indeed obligation in general" (EG 126). Heidegger goes on to say that reason, as "account giving," arises from such self-obligation, but he does not say how (EG 130–31). If we recall that Dasein responds to the call of conscience by "taking over being a ground," however, we can see that such responsiveness does not simply consist in committing myself to some course of action, but in making myself *accountable* for it—that is, in accounting for myself, giving reasons.

The possibility of everyday discourse ('communication') rests originally on this proto-act of offering reasons. To respond to the call—and a "free-floating call from which 'nothing ensues' is an impossible fiction when seen existentially" (BT 324/279)—to 'become accountable,' is to speak to the other, to communicate. When I give reasons and communicate as the one-self, this is a *trace* of my subjectivity, possible only for a creature that can be responsible, can answer the call of conscience. For Heidegger, as for Kant, then, giving reasons is the 'evidence' of first-person authority. Only 'I' can do it; the very notion only makes sense for a creature that is not simply a "reflection back from things," a practical identity absorbed in the world.[42] By opening up a space in which I can recognize something like a 'claim,' my response to the call transforms the 'thrownness' that I share with all conforming herd-animals into a *world* of meaning. In this way, intentionality, 'ontic transcendence,' finds its ultimate condition in first-person authority.[43]

Notes

1. Martin Heidegger, *History of the Concept of Time: Prolegomena*, trans. Theodore Kisiel (Bloomington: Indiana University Press, 1985), 110; *Prolegomena zur Geschichte des Zeitbegriffs*, Gesamtausgabe 20, ed. Petra Jaeger (Frankfurt: Klostermann, 1979), 152.

2. John Haugeland, "The Intentionality All-Stars," in *Having Thought* (Cambridge, MA: Harvard University Press, 1998), 127–70, here 132, 147. Haugeland concludes his article by acknowledging that all the positions he has examined "are alike in confronting intentionality only from the outside—in the 'third-person,' as it were," and notes that an approach from the first-person would require "entirely different strategies and considerations" (162). This chapter suggests one such consideration.

3. An example of the first would be Jerry Fodor, *The Language of Thought* (New York: Crowell, 1975); an example of the second, Hilary Putnam, "The Meaning of Meaning," in *Mind, Language, and Reality: Philosophical Papers*, vol. 2 (Cambridge: Cambridge University Press, 1975), 215–71.

4. This is the position Haugeland, "Intentionality All-Stars," op. cit., 147, describes as "neopragmatism," under which he includes Robert Brandom, Wilfrid Sellars, Hubert Dreyfus, and himself. He also includes Heidegger, though in a note appended at a later date he admits that "there is a 'pragmatist' strain *at most* in Division I of *Being and Time*. Certainly the larger tendency of the work is profoundly non-pragmatist." See also Mark Okrent, *Heidegger's Pragmatism* (Ithaca, NY: Cornell University Press, 1988).

5. For example, in *Being and Nothingness* Sartre makes this point in *criticism* of Heidegger, while Mark Okrent, in *Heidegger's Pragmatism*, op. cit., makes the same point in *praise* of Heidegger.

6. Heidegger uses this phrase occasionally to identify the topic of his *Daseinsanalytik*, most frequently when he is comparing it to Kant's project. See, for example, Martin

Heidegger, *Being and Time*, trans. John Macquarrie and Edward Robinson (New York: Harper & Row, 1962), 45; *Sein and Zeit* (Tübingen: Niemeyer, 1976), 24. Henceforth, references to *Being and Time* will be cited in the text with English, followed by German, pagination. At times I have altered the translation without comment.

7. John Haugeland has introduced a first-person notion of 'commitment' as a necessary condition on intentionality. I take my account to be compatible with his, though if 'commitment' is understood as rendering Heidegger's *Entschlossenheit,* my concern in this chapter is with a condition of commitment itself: the care structure as it is revealed in the collapse of practical engagement in the world. See John Haugeland, "Truth and Rule-Following," op. cit., 305–61, esp. 339–43; and "Truth and Finitude: Heidegger's Transcendental Existentialism," *Heidegger, Authenticity, and Modernity: Essays in Honor of Hubert Dreyfus,* vol. 1, ed. Mark Wrathall and Jeff Malpas (Cambridge, MA: MIT Press, 2000), 43–78.

8. *Martin Heidegger/Karl Jaspers Briefwechsel 1920–1963,* ed. Walter Biemel and Hans Saner (Frankfurt: Klostermann, 1990), 71. Letter of December 16, 1926.

9. David Carr, *The Paradox of Subjectivity* (Oxford: Oxford University Press, 1999), 77.

10. Hubert Dreyfus, *Being-in-the-World: A Commentary on Heidegger's* Being and Time, *Division I* (Cambridge, MA: MIT Press, 1991), 13, 74–75, 147. Frederick A. Olafson, *Heidegger and the Philosophy of Mind* (New Haven, CT: Yale University Press, 1987), 27, in contrast, argues that Heidegger does seek a "reconstructed concept of the subject," that is, of the "subject-entity as that for which other entities exist as such" (32). For a critical discussion see Frederick A. Olafson, "Heidegger *à la* Wittgenstein, or 'Coping' with Professor Dreyfus," *Inquiry* 37 (1994), 45–64; Taylor Carman, "On Being Social: A Reply to Olafson," *Inquiry* 37 (1994), 203–24; and Frederick A. Olafson, "Individualism, Subjectivity, and Presence: A Reply to Taylor Carman," *Inquiry* 37 (1994), 331–38.

11. Dreyfus, *Being-in-the-World,* op. cit., 57.

12. Martin Heidegger, *The Basic Problems of Phenomenology,* trans. Albert Hofstadter (Bloomington: Indiana University Press, 1982), 159; *Grundprobleme der Phänomenologie,* Gesamtausgabe 24, ed. Friedrich-Wilhelm von Herrmann (Frankfurt: Klostermann, 1975), 227.

13. See Friedrich-Wilhelm von Herrmann, *Subjekt und Dasein* (Frankfurt: Klostermann, 1974), 65.

14. See, for example, Charles Siewert, *The Significance of Consciousness* (Princeton, NJ: Princeton University Press, 1998); and David Chalmers, *The Conscious Mind* (New York: Oxford University Press, 1996).

15. About Husserl's own investigation into consciousness Heidegger notes that "a 'formal phenomenology of consciousness'" is a legitimate "phenomenological problematic in its own right" (BT 151/115), but he doesn't tell us what its relation to his own existential analytic would be. Similarly, in *History of the Concept of Time,* op. cit., 108 (*Prolegomena zur Geschichte des Zeitbegriffs,* 149), Heidegger admits that "this consideration [of consciousness as object of a science] is in fact possible."

16. My discussion in this section is greatly indebted to conversations with Mark Okrent, whose forthcoming book on intentionality makes illuminating use of the

concept of "type." See also Dreyfus, *Being-in-the-World*, op. cit., chapter 4, and Haugeland, "The Intentionality All-Stars," op. cit., 147–53, on conformism and normativity.

17. I borrow this strategy from Dan Zahavi, who employs it in his exemplary book, *Self-Awareness and Alterity: A Phenomenological Investigation* (Evanston: Northwestern University Press, 1999), chapter 1. I have also found Tomis Kapitan, "First-Person Reference," and James Hart, "Castañeda: A Continental Philosophical Guise," to be helpful here. Both are found in Hector-Neri Castañeda, *The Phenomeno-logic of the I: Essays on Self-Consciousness*, ed. James Hart and Tomis Kapitan (Bloomington: Indiana University Press, 1999).

18. Of course, I can be wrong about what I feel, but not about the fact that it is *I* who feel it. Zahavi, *Self-Awareness and Alterity*, op. cit., 5.

19. Zahavi, *Self-Awareness and Alterity*, 7.

20. Zahavi, *Self-Awareness and Alterity*, 8.

21. Zahavi, *Self-Awareness and Alterity*, 9–10. Ernst Tugendhat, *Self-Consciousness and Self-Determination*, trans. Paul Stern (Cambridge, MA: MIT Press, 1986) misses just this point when he argues that 'I' can be defined simply as the term "each of us uses to refer to himself." This leads him to the claim that "I cannot identify myself by the use of the word *I*" since "the word *I* designates the ultimate reference point of all identification, though the person referred to by it—the speaker—is not identified; but he is referred to as identifiable from the 'he' perspective" (73). In other words, all identification is criterial, by way of public, third-person descriptions. What is missing is a grasp of the kind of self-awareness entailed in the very *meaning* of 'I.' This kind of self-'identification' is not an answer to the question "Who am I?"—as Tugendhat supposes (209)—but rather an encounter with what generates the asymmetry between my *being* the "ultimate reference point of all identification," on the one hand, and the "person . . . identifiable from the 'he' perspective" on the other. This first-person self-awareness does not depend on my identifying myself in terms of any third-person descriptions of 'who' I am.

22. The relation between the transcendental and the empirical ego in Husserl is notoriously disputed, but for some recent discussions see Dan Zahavi, *Self-Awareness and Alterity*, op. cit., 138–56, and Robert Sokolowski, *Introduction to Phenomenology* (Cambridge: Cambridge University Press, 2000), 112–29. For discussions that include Heidegger's stance toward the problem, see David Carr, *The Paradox of Subjectivity*, op. cit., and Steven Crowell, *Husserl, Heidegger, and the Space of Meaning: Paths Toward Transcendental Phenomenology* (Evanston: Northwestern University Press, 2001), chapters 9 and 13.

23. Like Wittgenstein, Tugendhat, *Self-Consciousness and Self-Determination*, op. cit., 56–76, denies that the 'logic' of 'I' has any ontological relevance, while Taylor Carman, "On Being Social: A Reply to Olafson," op. cit., 216, uses Wittgenstein's dictum that "nothing in the visual field warrants the conclusion that it is seen from an eye" to gloss Heidegger's supposed non-subjective account of the 'mineness' of everyday coping.

24. Dreyfus, *Being-in-the-World*, op. cit., 161.

25. In spite of Heidegger's aversion to the language of 'subjectivity,' there is even some textual warrant for my terminological preference. For Heidegger notes that the existential analysis of conscience "does justice to the 'objectivity' of the appeal for the first time by *leaving it its 'subjectivity,'* which of course denies the one-self its dominion" (BT 323/278). Conscience defines the domain of 'subjectivity,' but this is not an inner space of mental representations. As Heidegger explicitly states, "neither the call, nor the deed which has happened, nor the guilt with which one is laden, is an occurrence with the character of something present at hand which runs its course" in the stream of *Erlebnisse* (BT 337/291).

26. This point is elaborated in Steven Crowell, "Authentic Historicality," in David Carr and Chan-Fai Cheung (eds.), *Space, Time, and Culture*, Contributions to Phenomenology, vol. 51 (Berlin: Springer, 2004).

27. This does not mean that Heidegger provides a complete account of reason, but he does indicate the ontological place for such an account. Thus it is not true, as Tugendhat, *Self-Consciousness and Self-Determination*, op. cit., 215, states, that Heidegger's account of resoluteness is "an attempt to banish reason from human existence and in particular from the relation of oneself to oneself." Tugendhat recognizes that "Heidegger's concept of self-determination not only admits of extension through a relation to reason but also demands this extension on its own grounds" (215), but because he never considers the analysis of conscience, he conceives this "extension" as coming from outside the Heideggerian project. On the other hand, to specify such a "relation to reason" immanently, by employing the concept of *phronesis*—as does Einar Øverenget, *Seeing The Self: Heidegger on Subjectivity* (Dordrecht: Kluwer, 1998), 223–31—is to ignore the fact that this sort of 'practical' reason cannot account for its own 'rationality.' Tugendhat, in contrast, clearly recognizes that the 'autonomy' analyzed in Division II is what makes possible the step from normativity to validity, from conformity to criticism, from understanding to reason.

28. Martin Heidegger, "The Question Concerning Technology," in *The Question Concerning Technology and other Essays*, trans. William Lovitt (New York: Harper & Row, 1977), 19.

29. Martin Heidegger, *Platon: Sophistes*, Gesamtausgabe 19, ed. Ingeborg Schüßler (Frankfurt: Klostermann, 1992), 143, 156–64.

30. In *Being and Time* Heidegger "formalizes" the notion of 'sight' to signify "access in general" (BT 187/147) and argues that everyday coping is not "blind"; it "has its own sight." That this is not merely a matter of the physiology of the optical organ is clear: "Dealings with equipment subordinate themselves to the manifold assignments of the 'in order to.' And the sight with which they thus accommodate themselves is *circumspection [Umsicht]*" (BT 98/69).

31. What Heidegger is getting at here reflects Korsgaard's distinction between "criteria of explanatory and normative adequacy": "The difference is one of perspective. A theory that could explain why someone does the right thing—in a way that is adequate from a third-person perspective—could nevertheless fail to justify the action from the agent's own, first-person perspective, and so fail to support its normative claims."

Christine Korsgaard, *The Sources of Normativity* (Cambridge: Cambridge University Press, 1996), 14.

32. Nietzsche, one source for this idea, emphasizes that conscience, as internalization of punishment, gives rise to an "uncanny illness." But it also creates the world's first *interesting* animal: "[T]he existence on earth of an animal soul turned against itself, taking sides against itself, was something so new, profound, unheard of, enigmatic, contradictory, and *pregnant with a future* that the aspect of the earth was essentially altered." Friedrich Nietzsche, *On the Genealogy of Morals*, trans. Walter Kaufmann (New York: Vintage, 1969), 85 (second essay, section 16).

33. See, e.g., Martin Heidegger, *Metaphysical Foundations of Logic*, trans. Michael Heim (Bloomington: Indiana University Press, 1984), 184; *Metaphysische Anfangsgründe der Logik*, Gesamtausgabe 26, ed. Klaus Held (Frankfurt: Klostermann, 1978), 237; and also the essay "Vom Wesen des Grundes," to be discussed below.

34. The fact (which Heidegger emphasizes in his critique of rationalism) that giving reasons at some point 'gives out' is no argument against the claim that the practice of giving reasons—a practice that originates not with normativity as such but with normativity in relation to a creature capable of the first-person perspective—is constitutive of 'worldhood' as the space of intelligibility.

35. I take a stand on them in Steven Crowell, "Facticity and Transcendental Philosophy," in Jeff Malpas (ed.), *From Kant to Davidson: Philosophy and the Idea of the Transcendental* (London: Routledge, 2002).

36. John McDowell, *Mind and World* (Cambridge, MA: Harvard University Press, 1994), 71, n. 2. In this comparison I am not committing myself to the details of McDowell's account, but only to something like this distinction. Compare Haugeland, "Intentionality All-Stars," op. cit., 151: "To say that biological and social categories are 'emergent' is not to say, of course, that they are incompatible with vapid materialism or exempt from the laws of nature. Quite the contrary: it is only because conformism is itself in some sense a 'causal' process that the emergent social pattern is nonaccidental in the sense required for intentionality." On the problem of 'double grounding' implied in Heidegger's discussion, see Crowell, *Husserl, Heidegger, and the Space of Meaning*, op. cit., chapter 12.

37. The entire passage would be relevant for my argument, but I can only cite it here without detailed commentary: "Der Nichtcharakter dieses Nicht bestimmt sich existenzial: *Selbst* seiend ist das Dasein das geworfene Seiende *als* Selbst. *Nicht durch* es selbst, sondern *an* es selbst *entlassen* aus dem Grunde, um *als dieser* zu sein. Das Dasein is nicht insofern selbst der Grund seines Seins, als dieser aus eigenem Entwurf erst entspringt, wohl aber ist es als Selbstsein das *Sein* des Grundes. Dieser ist immer nur Grund eines Seienden, dessen Sein das Grundsein zu übernehmen hat."

38. Heidegger's position here is quite close to Kant's, well captured by Korsgaard: "According to Kant it follows from the fact that a rational being acts 'under the idea of freedom' . . . that she acts for a reason or on a principle which she must regard as voluntarily adopted. The point here has to do with the way a rational being must think of her actions when she is engaged in deliberation and choice. When you make a choice, you do not view yourself simply as impelled into it by desire or impulse. Instead, it is

as if there were something over and above all of your desires, something that is *you*, and that decides which if any of your desires to gratify" (Christine Korsgaard, *Creating the Kingdom of Ends* [Cambridge: Cambridge University Press, 1996], 57). See also Korsgaard, *Sources of Normativity*, op. cit., 94: "If the bidding from outside is desire, then the point is that the reflective mind must endorse the desire before it can act on it, it must say to itself that the desire is a reason. As Kant put it, we must *make it our maxim* to act on the desire. Then although we may do what desire bids us, we do it freely." For Dasein, nothing is a mere 'determinant' but is always subject to the measure of the possible.

39. Martin Heidegger, "What is Metaphysics?" trans. David Farrell Krell, in *Pathmarks*, ed. William McNeill (Cambridge: Cambridge University Press, 1998), 93.

40. Heidegger makes the connection explicit between Kant's notion of the *personalitas moralis* as an end-in-itself and his own concept of Dasein as ultimate 'for the sake of which' in *Basic Problems of Phenomenology*, op. cit., 122–76; *Gründprobleme der Phänomenologie*, 173–251.

41. Martin Heidegger, "On the Essence of Ground," trans. William McNeill, in *Pathmarks*, ed. William McNeill (Cambridge: Cambridge University Press, 1998), 125. Henceforth cited in the text as EG.

42. This implies that the first-person is the ground of dialogical (and thus also of dialectical) rationality, rather than the reverse. To argue this fully would take a separate paper, but see Steven Crowell, "The Project of Ultimate Grounding and the Appeal to Intersubjectivity in Recent Transcendental Philosophy," *International Journal of Philosophical Studies* 7 (1999), 31–54.

43. This paper was first delivered at a conference on "Phenomenology in the Nordic Countries" in Copenhagen, Denmark, and again at the third annual meeting of the International Society for Phenomenological Studies, in Asilomar, California. I thank the participants at both conferences for valuable criticism.

8

Can There Be a Better Source of Meaning than Everyday Practices? Reinterpreting Division I of *Being and Time* in the Light of Division II

Hubert L. Dreyfus

I. Average versus Primordial Understanding

In Division I of *Being and Time* Heidegger says that "publicness primarily controls every way in which the world and human beings get interpreted, and it is always right" (165).[1] This seems to follow from three basic theses: (1) people have skills for coping with equipment, with other people, and for taking up public roles like student or teacher; (2) to make sense, these everyday coping practices must conform to public norms; and (3) these public norms are the basis of average everyday significance or intelligibility. In Heidegger jargon: "The one articulates the referential context of significance" (167). That is, norms tell us what *one* normally does.

For Heidegger then, as for Wittgenstein, the source of the intelligibility of the world and of human life is our shared, everyday, public practices. But we must beware of concluding from the *basis* of intelligibility in everyday practices, that, for Heidegger, as for Wittgenstein and pragmatists such as Richard Rorty, there is no superior source of meaning than the everyday; for Heidegger also says that "by publicness everything gets obscured" (165), and adds that Division I of *Being and Time* provides a phenomenology only of everyday *average* understanding and so will have to be revised in the light of the more "primordial understanding" (212) he describes in Division II.

But how can Heidegger account for a higher form of intelligibility than the public, average intelligibility provided by the social norms? Like Wittgenstein and Rorty, he rejects any of the forms of higher metaphysical intelligibility claimed by philosophers. It looks like for Heidegger, as for Wittgenstein, there simply couldn't be any higher intelligibility than that provided by our shared everyday practices. As Wittgenstein says, explanations have to stop somewhere, and then we simply have to say this is what we do. Yet Heidegger clearly holds that there is a form of understanding of situations, on the one hand, and of human being, on the other, that is superior to everyday understanding. What could such a more primordial understanding be?

To get a clue, it helps to recall what we learn from Theodore Kisiel's research into the sources of *Being and Time*. According to Kisiel, the book grows out of Heidegger's work on Aristotle: Division I elaborates on *techne*, everyday skill, and Division II on *phronesis*, practical wisdom.[2] But just what phenomena do Aristotle and Heidegger have in mind with *techne* and *phronesis*? The way to find out is to let these phenomena show themselves as they are in themselves, so I will take a moment to review, in a very abbreviated way, four of the five stages of skill acquisition. Then I'll describe what more is needed for a skilled learner to gain practical wisdom—a mastery of his or her culture's practices. Finally, I'll suggest that, at the end of *Being and Time*, Heidegger drew on Kierkegaard's Christian understanding of being reborn, to introduce an even higher skill than could be understood by Aristotle and the Greeks.

II. A Phenomenology of Skill Acquisition[3]

Stage 1: Novice

Normally, instruction begins with the instructor decomposing the task environment into context-free features that the beginner can recognize without the desired skill. The beginner is then given rules for determining actions on the basis of these features.

For example, the child who is learning how to behave appropriately in his or her culture may be given the rule: "Never tell a lie."

Stage 2: Advanced Beginner

But as the novice gains experience actually coping with real situations, he sees that the rules don't work and learns to see meaningful additional aspects of the situation. Instructional *maxims* can then refer to these new *situational aspects*.

The policy "Never tell a lie" will get a child into fights and excluded from important events so, with the coaching of their parents, children learn to tell their friends when leaving their homes that they had a good time, regardless of the truth. Thus, the child learns to replace the rule "Never lie" with the maxim "Never lie except in situations when making everyone feel good is what matters."

Stage 3: Competence

But there are many types of social situations, so children must learn to choose a perspective that determines which elements of the situation will be treated as important and which ones will be ignored.

Thus a young person learns that there are situations in which one must tell the truth and others in which one lies. Although this is daunting, the adolescent has to decide whether the current situation is one of building trust, giving support, manipulating the other person for his or her own good, harming a brutal antagonist, and so forth. If, for instance, trust is the issue, the young person has to decide when and how to tell the truth.

Since such decisions are risky, they give rise to the anxiety that goes with free choice. In the face of this anxiety the learner is tempted to seek the security of standards and rules. For example, if a risk-averse young person decides that a situation is one of trust and so tells a friend more than the friend can bear and thereby loses the friendship, he may decide on the rule, "Never tell more truth than is absolutely necessary." This rule may prevent new breakdowns in similar situations, but it will also prevent further skill refinement. In this case, it will prevent frank and flexible friendships. In general, if one seeks to follow rules one will not get beyond competence.[4] There is no substitute for taking risks.

But this means there is no way to avoid anxious involvement. Prior to this stage, if the rules and maxims don't work, the performer could rationalize that he has not been given adequate guidelines. Now, however, the learner feels responsible for his choices, and often his choice leads to confusion and failure. Of course, sometimes things work out well, and the competent performer experiences a kind of elation unknown to the beginner. Thus, learners at this stage find themselves on an emotional roller coaster.

Of course, not just any emotional reaction such as enthusiasm, or fear of making a fool of oneself, or the exultation of victory, will do. What matters is taking responsibility for one's successful and unsuccessful choices, even brooding over them; not just feeling good or bad about winning or losing, but replaying one's performance in one's mind step by step. The point, however, is not to *analyze* one's mistakes and insights, but just to *let them sink in*. Experience shows that only then will one become an expert.

As the competent performer becomes more and more emotionally involved in his task, it becomes increasingly difficult for him to draw back and adopt the *detached* rule-following stance of the beginner. While it might seem that this involvement would interfere with rule-testing, and so would lead to irrational decisions and inhibit further skill development, in fact just the opposite turns out to be the case. If the detached stance of the novice and advanced beginner is replaced by involvement, and the learner accepts the anxiety of choice, he is set for further skill advancement.

Stage 4: Expertise

With enough experience and willingness to take risks, the learner becomes an expert who immediately sees what sort of situation he is in and what to do. In this way, most children grow up to be experts who have learned, among many other things, spontaneously to tell the truth or to lie, depending upon the situation. Most people grow up to be ethical experts responding in what is generally recognized as the right way to a wide range of interpersonal situations.

But although the virtuous person does the right thing according to the standards of the one, this isn't the whole story. While most of us are ethical experts in many domains such as truthfulness, according to Aristotle a few superior people go beyond ethical expertise. They are admired for their *phronesis* or practical wisdom. Let us call this stage mastery.

Stage 5: Mastery

We have so far seen that, if the learner stays emotionally involved and has enough experience, he will become an expert who responds intuitively to the current situation. That means that the average person is an expert in many domains, from dressing to driving to ethical behavior. As long as the situation remains stable, such expertise does not require constant learning. And, as reflection and observation shows, most experts become satisfied with a given level of success, and stop responding emotionally to each new experience. A few people, however, at least in areas important to them, are never satisfied that they have done the right thing, even if public opinion assures them it was right. They sense that there is no one right thing to do and that they can always improve.

Such continually anxious experts are never complacent. But, happily, if they brood over their successes and failures, replaying them over and over in their mind, they will reach a new level of skillful coping beyond expertise. Just as the beginner can go on to become aware not just of context-free features but

also of meaningful situational aspects, the expert can progress from responding immediately to *specific situations* to responding immediately to the *whole
meaningful context.* Thus the constantly anxious expert develops a masterful
grasp of the whole unfolding activity—a grasp that the complacent expert can
never achieve. According to Heidegger, this is the higher skill Aristotle called
phronesis, practical wisdom.

Considering some examples can help us see how mastery goes beyond expertise. The average carpenter can be counted on to be an expert who will
put wood together in the standard way and hit the nails appropriately for the
kind of wood he is using. The master craftsman, however, is responsive to
the specific grain of the piece of wood he is using and to the whole situation,
both architectural and social, into which his work is to fit.[5] In team sports, the
normal expert takes account of the current location of the other players, but
there are rare players, such as Larry Bird, who are gripped by the game and are
never satisfied with doing the standard thing. They go on to develop a feel for
the whole evolving situation in the overall game. Bird thus could respond to
possibilities on the court that others couldn't see.

The same distinction between the expert and the master shows up outside
of sports. A colleague of mine, who is generally recognized to be a master
teacher, is never satisfied with her teaching. In her lectures she learns from
her interactions with the students, and after each lecture replays them in her
mind, feeling elated at the moments when things went well and she and the
students learned together, and discouraged when a long discussion led nowhere.
Colleagues are amazed to find that as she walks about the campus listening to
her Walkman she is listening not to music but to her lecture from the previous
year. But she is not giving herself rules for how to avoid mistakes and do better
next time; that sort of detachment would lead to a regression to competence.
She is simply letting the classroom interactions and the connected emotions
sink in. Her brain then takes over and does the rest outside of consciousness;
the result is that each year she is an even more masterful teacher.[6]

III. How a Resolute Response to the Anxiety of Guilt Makes *Phronesis* Possible

But why do some people constantly replay what they have done and let their
joy at their successes and sadness at their failures obsess them? Why aren't they
satisfied by knowing they have done what is publicly recognized as the right
thing? Heidegger can help us here. He notes in Division I that there is no right
way to act, but that the average way of acting avoids this unsettling fact by doing

what everyone agrees is the right thing. Heidegger calls such "lostness in the one" "tranquilized," and describes it as following "rules and standards" (312).

In Division II, however, Heidegger introduces the anxiety of guilt as a positive corrective to this tranquilized state. Ontological guilt in *Being and Time* does not mean what guilt normally is taken to mean. It is not a sense of having done something wrong but rather a structural characteristic of all human beings. Guilt is defined as the fact that one is indebted to the norms of one's culture, but that one can't get behind this cultural thrownness so as to make these norms explicit and justify them.

There is no reason why *our* way of doing things is right; it is just what we do. The anxious realization of the ungroundedness of the rules and standards of the public's average understanding undermines the expert's complacency. If a person faces the anxiety caused by his ontological guilt he can act with what Heidegger calls resoluteness, which Heidegger defines as "self projection upon [my] ownmost being-guilty, in which [I am] ready for anxiety" (343).

Thus Heidegger's *resolute* individual deviates both from the beginner's rules and the public's standards. In Heidegger's terms, *irresolute* Dasein responds to the *general situation* (*Lage* in German), whereas *resolute* Dasein responds to the *concrete Situation* (*Situation* in German). As Heidegger puts it: "for the one ... the [concrete] Situation is essentially something that has been closed off. The one knows only the 'general situation'" (346), while "resolute Dasein" is in touch with the "concrete Situation of taking action" (349). We can now see that response to the concrete Situation refers to the broader contextual understanding of the unfolding situation characteristic of the master. Heidegger says in his discussion of *phronesis* in his 1925 *Sophist* lectures:

> [The *phronimos*] ... is determined by *his situation in the largest sense*.... The circumstances, the givens, the times and the people vary. The meaning of the action ... varies as well.... It is precisely the achievement of *phronesis* to disclose the [individual] as acting *now* in the *full situation* within which he acts.[7]

Heidegger adds: "Our concrete interpretation of *phronesis* shows how actions are constituted in it. Namely in terms of the *kairos*."[8] *Kairos* is Aristotle's term for the decisive moment in which the *phronimos* grasps the whole temporally unfolding concrete Situation. It is "ultimately an immediate overall view of the moment from the point of view of the end of the action in question."[9]

Of course the actions of the *phronimos* are the result of the gradual refinement and enlargement of what starts out as general responses to the general situation. Mastery grows out of long, involved, anxious experience acting within the shared cultural practices. Thus, in discussing *phronesis* Heidegger quotes Aristotle's remark that "Only through much time... is life experience possible."[10] And in *Being and Time* he is explicit that the intelligibility of the (concrete) Situation disclosed by resolute action is a refinement of the everyday:

> The "world" which is available does not become another "in its content" nor does the circle of others get exchanged for a new one; but both being toward [equipment] understandingly and concernfully, and solicitous being with others, are now given a definite character. [344]

Or, more clearly, given our concern with the one:

> Resolution does not withdraw from "actuality" but discovers first what is factically possible; and it does so by seizing upon it in whatever way is possible for it as its ownmost *ability-to-be in the "one."* [346, my italics]

IV. From *Kairos* to *Augenblick*

Kisiel's claim that Heidegger's resoluteness is a working out of Aristotle's phenomenology of practical wisdom is thus convincing. But Kisiel's plausible way of understanding the passages in question is disputed by another group of interpreters who point out that Heidegger's account of resoluteness is based on his early interest in the account of radical transformation in St. Paul, Luther and Kierkegaard.[11] These interpreters understandably focus not on the Greek *kairos*, as the decisive moment in masterful action, but on Heidegger's use of the Kierkegaardian term for radical transformation, the *Augenblick,* translated as the "Instant."

Heidegger would agree with both parties to this dispute. He distinguishes the *phronimos's* understanding of the *concrete Situation* revealed by guilt from what he calls the *limit-situation* revealed by death. He introduces the *Augenblick*: Dasein "gets brought back from its lostness by a resolution, so that both the *concrete Situation* and . . . the primordial *'limit-Situation'* of *being-towards-death*, will be disclosed as an *Augenblick* that has been held on to" (400). Heidegger adds: "What we here indicate with 'Augenblick' is what Kierkegaard was *the first to really grasp in philosophy*—a grasping which *begins the possibility of a completely new epoch in philosophy for the first time since Antiquity*."[12]

Clearly there is something crucially important that Aristotle's account of *phronesis* could not capture. To understand this new level of skill introduced by Christianity and first fully articulated by Kierkegaard, we need to return to the phenomena and introduce a sixth stage of skill enhancement.

Stage 6: World Transformer

Mastery is as good as one can get in the stages of skill acquisition in a settled domain, but there is a further form of skill that is usually called creativity. Then the skilled practitioner doesn't merely *intuitively* cope as most of us do when we are experts in a domain, or even manifest a deep *insight* into the domain as masters do; rather I have a *vision* of the skill domain so original that it changes my world. Revolutionary scientists such as Galileo, leaders such as Martin Luther King, Jr., and entrepreneurs such as Ford change their world in this way.

But there are less dramatic versions. Perhaps the clearest examples can be found in sports. In basketball, Larry Bird never went beyond mastery and was recognized as one of the best team players who ever played, but Michael Jordan expressed his style of life in his play. He played basketball not as a team player but as an individual. At first people thought that this undermined the teamwork essential to the sport, but it worked, and that changed the way the game is now played.[13]

Outside sports, we find the same phenomenon in visionaries who see the possibilities of new technologies. For example, Alan Kay, back in the late sixties when computers filled whole rooms, began to develop the laptop computer with the desktop interface. Kay is interesting because he sees our culture's normal way of doing things not as sensible and natural, but as purely contingent. He is thus fascinated by history. For example, when working on what he called his "dynabook," the latest version of which is Apple's "PowerBook," he read the history of books so as to loosen up what people normally take for granted about them. He was interested in why books are the size they are, how they came, rather late in the game, to have page numbers, etc.

Thus, world transformers somehow sense that the whole currently accepted way of doing things is arbitrary, and have a vision that what is now being done could be done in an entirely different way, which would even change what counted as doing things better. They are often sensitive to the fact that people aren't doing what they think they are doing. Rather than ignoring or covering up or explaining away such anomalies, they hold onto and elaborate them. Especially if these anomalies reveal other ways of doing things left over from the past.[14]

V. The Greek Cultural Master vs. the Christian World Transformer

Given the phenomenology of world disclosing, we can now see that there are two totally different levels of skill beyond the expertise described in Division I of *Being and Time*. As we have already seen, according to Heidegger, anxious, *guilty* resoluteness—Dasein's sense of its thrownness—makes possible the mastery exhibited by the *phronimos* who, because he has held onto anxiety, and so no longer takes for granted that the standard public way of acting is "always right," can go on learning and master broader and broader situations. But, according to Heidegger, the Aristotelian *phronimos* has not sensed the ungroundedness of the Greek understanding of what it means to be a human being. In fact, the Greek *phronimos* could, if he had taken Aristotle's ethics course,[15] learn that what one does when one is a Greek expresses the essential rational character of human nature. The *phronimos*, therefore, although admired for his wisdom, is not *fully* authentic.

Besides the *masterful coping* of the *phronimos,* made possible by a grasp of the concrete *Situation in the widest sense*, there is a *"fully authentic"* way of acting made possible by Dasein's *"primordial understanding"* of *its own way of being*. This fully authentic way of acting is a more complete form of resoluteness in which Dasein not only faces the anxiety of guilt, viz., the sense that the everyday norms of its society are thrown rather than grounded and so have no final authority; it also faces the anxiety of the limit-situation of death, where death, like guilt, is given a new "ontological meaning." In *Being and Time*, death does not mean an event at the end of one's life, but rather the sense that my identity and world are ungrounded, and so can be totally transformed. Ontological death, then, is a prerequisite for the possibility of being reborn.

Once we see that there are two phenomena, masterful response to the concrete Situation and radical transformation of the self and world, we can begin to see that Heidegger is distinguishing and relating two basic experiences of the source, nature, and intelligibility of decisive action—the Greek experience of the *kairos*, arising from a sense of the ungroundedness of public norms, that makes possible *masterful coping **in** the world,* and the Christian experience of the *Augenblick*, arising from *a primordial understanding of Dasein* itself as ungrounded, that makes possible *a transformation **of** the world*.

This enables Heidegger to distinguish two kinds of resoluteness. As he puts it:

> We have defined "resoluteness" as a projecting of oneself on one's ownmost being-guilty. . . . Resoluteness gains its authenticity as *anticipatory* resoluteness. In this, Dasein understands itself with regard to its ability-to-be, and it does so in such a manner that it will go right under the eyes of Death in order thus to take over in its thrownness that entity which it is itself, and to take it over wholly. [434]

In other words, the resolute *phronimos* merely experiences the thrownness of everyday norms and so has the sense that they do not provide rules to be rigidly followed nor shared standards of what is right that can guide performance.

He therefore gives up *a general understanding* of the situation and responds to the *full concrete Situation.* In anticipatory resoluteness, however, anxiety in the face of death frees Dasein from taking for granted even the agreed-upon current cultural concerns. That is, in *anticipatory resoluteness,* Dasein has to be ready at all times to give up its identity and its world altogether. In such an understanding, Dasein manifests "its authenticity and its totality" (348).

This readiness makes it possible for Dasein to change history by what Heidegger calls *repetition.*

> Repetition makes a reciprocal rejoinder to the possibility of existence that has-been-there. . . . But when such a rejoinder is made to this possibility in a resolution, it is made in an *Augenblick*; and as such it is at the same time *a disavowal of that which in the today, is working itself out as the "past."* [438, my italics]

What Heidegger is suggesting here is an original account of cultural creativity. In an instant of decisive action—which, of course, can take years to be carried out—authentic Dasein can take over *marginal practices from the past* and by making them central in the current context can exhibit a new understanding of the past and a new form of life that can transform his culture's fate.

Heidegger tells us that fate "is how we designate Dasein's primordial historizing, which lies in authentic resoluteness and in which Dasein *hands* itself *down* to itself, free for death, in a possibility which it has inherited and yet has chosen" (435). The most striking example of such a transformation is the Christian experience of Jesus as a world-transformer. We are told that the Jews followed the Law. One was guilty for one's overt acts. Jesus changed all this when, in the Sermon on the Mount, he said that everyone who looks at a woman lustfully has already committed adultery with her in his heart. He also said that He had fulfilled the Law and so could practice healing even on the Sabbath. On his new account the Law is only marginal, and what really matters is that one is guilty for one's desires. Purity, not rightness of action, is required, and in that case one can't save oneself by will power, but only by throwing oneself on the mercy of a Savior and being reborn.

It might seem that this cannot be a such radical change from Judaism, since the eighth commandment already enjoins one not to covet anything that is your neighbor's, and coveting is surely a case of desire, not overt action. But Heidegger would point out that if Jesus had not had some basis in the tradition no one would have had a clue as to what he was talking about, so it is important that he take up and make central a marginal practice already in the culture.

As Heidegger puts it in *Being and Time,* an authentically historical individual transforms his generation's understanding of the issue facing the culture and thereby produces a new authentic "we." Such a history maker thus goes beyond not only the ethical expertise of his peers, but even beyond the full Situational understanding of the *phronimos*.[16]

Since all intelligibility must be grounded in shared everyday practices, however, such a charismatic leader will have to change common sense. Such a world transformer can *show* a new style and so be *followed*, as Jesus was followed by his disciples, even though they did not fully understand the meaning of what they were doing. But he will not be fully intelligible to the members of the culture until his new way of coordinating the practices is articulated in a new public language and preserved in new public institutions. So, as Heidegger says, no matter how publicness covers up radical originality, "even resoluteness remains dependent upon the one and its world" (345).

Conclusion

In summary, according to Division II of *Being and Time*, public, average, everyday understanding is necessarily general and banal. Nonetheless, this leveled, average understanding is necessary in the early stages of acquiring expertise and as the background for all intelligibility. It is thus both genetically and ontologically prior to any more primordial understanding.

Once, however, an individual has broken out of the one's reassuring everyday rules by anxiously facing his freedom to choose without guidelines among alternative interpretations of his situation, by repeated risky experience in the everyday world he can become sensitive to the discriminations that constitute *expertise* in the concrete local situation. Then, with further involved experience facing resolutely the anxiety of groundlessness, he can go on to become a *phronimos*, a cultural master, who responds to the whole situation in a broader and deeper way than any expert. Finally, by facing the anxiety of death in anticipatory resoluteness, and so seeing that his identity and that of his culture is ungrounded and could be radically changed, a fully authentic Dasein can disclose an even higher kind of intelligibility. He can take up marginal possibilities in his culture's past in way that enables him to change the style of a whole generation and thereby disclose a new world.[17]

All of this shows that the shared intelligibility of the one, even though it "obscures everything," can be deepened and even radically transformed but can never be left behind. So the public norms described in Division I are never abandoned, but in Division II they turn out to be the basis of two important positive phenomena—mastery and world-transforming—understood by the Greeks and the Christians respectively, but never dreamed of in the philosophy of pragmatists and Wittgensteinians.

Notes

1. Page references in the text refer to the standard English translation: Martin Heidegger, *Being and Time*, trans. John Macquarrie and Edward Robinson (New York: Harper & Row, 1962). This translation and others have occasionally been modified.

2. Theodore Kisiel, *The Genesis of Heidegger's "Being and Time"* (Berkeley: University of California Press, 1993), 9. Kisiel says: "The project of BT thus takes shape in 1921–24 against the backdrop of an unrelenting exegesis of Aristotle's texts . . . from which the . . . *pre*theoretical models for the two Divisions of BT, the *techne* of *poiesis* for the First and the *phronesis* of *praxis* for the Second, are derived."

3. For a more detailed account see Hubert L. Dreyfus and Stuart E. Dreyfus, *Mind over Machine* (New York: Free Press, 1988), and *The Road to Mastery and Beyond* (Cambridge, Mass.: MIT Press, forthcoming).

4. Patricia Benner has described this phenomenon in *From Novice to Expert: Excellence and Power in Clinical Nursing Practice* (Menlo Park, Calif.: Addison-Wesley, 1984), 164.

5. "[A] true cabinetmaker . . . makes himself answer and respond above all to the different kinds of wood and to the shapes slumbering within wood—to wood as it enters into man's dwelling with all the hidden riches of its nature. In fact, this relatedness to wood is what maintains the whole craft." Martin Heidegger, *What Is Called Thinking?* trans. J. Glenn Gray (New York: Harper & Row, 1968), 14–15. The same story with more details is presented in Heidegger's account of the "four causes" involved in the making of a silver chalice: Martin Heidegger, "The Question Concerning Technology," in *The Question Concerning Technology and Other Essays*, trans. William Lovitt (New York: Harper & Row, 1977), 6–8.

6. One might object that this account has the role of involvement reversed; that the more the beginner is emotionally committed to learning the better, while an expert could be, and, indeed, often should be, coldly detached and rational in his practice. This is no doubt true, but the beginner's job is to follow the rules and gain experience, and it is merely a question of motivation whether he is involved or not. What is important is that the novice is not emotionally involved in *choosing* an action, even if he is involved in its outcome. Only at the level of competence is there an emotional investment in the *choice of action*. Then emotional involvement seems to play an essential role in switching the learner over from what one might roughly think of as a left-hemisphere analytic approach to a right-hemisphere holistic one. That amateur and expert chess players use different parts of the brain has been confirmed by recent MRI research. Researchers report that:

> activity is most evident in the medial temporal lobe in amateur players, which is consistent with the interpretation that their mental acuity is focused on analyzing unusual new moves during the game. In contrast, highly skilled chess grandmasters have more γ-bursts in the frontal and parietal cortices.... These marked differences in the distribution of focal brain activity during chess playing point to differences in the mechanisms of brain processing and functional brain organization between grandmasters and amateurs.

See Ognjen Amidzic, Hartmut J. Riehle, Thorsten Fehr, Christian Wienbruch, and Thomas Elbert, "Patterns of focal γ-bursts in chess players: Grandmasters call on regions of the brain not used so much by less skilled amateurs," *Nature* 412, 9 August 2001, 603.

7. Martin Heidegger, *Plato's "Sophist,"* trans. Richard Rojcewicz and André Schuwer (Bloomington: Indiana University Press, 1997), 101 (my italics). In his *Sophist* course, Heidegger has not yet made a clear distinction between *Lage* and *Situation*. He uses both terms interchangeably to refer to the concrete situation. See, for example, page 102: "out of the constant regard toward that which I have resolved, the situation [*Situation*] should become transparent. From the point of view of the *proaireton*, the concrete situation [*konkrete Lage*] . . . is covered over."

8. Martin Heidegger, *Supplements: from the Earliest Essays to "Being and Time" and Beyond*, ed. John van Buren (Albany: State University of New York Press, 2002), 134.

9. Ibid., 134, 135.

10. Ibid., 97.

11. However, in 1924 Heidegger also uses the term *Augenblick* to describe the *phronimos's* instantaneous insight into the Situation: "in *phronesis* . . . in a momentary glance [*Augenblick*] I survey the concrete situation of action, out of which and in favor of which I resolve [*entschliesse*] myself": *Plato's "Sophist,"* 114. This reading is confirmed by *Basic Problems*, where the *Augenblick* is equated with Aristotle's *kairos*, the moment of appropriate skillful intervention. "Aristotle saw the phenomenon of the *Augenblick*, the *kairos*": *The Basic Problems of Phenomenology*, trans. Albert Hofstadter (Bloomington: Indiana University Press, 1982), 288. Still, *Augenblick* is also Luther's translation of St. Paul's instant in which we shall be changed in a "twinkling of an eye." So John van Buren says rather darkly and unhelpfully that "Heidegger took the movement that concentrates itself at the extreme point (*eschaton*) of the *kairos* to be the kairological time that he had already discovered in the Pauline eschatology": *The Young Heidegger: Rumor of the Hidden King* (Bloomington: Indiana University Press, 1994), 231. To make sense of this we will have to stay close to the two phenomena Heidegger is distinguishing and relating.

12. Martin Heidegger, *The Fundamental Concepts of Metaphysics: World, Finitude, Solitude*, trans. William McNeill and Nicholas Walker (Bloomington: Indiana University Press, 1995), 150 (translation modified). (Kisiel clearly distinguishes the Aristotelian and Pauline meanings of *Augenblick*: *The Genesis of Heidegger's "Being and Time,"* 437.)

13. It is important to contrast entrepreneurs, like Ford, and style-changers like Michael Jordan with inventors such as Edison. Ford had a vision of a new form of production that would not try to make perfect cars for the rich like Rolls and Royce, but simple, reliable cars for everyone. His success changed the world. Edison changed the world too, but, even when he invented the electric light bulb, he had no vision of a new style of life it would bring about. He was just seeing what new gadgets he could make. We thus need to distinguish Ford as a *world transformer* from Edison as an *innovator*. In sports too there are not only *style changers* like Michael Jordan, who express their way of life in their actions, but also *innovators* like Dick Fosbury. Unlike Jordan, Fosbury wasn't trying to change the high jump so as to better express his sense

of the sport; he was only trying to find a way to jump that felt better. He thus changed the technique but not the point or style of the sport.

14. We can also return to our examples of mastery to see what they would be like if they were to become world-transformers. A master craftsman, drawing on historical practices such as the love of nature practiced by the Romantics, who treated nature as somehow sacred, might sense that the issue for our time is saving the environment. So to resist our current tendency to think of nature as a resource to be used and then thrown away, he might start a movement to make only things that can be transformed and recycled. The masterful teacher might realize that what is most important in education is not course content, but passing on the positive way of facing the anxiety of thrownness that makes one capable of being a *phronimos,* and of facing the anxiety of death that makes one capable of being a world transformer. She might then draw on the way scientists in their post-doctoral years become apprentices to masterful scientists to change the ways university education is taught so as to emphasize the way teaching assistants learn as apprentices.

15. See M. F. Burnyeat, "Aristotle on Learning to be Good," in *Essays on Aristotle's Ethics,* ed. Amélie Oksenberg Rorty (Berkeley: University of California Press, 1980).

16. The phenomenon of world disclosing is described and illustrated in Charles Spinosa, Fernando Flores, and Hubert L. Dreyfus, *Disclosing New Worlds* (Cambridge, Mass.: MIT Press, 1997).

17. Heidegger sensed that such a fully authentic Dasein's anxious reinterpretation of what his generation stands for allows him to transform the cultural understanding of his time, but, in *Being and Time,* Heidegger could not yet see how radically a culture's understanding could be transformed. Only when he had understood that the style of a culture—its whole understanding of being—could change, could he fully grasp what it would be like for cultural paradigms such as statesmen, works of art, gods, and philosophers to disclose new worlds. See Martin Heidegger, "The Origin of the Work of Art," in *Poetry, Language, Thought,* trans. Albert Hofstadter (New York: Harper & Row, 1971).

9

Genuine Timeliness, from *Heidegger's Concept of Truth*

Daniel O. Dahlstrom

WITH THE INTERPRETATION of the world's manner of being, a manner of being that is constituted by "not-announcing-itself," Heidegger launches his first salvo at the traditional conception of being, namely, the presumption of its equivalence to presence in the sense of something persistently on hand. The work-world, like the implements and network of references that compose it, is not something on hand. To the contrary, not being on hand (or being absent in a particular sense) is constitutive of its manner of being. Nevertheless, traditional assumptions about being can be explained, Heidegger suggests, by the phenomenon of the "crowd" and our tendency, in being-here (*Dasein*), to self-evasion. At the same time, the traditional conception of being (with which the logical prejudice makes common cause) becomes untenable, he argues, in the light of what basically characterizes every dimension of being-here: the phenomenon of care. To be-here is not to run around aimlessly without origins or prospects, nor is being-here a senseless play of presences and absences. To be-here is to be someone thrown into the world and falling prey to it, yet for whom what "always already and always still" matters is for her herself to be. "The being disclosed is that of an entity for whom what matters is this being."[1] Yet since it is possible to be-here authentically or inauthentically, a complete analysis of this manner of being must include a determination of the sense of genuine (authentic) existence. In this way Heidegger attempts to insure the desired differentiation of being-here from being merely handy or on hand.

However, there is a final and decisive step that must be taken to disestablish the conceptions of being and truth—the ontology and alethiology—

traditionally underlying the logical prejudice. The central ontological assumption of the logical prejudice is the equation of being with the presence of things. Being is accordingly interpreted in terms of the present.[2] Heidegger is intent on (a) exposing the largely unreflected, temporal character of this ontological determination and (b) challenging the hegemony of this specific temporal determination. But he himself contends that a certain timeliness (*Zeitlichkeit*) provides the horizon against which it is meaningful to speak, not only of nature's manner of being-on-hand or, for that matter, a tool's way of being-handy, but even a human being's way of being-here. This temporal determination might, of course, simply mean that "being" stands for an occurrence or presence in a succession of nows that are on hand (either singly or in some ideal series). Yet if it did, being-here would be reducible to being-on-hand. The central ontological (=temporal) supposition of the logical prejudice would be corroborated and neither the difference between perceptual or propositional truth and the allegedly original truth (disclosedness) of being-here nor the difference between authentic and inauthentic ways of being-here could be upheld. For all these reasons, Heidegger's campaign against the logical prejudice's central ontological assumptions must include an examination of the distinctive timeliness of human existence. More specifically, in order to establish that being-here is not something merely on hand and cannot be adequately understood in terms of things on hand, he must show how timeliness constitutes the sense of being-here and how this timeliness, far from depending upon a sequence of on-hand nows ("being-within-time": *Innerzeitigkeit*), gives rise to such a conception of time. Heidegger must show, in other words, how the very notion of time that lends credence to the equation of being with presence is derivative of the timeliness of being-here.

But there is a further reason why Heidegger must turn to the question of time. It should be clear by now that Heidegger is arguing that the disclosedness that constitutes being-here is the original, existential truth. The manners of being (that of the on hand [*vorhanden*], the handy [*zuhanden*], others, and one's own) disclose themselves prethematically to being-here, which is, at bottom, this disclosure if it is anything. But the questions then arise: What is the sense of this disclosure? What is the horizon against which these manners of being disclose themselves? What gives these various manners of being their sense? What is the sense of being that this existential truth discloses? Since timeliness is Heidegger's answer to these questions, it is necessary for him to elaborate the content of this original, existential truth if he is to make good on his claim that it is more basic than propositional or perceptual truths.

Conceptions of being and truth are typically anchored in a view of time. The logical prejudice and its ontological presuppositions represent one such anchoring, Heidegger's existential analysis another. In order to demonstrate that the timeliness disclosed by being-here is more fundamental than the concept of time underlying the logical prejudice and its assumptions, Heidegger must first establish what that timeliness is. He begins by taking his cues from an analysis of the genuine manner of being-here, as he unpacks five aspects of "genuine timeliness."

To be-here resolutely is to hear one's conscience and project oneself onto the possibility that is most truly one's own: one's death. Because resolutely, genuinely being-here amounts to anticipating this possibility (the end of one's possibilities), it can be described as a way of coming to the potential that is most properly one's own, and, in that sense, authentically becoming or, as it might be put more colloquially, "genuinely coming into one's own." "*Zukunft*," the German equivalent to "future," is composed of the roots "to" or "at" (*zu*) and "coming" (*kunft*), such that the term might be read as a nominalization of "coming to." Heidegger plays on this etymology as he derives "the original phenomenon of the future" from authentically, i.e., resolutely, being-here.

> [B]eing resolute in anticipating [death] is a way of *being toward* a potential way of being that is extraordinary and most one's own [*Sein zum eigensten ausgezeichneten Seinkönnen*]. Something of this sort is only possible in that being-here *can* come to itself *at all* in this possibility that is most its own, and hold out the possibility in this manner-of-allowing-itself-to-come-to-itself as a possibility (or, in other words, in that being-here exists). Holding out that extraordinary possibility and allowing itself to come to itself is the original phenomenon of the future. (SZ 325)

The original phenomenon of the future thus consists in someone holding out the possibility of her death, allowing this potential that is most her own to come to her. In effect, she comes to be or becomes existentially who she already is becoming existentially. What does it mean to allow this direst of possibilities to come to us? It means not running away from death. An inkling of what is meant can be gathered from the commonplace observation at funerals that death puts everything into perspective, as we see it coming, inevitably, to us. Inasmuch as a person allows herself—her genuine manner of being-here—to come to her in this way, she anticipates it. Heidegger accordingly calls this genuine future "anticipating" or, more literally, "running ahead" (*Vorlaufen*: SZ 336). This anticipating ("a more original way of being toward death than a concerned expectation of it") is only possible because being-here is "always already coming to itself," something that cannot be said for what is merely handy or on hand (SZ 325).

This manner of "coming-to-oneself" is the original and genuine phenomenon of the future. In other words, whatever else might be said about the future, it is at bottom the "becoming" exemplified or, better, authenticated by a resolute anticipation of death. By contrast, the expression of the first structural aspect of care, namely, "being ahead-of-itself," is "the formally indifferent term for the future" (SZ 337). In any case, however, the future as a "becoming" is the fundamental sense of being-here. The fact that to be-here is always to be ahead of ourselves, that we know what matters in advance of any theory or practice (*vortheoretisch und vorpraktisch*), that in each case we have already projected and, as long as we exist, continue to project ourselves unthematically onto possibilities, that our very existing is this thrown project of being-here— these various dimensions of understanding rest ultimately on the fact that to be-here is to come to or "become" oneself and in this way to be preeminently futural.[3]

To be-here resolutely is to take over and disclose ourselves precisely as each of us respectively is already (SZ 325f). "To be ahead of oneself genuinely," projecting oneself onto the possibility that is most properly one's own ("death"), is to come back to the very possibility into which one has already been thrown and in that sense already is. "Only insofar as being-here generally *is*-as-I-*am*-having-been [*als ich bin-gewesen*], can it come to itself in a futural sense such that it comes-*back*" (SZ 326). The hyphenated expression "is-as-I-*am*-having-been" is a clumsy way of conveying the expression *bin-gewesen*. Without the hyphen, the use of *gewesen*, the past participle of *sein*, can signal something that is over, an event or state of affairs completed in the past. It might also signify a past event that reaches into the present (though in some of these cases the "imperfect" is used instead).[4] Thus, without the hyphens, "*ich bin gewesen*" translates simply "I was" or "I have been." But Heidegger makes it perfectly clear that the expression *bin-gewesen* does not refer to something "past" (*vergangen*), that is, something no longer on hand, or to those effects of it that remain on hand (SZ 380). Thus, the hyphenated expression "*is*-as-I-*am*-having-been" indicates neither something over and done with nor something still lingering like a nasty hangover. Instead the expression signifies, as Thomas Sheehan has aptly put it, "that which at any given moment is always prior to and beyond our determination."[5] It signifies not a passing that is not past—like retention in Husserl's analysis of time-consciousness—but instead the manner in which being-here is always "already" and, indeed, always already "foregone" (*Vorbei*) in more than one sense of the word.[6] Just as Heidegger employs the awkward expression *Gewesensein* (usually translated "alreadiness" here) in contrast to *Vergangenheit* (past), so, too, he speaks of "the a priori perfect," presumably in contrast to the normal, a posteriori uses of the perfect that are registered in grammars (SZ 85). To be-here authentically, in other words, is to be who one is "already," and "one can only *be* genuinely already [*gewesen*]" insofar as one projects or anticipates that one is, indeed, in a sense already "gone" (SZ 326).

In a way that clearly resonates with themes of Schopenhauer, Kierkegaard, and Nietzsche (though without mention of these philosophers), Heidegger depicts authentically being what one already is as something that springs from the genuine future in the form of a "repetition" or "retrieval" (*Wiederholung*). "In anticipating, being-here retrieves or brings itself back to the potential-to-be that is most proper to it" (SZ 339).

Being-here can thus "retrieve" itself only by virtue of the fact that, in its being, it is "fore-gone" (in the distinctive sense indicated) and "abides" as such, i.e., existing as its "alreadiness" (at times, e.g., to capture the gerund *gewesend*, the term "abiding" is used instead of "alreadiness").[7] Coming to oneself (the authentic sense of the future) means, at the same time, coming *back* to who one already is. "Being-here is genuinely with itself, it is truly existent, if it holds itself in this anticipating."[8] The second structural aspect of care—"being-already-in (a world)"—expresses the thrownness disclosed through disposition and grounded in this original "alreadiness." Thus, our dispositions (the way that we prethematically, even instinctively turn toward some things and away from others) disclose our manners of being to us by bringing us back to how we already are. The point, Heidegger cautions, is not that the manners of being disposed (e.g., fear or anxiety) are to be deduced from timeliness but that they are only possible on the basis of it (SZ 340–46).

In the anticipating resoluteness, being-here is ahead of itself in an authentic way and genuinely comes back to its thrownness, its abiding mortality, in such a way that it first finds itself in its genuine situation. Resoluteness discloses the respective, genuine potential-to-be of being-in-the-world in a *moment* (*Augenblick*) that springs from genuinely coming-to-oneself and thus to who one is already. The moment is the authentic present as the authentic encounter with things, a way of being present to them such that they can present themselves. This moment is thus not so much a way of rendering something present (*Gegenwärtigen*) as it is a matter of giving full attention to what is encountered in being-here, "genuinely attending to it" (*eigentliche Gegen-wart*). "In resoluteness, the present is not only fetched back from the dispersal into concerns nearest at hand, but instead is held in the future and alreadiness" (SZ 338). In this moment, a human being is first genuinely involved in (*bei*) his world.[9]

Genuine timeliness as this "retrieving-momentous anticipating" is the existential-ontological sense of genuine care (genuinely being-here), that is, the way in which it discloses. Five different aspects of this sense of timeliness deserve mention. First, timeliness cannot be broken down into separate parts, as if genuinely being who one already is, being-involved-in-the-world, or coming to oneself could be on hand somehow without one another. The genuine way of being-already (the "retrieval" or "repetition") and the genuine way of being in the moment ("attending to" the world and letting it present itself) are connected with the genuine future (the "anticipating") without being fully dependent upon it. Each "dimension" of time is dependent upon the others in an integrated whole that makes up timeliness.

This integrated character with its reciprocal complementarity does not, however, mean that some sort of equilibrium reigns within genuine timeliness akin, for example, to that achieved when forward and reverse chemical reactions occur at the same rate. The "retrieval" or "repetition" characteristic of authentically being who one already is springs from the manner in which being-here is authentically ahead of itself, and authentically being-here in the situation of the moment reveals itself only on the basis of this retrieval. These considerations point to a second feature of genuine timeliness: the primacy enjoyed by the future ("becoming"). "*The basic phenomenon of time is the future.*"[10]

From the primacy of the future, the third aspect of genuine timeliness follows: its finitude. In order to forestall misunderstandings that accompany this aspect, it is necessary to point out that this "finitude" does not refer to an end or punctuated interval in a series of elapsing nows. The genuine future (that "coming-to-oneself" described above) is not a possibility simply not yet on hand, that "springs forth" at some undetermined point of time within a now-sequence or occupies its place in the like. Death, it bears recalling, is the inevitable possibility, not of anything on hand, but of the impossibility of being-here (SZ 262). "The original and genuine future" is being-here's manner of allowing this possibility to come to it, "existing as the possibility of nothingness, a possibility that cannot be overtaken" (SZ 330).

The fourth aspect of genuine timeliness concerns the relation of timeliness to being-here. Genuine care is a phenomenal expression of genuine timeliness or, in more inflated terms, timeliness is the (transcendental) condition of the possibility of care. That is to say, genuine timeliness provides the "sense" of genuine care; it constitutes in a concrete way the transcendence signified by "care" and "being-in-the-world." "Sense" for Heidegger is that "upon" or "over against which" something is projected; without this "horizon" what is projected would not be visible or sensible (ambiguity intended), even if in the process the horizon itself in a certain sense is not regarded (see SZ 151, 324). Seen in this light, genuinely being-here only makes sense (*sinnvoll*) in view of timeliness as the sort of "anticipating" (*Vorlaufen*) that "retrieves" or brings me back to myself (*wiederholend*) and in the process makes my situation present to me in the decisive "moment" or "momentously" (*augenblicklich*).

As far as talk of "sense" as a horizon is concerned, it is only natural to think of the following pairs: foreground/background, figure/ground, or melody/accompaniment. These examples are instructive but also misleading (and no less instructive because they are misleading). In certain respects it hardly seems possible for us to direct our attention only at the foreground of a picture; without a ground against which a figure cuts a profile, the figure would never be apparent. So, too, some musical accompaniments seem to fade out, thereby allowing the melody to stand out all the more. In corresponding fashion, genuine timeliness does not merely constitute respective ways in which to be-here is to stand out or ex-ist and thus disclose (namely, "running-ahead" or "anticipating," "retrieving" or "repeating," and "involvement in the moment"). Genuine timeliness also includes the horizon for these timely constitutions of existence, though the horizon is different in each case.[11]

In order to appreciate Heidegger's interpretation of timeliness as the horizon or sense of being-here, it may be helpful to recall that being-here is intentionality or, better, the paradigm of intentionality, a categorial perception, viewed "from the inside," to use Heidegger's own trope. As a means of capturing the originally timely character of being-here, of being-in-the-world as the ground level of intentionality, Heidegger construes the modes of timeliness—anticipating, retrieving, and the moment—as "ecstases" (*Ekstasen*). This use of "ecstasis" (from *ek:* out, and *histemi:* to place) plays on original uses of the Greek term in the sense of displacement, literally and figuratively, as well as on modern connotations of those figurative senses. We say, for example, that someone is ecstatic when she is "beside herself" with joy or pleasure and so given up to the experience that she gives little or no thought to herself or even to what she is doing. Being ecstatic, one is on the verge of being unconscious, but precisely because one is so focused, so intently engaged in and, in that active sense, given up to the moment. Heidegger's appeal to these associated meanings is meant to convey how those modes of timeliness—those ecstases—jointly constitute the most basic level of being-here or, in other words, the prethematic process of being-here in the sense of being *outside oneself*. Again, as in the case of "being-here," Heidegger exploits a term with an unmistakably spatial root, while at the same time insisting on the fundamentally temporal significance of the phenomenon so designated. The term ecstasis is used to translate *Ekstase* because it is an English word, roughly synonymous with 'ecstasy,' albeit far less common, and because Heidegger himself uses a term similar in meaning to ecstasy—*Entrückung* (rapture)—as a means of elaborating the meaning of *Ekstase*. "Ecstasis" seems an apt translation since it brings to mind the normal connotations of ecstasy, but, thanks to its uncommonness, also deflects any quick identification of the usual senses with the sense introduced by Heidegger to convey how timeliness constitutes being-here.

With this notion of ecstasy in mind, the horizonal character of timeliness must be understood in two respects (SZ 324ff, 365). In one respect, genuine timeliness provides the horizon for genuine care as a whole, and thereby the "sense" of genuine human existence. In another, closely related respect, each mode of genuine timeliness—what Heidegger dubs the "ecstases" or, literally, ways of "standing out" from itself in "anticipating," "retrieving," and the "moment"—has its own respective horizon. Genuine timeliness comprises the horizon of care and thereby the sense of existence by integrating the horizons for the "ecstases" of anticipating, retrieving, and moment that respectively constitute the genuine future, past, and present.

Yet in either of these respects, the horizonal metaphor can be misleading. For example, the horizon for "anticipating"—the "for-the-sake-of-oneself"—does not merely accompany it like some neutral background. Instead the horizon structures the genuine projection, pulling and guiding it. Yet this does not mean that the horizon somehow obtains independently of the projection. "*The move-away* [*Entrückung*, that is of the essence of each "ecstasis"] *opens this horizon and holds it open*" (GP 378). Genuine timeliness is a projecting (i.e., an anticipating) from which (as already discussed) a genuine way of "already being" (retrieving) and a genuine way of "attending to things" (in the moment) spring. But it is always a projecting "toward something" ("for the sake of oneself, one's being-here") and this directionality is decisive.

Mention has already been made of the integral character of timeliness. Each "ecstasis" of genuine timeliness "reaches" or "stands out" to the other two, which form part of that aspect's horizon (not unlike Husserl's longitudinal and transversal time-consciousness). Thus, for example, the nexus of anticipating and retrieving forms part of the horizon of the moment, namely, the genuine possibilities that being-here attends to in its situation. The anticipating or forerunning, the retrieving or repeating, and presenting in the moment are, in Heidegger's formulation, "ecstases of timeliness"; he labels the respective direction or horizon of the ecstasis its "horizonal schema" (SZ 365, 329). In view of the fact, first, that genuine timeliness constitutes the horizon of care and thus the sense of human existence and, second, that each ecstasis of genuine timeliness has a respective, leading horizon, Heidegger speaks of the "ecstatic-horizonal" character of timeliness.

The purpose of this account of timeliness, it bears recalling, is to articulate the sense of "being-here" and "being-in-the-world," Heidegger's terms for what Husserl allegedly describes "from the outside" as intentionality. Heidegger's account of ecstatic-horizonal timeliness is thus supposed to capture the concrete transcendence that receives, in his view, only muted and inadequate elaboration in the sort of theoretical and perceptual orientation that Husserl gives to the doctrine of intentionality. In pursuit of this objective, Heidegger uses typically spatial adverbial expressions to designate the horizons (e.g., *Wohin*) and nominalizations of active verbs typically ascribed to a human agent for the respective ecstases (e.g., *Vorlaufen*). Though they appear to the reader as "mixed metaphors," the combinations of these two sorts of locutions are designed to indicate a presubjective yet ecstatic unfolding (later dubbed "time-space") as the original significance of "being." "There is, as part of the ecstasis, a peculiar *openness*, which is given with the 'outside-itself.' That toward which each ecstasis is, in a specific way, in itself open, we designate as the 'horizon of the ecstasis'" (GP 378). The horizons are thus related to the ecstases as the world is related to the existentials making up "being-in-the-world." More precisely, the horizonality of ecstatic timeliness is the original significance of the "world." "The world is neither on hand nor handy but instead unfolds (*zeitigt sich*) in timeliness. It 'is here' with the outside-itself of the ecstases. If no *being-here* exists, no world is also 'here'" (SZ 365).

In this way Heidegger introduces the transcendental dimension of the analysis of timeliness. "Resting on the horizonal unity of ecstatic timeliness, the world is transcendent" (SZ 366). For example, precisely in the "moment" that springs from genuinely coming-to-ourselves, we bring ourselves, being-here, face-to-face with our respective situations. On the basis of genuine timeliness, we encounter others, what is handy, and what is on hand. Regarded in this way, genuine timeliness is the condition of the possibility of genuinely being-in-the-world, encompassing the worldliness of the work-world, being-with-others, and being-oneself and thereby allowing for an authentic encounter with intraworldly entities.

Given that (a) the disclosedness of the sense of being-here is the original truth, (b) the ecstatic-horizonal timeliness is the sense that is thereby disclosed, and (c) timeliness in the manner elucidated thus constitutes the care (existence) of being-in-the-world, timeliness might be labeled "the transcendental truth." The word "ecstatic" accordingly indicates that timeliness is "the original 'outside-itself' in and of itself" and precisely in this sense, as the "woof and warp" of being-in-the-world, it can be said to be the condition of the possibility of being-in-the-world.[12] Being-here (being-in-the-world, concerned, caring about others and about oneself) is "outside-itself." The original "outside-itself" is the timeliness by means of which it is "here" (*da*). It scarcely needs to be added that Heidegger's explanation of how genuine timeliness (*wiederholend-augenblickliches Vorlaufen*) constitutes the sense of genuine care would be misunderstood from the ground up if it were conceived as a property or determination that happens to accrue to some care that is otherwise on hand. To be here is to care, and caring is timely through and through, that is, ecstatically unfolding against a horizon.[13]

The fifth and final point to be made about timeliness springs from its ecstatic-horizonal character. A thing that is handy or on hand is an entity that surfaces in time; being-here is that entity the sense of which, namely, care, is grounded in timeliness. Since timeliness constitutes the sense of being-here and thereby underlies any sense of being handy or on hand, it would be a category mistake to define timeliness itself as an entity or to maintain that timeliness itself "is." As a means of avoiding such category mistakes and emphasizing the dynamic, unified phenomenon of timeliness as the original "outside-itself," Heidegger speaks of the *Zeitigung* of timeliness, a term that might be translated "ripening," "unfolding," or even "timing."[14] While Heidegger, perhaps ill-advisedly, construes timeliness transcendentally, as a condition of the possibility of being-here, he does not understand it as something that somehow obtains apart from being-here. Instead, timeliness is the sense of being-here. Every existential is, in the last analysis, a complex kind of timing or a matter of timing. For example, "coming-to-oneself"—the original and genuine sense of the future—is the timeliness that constitutes and is disclosed by the basic existential of understanding/projecting; the way we are always already disposed in the thrownness of our existence is also a matter of timing, a certain kind of abiding or "alreadiness."

The chart below summarizes the foregoing sketch of five aspects of genuine timeliness. On the basis of that sketch, it becomes clear how they are connected with one another. The original timeliness has that ecstatic-horizonal character (*das ursprüngliche Außer-sich an und für sich selbst*), above all because the ecstases constantly complement one another, but in such a way that the future is *primus inter pares*. The finitude of genuine and original timeliness is also connected to the fundamental futurity—the "coming-to-oneself"—of timeliness's ecstatic-horizonal character. Timeliness "is" not, but instead "unfolds" (*zeitigt*) and its "timing" lies ontologically in advance of every sense of being (being-here, being-with, being a world, being-handy, being-on-hand). In the timing that constitutes the sense of being-here, of caring, what it means "to be" is originally disclosed.

Five Aspects of Genuine Timeliness

1. The integrated character of its modes (the retrieval, the moment, and the anticipation are unified and inseparable—like the Trinity).
2. The primacy of the future: the original past (the retrieval) and present (the moment) spring from the original future (coming-to-oneself, becoming who one genuinely is by anticipating the possibility most one's own).
3. The finitude: the genuine future is the anticipation of death.
4. The ecstasis and horizon: genuine timeliness comprises ecstases, that is to say, ways in which to be-here is to be "outside" or even "beside oneself" and horizons (that on which the projection is projected), in view of which being-here is "ecstatic"; this ecstatic-horizonal character of timeliness is the sense of the manner of being defined as "being-here" (care, existence) *and* the transcendental condition of being-in-the-world (longitudinal and transversal, respectively).
5. The unfolding: genuine time is not, but instead "unfolds" and that is precisely what it means to be "the original 'outside-itself' in and for itself."

Notes

1. *Sein und Zeit* (=SZ), 12th ed. (Tübingen: Niemeyer, 1972), 325. Translations from SZ are my own.

2. The equation of an entity's being with its presence is also meant to convey that it is in a place and available. The ontological significance of "presence" thus embraces all the senses of the term conveyed in the statement: "Presently present, she presents herself to the Queen" (="Now here, she makes herself available to the Queen"). Yet the appeal to the preeminently temporal modality of presence is appropriate if Heidegger can make good on his contention that a certain timeliness explains this multilayered, ontological significance of "presence" as well as the ontological significance of other ways of being.

3. *Logik: Die Frage nach der Wahrheit, Gesamtausgabe* (=GA) 21, 413; here Heidegger observes that the ontic phrase "Become what you are!" (from Pindar) is only possible if, in an ontological sense, I am what I become. Sheehan has called attention to this observation and, in general, to the advisability of construing the future as "becoming"; cf. Thomas Sheehan, "Heidegger's New Aspect: On *In-Sein, Zeitlichkeit,* and *The Genesis of Being and Time,*" *Research in Phenomenology* 25 (1995), 216f.

4. Sheehan rightly notes the novelty of what Heidegger calls "das apriorische Perfekt" (SZ 85) in contrast to the empirical perfects of grammar. It is worth noting, however, that, in addition to expressing some completed event or one that, while over, continues to be significant, the perfect can also be used to indicate something that is only completed in the future ("Wenn Richard seine Prüfung gemacht hat, fährt er in seine Heimat zurück"). Cf. Dora Schulz and Heinz Griesbach, *Grammatik der deutschen Sprache* (München: Hueber, 1972), 46ff.

5. Sheehan, "Heidegger's New Aspect," 317; Dylan Thomas gives expression to something akin to what Heidegger means by "authentic alreadiness" in the first stanza of his poem "This Side of the Truth": "This side of the truth, / You may not see, my son, / King of your blue eyes / In the blinding country of youth, / That all is undone, / Under the unminding skies, / Of innocence and guilt / Before you move to make / One gesture of the heart or head, / Is gathered and spilt / Into the winding dark / Like the dust of the dead." *The Poems of Dylan Thomas,* ed. Daniel Jones (New York: New Directions, 1971), 192.

6. For the use of *Vorbei* in this connection, cf. Heidegger, *The Concept of Time,* trans. William McNeill (Oxford: Blackwell, 1992), 12–15. Once again, as Heidegger grinds out his account, he is critically reworking Aristotelian and Hegelian themes. Cf. Aristotle's *to ti en einai* ("the what it was and continues to be") in, for example, *Metaphysics* 1029b1–1030b13, an expression that is frequently translated "essence" or "*Wesen*"; cf. Joseph Owens, *The Doctrine of Being in the Aristotelian Metaphysics* (Toronto: Pontifical Institute of Medieval Studies, 1957), 352–58; G. W. F. Hegel, "Die objektive Logik" (1812/1813), in *Wissenschaft der Logik,* ed. Friedrich Hogemann and Walter Jaeschke (Hamburg: Meiner, 1978), 241: "Die Sprache hat im Zeitwort *Sein* das Wesen in der vergangenen Zeit 'gewesen' behalten; denn das Wesen ist das vergangene, aber zeitlos vergangene Sein." Heidegger is, in effect, deconstructing these senses

of "essence" (*Wesen*) in favor of that of the "already" (*gewesen*). In this regard, see Heidegger, *Vom Wesen der Wahrheit*, 4th ed. (Frankfurt am Main: Klostermann, 1978), 26 (="On the Essence of Truth," in *Pathmarks*, ed. William McNeill [Cambridge: Cambridge University Press, 1998], 153): "The question of the essence of truth finds its answer in the sentence: *the essence of truth is the truth of the essence.*"

7. The translation "alreadiness" is suggested by Thomas Sheehan; see his "How (Not) to Read Heidegger," *American Catholic Philosophical Quarterly* 69 (1995): 275–94; esp. 290ff. When the term "abiding" is used in the remainder of this chapter, it is meant as a synonym for "alreadiness," i.e., the "a priori perfect," and not the persistence (in one sense or the other) of something previously on hand. It should be noted that Heidegger muddies the waters on this score somewhat in GA 24, *Die Grundprobleme der Phänomenologie* (=GP), where he is less clear about the distinction between alreadiness and a kind of past; cf. GP 375. (The German pagination is also provided in *The Basic Problems of Phenomenology*, trans. Albert Hofstadter [Bloomington: Indiana University Press, 1982]. Translations from GP are mine.) Retrieving possibilities that have come down to us and retrieving one's authentic alreadiness by "handing oneself over to it," i.e., freeing oneself for it, are distinct but combined in "historicity" (*Geschichtlichkeit*). For a brief but lucid review, see Sheehan, "Heidegger's New Aspect," 220f.

8. *The Concept of Time*, 13; cf. ibid., 12–13: "Anticipating [or running toward: *Vorlaufen*] being-gone is being-here's running approach [*Anlaufen*] toward its most extreme possibility; and insofar as this 'running approach' is serious, it is thrown back, in this running [*Laufen*], upon its still-being-here itself. It is being-here's manner of coming back to its everydayness. . . . " (Translations mine.)

9. For a valuable reading of *Augenblick*, with an emphasis on its connection with "originary praxis in its full ethical and political character," see William McNeill, *The Glance of the Eye: Heidegger, Aristotle, and the Ends of Theory* (Albany: SUNY Press, 1999), esp. 116: "These remarks on conscience also indicate that the *Augenblick* or 'glance of the eye,' as we have preferred to translate it, is not to be understood as a 'moment of time' in the sense of an 'instant.' Rather, it refers to the unfolding disclosure of the presencing of a situation *in the duration appropriate to it.*" Elaborating the connection between Heidegger's concept of *Augenblick* and interpretation of the doctrine of *phronesis* in the *Nicomachean Ethics*, McNeill relates how the actual end of an action, the means pursued by deliberation, the time of the deliberation, and the right moment to act, "*all* depend upon *what is called for by the concrete circumstances of the moment*, as disclosed in the practical *aisthesis* or *Augenblick*" (ibid., 118).

10. *The Concept of Time*, 14.

11. Heidegger describes these horizons formally, i.e., irrespective of whether the manner of being-in-the-world is authentic or not. The horizon for coming-to-oneself (the future) is "the 'for-the-sake-of-oneself'" (*das "Umwillen seiner"*); the horizonal schema for alreadiness is the "for-what" or "in-the-face-of-what" (*das Wovor*, as in "what do you fear for?"); and that for rendering present is the "in order-to" (*Um-zu*): SZ 365; GP 377f.

12. SZ 329; GP 377f. As these passages demonstrate, the expression "ecstatic-horizonal" is fraught with spatial metaphors, again raising the questionableness, later

conceded by Heidegger, of his efforts to ground the spatiality of being-here in timeliness. The ecstatic feature, it bears noting, is similar to Husserl's view of the transcendence in time-consciousness itself; that is to say, by virtue of the retentional-primal impression unity of abiding, every now transcends or "has a fringe." A different but related ecstatic feature can be found in the bodiliness and motivated perception discussed in *Ideas II.*

13. "In the flight from [or in the face of: *vor*] itself, time remains time." Heidegger, *History of the Concept of Time: Prolegomena,* trans. Theodore Kisiel (Bloomington: Indiana University Press, 1985), 227.

14. SZ 328–31. As a translation of "*zeitigen,*" "unfold" has the advantage of being transitive, intransitive, and reflexive, like the German word; it also captures the sense of movement and the dually ecstatic-horizonal character of timeliness (see below). The term has some misleading connotations as well, e.g., it might be taken in an unduly neutral sense (as opposed to "ripen") or in literally spatial senses.

10

Historical Meaning in the Fundamental Ontology of *Being and Time,* from *Martin Heidegger and the Problem of Historical Meaning*

Jeffrey Andrew Barash

A GAINST WHAT HE PERCEIVED AS TRADITION, Heidegger insisted that, because the question of Being is oriented throughout by the possibility of *Dasein*'s understanding of it, "[i]f we are to formulate our question explicitly and transparently, we must first give a proper explication of a being [*eines Seienden*]—that of the questioner [*des Fragenden*]—with regard to its Being."[1] In avowedly circular reasoning, Heidegger thus affirmed that it is in the Being of *Dasein* that a sense of Being per se must be sought. The main point of Heidegger's statement, however, was that *Dasein* could not be reduced to a fixed metaphysical essence or to some underlying substance, nor could it be comprehended by an unclarified ontology of human life.

As we will see more clearly, in *Being and Time,* Heidegger leaves open what *Dasein*—the guiding thread through which the question of Being per se is to be pursued—is. In essence, *Dasein* is to be determined nowhere else than in its unspoken decisions about what it means *to be.* For Heidegger, no meaning, whether in everyday existence or in the most ethereal theory, can be extracted from *Dasein*'s presupposition of what it means to be, however tacit.

If, in light of understanding what it means to be, there remains a margin of indeterminacy in the way in which *Dasein* orients its Being, this orientation never arises in the abstract. At several points in the introduction to *Being and Time,* Heidegger states that *Dasein*'s ways of Being are "factically" given and, as such, are always decided in relation to circumstances of *Dasein*'s concrete past and prefigure its future choices. In this regard, he stresses that "[i]n its factical Being, any *Dasein* is as it already was, and is 'what' it already was. It *is* its past, whether explicitly or not. ... *Dasein* 'is' its past in the way of its own *Being*, which, to put it roughly, 'historicizes' out of its future on each occasion. ... Its own past—and this always means the past of its 'generation'—is not something that *follows along* after *Dasein*, but each time already precedes it."[2]

This statement introduces a paradox. Heidegger claims to refer to the "universal sense of Being [*Sein überhaupt*]" or, as he wrote elsewhere, to philosophy as "universal ontology [*universale Ontologie*]."[3] Yet, if this were the case, how might his presupposition that *Dasein* is its past, from which its future choices are projected, yield more than just a partial, perspectival viewpoint—which would preclude any preoccupation with Being in the universal sense that Heidegger sought to disclose?

Even earlier than Heidegger, the critical theorists of history had carefully refined a century-old historicist turn away from traditional concepts of the Being of humanity as a metaphysical substance, and had attempted to understand the meaning of humanity in terms of choices elucidated in relation to the past. In stipulating that humanity came to understand and determine itself in history, none of the critical theorists was ready to embrace an ontological position. For them, the potentialities of individual cultures and of individual perspectives of truth expressed in them, while held together by a tissue of universally graspable coherence, nonetheless precluded definitive knowledge both of the Being of humanity and of humanity's variable, if continuous, advent in history.

How, then, does Heidegger hope to account for the Being of *Dasein* in the universal sense he is claiming to investigate in *Being and Time*? And, once the past is founded on a universal philosophy of Being, what becomes of the national or cultural unities theretofore considered the individual bearers of historical meaning, in the context of which normative values and standards of truth emerge and are sustained from generation to generation, and on whose mediation the very possibility of history itself depends?

* * *

A brief recapitulation of the theme of *Dasein*'s Being-in-the-world, and then what Heidegger viewed as a laying bare of the fundamental constitution of *Dasein*'s Being, will set in relief the universal claim through which he conceived the problem of historical meaning.

Heidegger's ontology, as analyzed through *Dasein*'s Being-in-the-world, unveiled what was for the times a reorientation of philosophy: abandoning the predominant conceptions of the world as the scene of objectifications of life or of values in the context of determinate societies or cultures, Heidegger made existence in the world in its most ordinary and mundane moments the starting point of philosophy. Philosophy of life and of worldviews, phenomenology of universal structures of consciousness, and the traditional neo-Kantianism and its reinterpretation in terms of symbolic forms by Ernst Cassirer all confronted a philosophy of the most everyday and banal aspects of a world where, according to Heidegger, the analytics of *Dasein* (*Daseinsanalytik*) had to find its immediate theme.

What, according to Heidegger, does the ordinary, everyday character of the world teach us ontologically? Everydayness (*Alltäglichkeit*) describes a familiar, immediate relation between *Dasein* and the world of people and of things before any process of abstraction has distinguished *Dasein* as an observer occupied with given objects. In this relation Heidegger discerned a basis for universal coherence in everydayness as such, beyond a record of single, ordinary situations or biographies depicting everyday life: the ordinary world is given as a unity through *Dasein*'s tendency to forget what it means to be in the immediacy of its preoccupations.[4]

Exploring this context of everydayness, Heidegger developed the line of argumentation for which *Being and Time* became renowned. The sense of what it means to be is ordinarily forgotten in an everyday environment (*Umwelt*) in which *Dasein*'s self-understanding is spontaneously involved in and extracted from the useful processes of a functionally interpreted world; it is neglected under the influence of everyday collective conventionalism, conformism, and anonymity, through which *Dasein* is ordinarily led to behold itself. The predominance of the style of rapport of the everyday collectivity (*Mitwelt*)—the common opinion (*communis opinio*) that "one" has prescribed—Heidegger termed "das Man."[5] The very familiarity of everyday Being-in-the-world is the obverse side of *Dasein*'s estrangement from itself.

In the course of *Being and Time*, Heidegger elaborates on the possibility of a limited transcendence of everyday Being-in-the-world. What *Dasein* is, decided in terms of what it means to be, essentially hovers between two fundamental choices: immersion in and acceptance of spontaneous forgetfulness of what it means to be, or the attempt to recover a sense of responsibility for its own Being from the spontaneous familiarity of an everyday world.

This dualism in Heidegger's ontology pinpoints in preliminary form the fundamental assumption underlying his universal claim. In stating that "*Dasein is* its past" in deciding the possibilities of its future, Heidegger is not primarily concerned with qualitative changes in a historically evolving *Dasein* (in the sense of an unfolding of cultural or world history). His statement that *Dasein*'s Being is not given in a fixed way must be carefully distinguished from the critical theorists' claim that humanity determines itself historically. Far from focusing on the critical analysis of changes in human perspective from period to period, Heidegger presumes that, whatever the alteration in perspective, "what *Dasein is*" is ontologically prefigured by the duality of possible directions its choices must take.

In the later sections of *Being and Time*, the possibility of delineating *Dasein*'s choices is grounded in what Heidegger describes as the fundamental constitution of *Dasein*'s Being. The way in which he frames this fundamental constitution—comprising the tripartite structure of "existence," "facticity," and "fallenness"—exposes the root assumption on which his universal claim is based, and adumbrates its intention vis-à-vis the problem of historical meaning.[6]

In dealing with *Dasein*'s existence, nowhere is Heidegger concerned with the particularity of *Dasein*'s perspectival view of the world in a given historical context, and the structural differences between this perspective and that of later generations. He relegates the specific differences constituting the objective context of the choices of existence, whether analyzed as the advent of given values and the remission of others or as the ebb and flow of worldviews in the process of history, to the level of secondary, "ontic" phenomena.

More fundamental than this, for Heidegger, are the dual possibilities of ontological choice illuminated by existence's finitude. This finitude, manifested in the untransferable, unavoidable eventuality of death, universally stands before the future possibilities of all existing *Dasein* and, underlying all specific circumstances, constitutes the sense of what it means to be. In the face of this future, *Dasein* may choose to blend into the spontaneous forgetfulness offered by present modes of Being-in-the-world, which Heidegger traces to a tacit collective need to forget the distinctiveness of existence—marked by personal death—and be calmed in the face of the impending end. This is the mark, for Heidegger, of inauthentic existence. Or it may accept authentic responsibility for its existence, recognizing that its distinctiveness bears the emblem of finitude, resolving to wrest the sense of what it means to be from ordinary interpretation, and orienting this meaning in accord with the finitude of its own decisions.

When dealing with facticity, nowhere does Heidegger specifically focus on facts (*Tatsachen*) themselves.[7] Rather than deal with particular factual events, Heidegger analyzes what he views as the necessity for all *Dasein* to exist "factically" in a contingent world in which understanding finds its point of reference. Because universally entangled in given perspectives limited by *Dasein*'s own transience, this understanding allows of no absolute starting point.[8]

Fallenness, Heidegger notes, is in no way meant to be taken as a judgment of specific moral circumstances. *Dasein* is fallen because its tendency to interpret the meaning of Being in the everydayness of an immediately given world is fundamental to the facticity of existence. In this mode of Being *Dasein*'s fall into the domination of *das Man* in the everyday environment and collectivity can never be fully overcome, but only resisted. Only through the effort to recover an individual, finite sense of what it means to be can each of us oppose a flight from the anxiety of death as our death, favored by the anonymity and conventionalism of tacit collective modes of seeking security and discharging the burden of finitude in face of the exigencies of current events.

Of itself, the universal claim involved in Heidegger's vision of the fundamental structures of *Dasein*'s Being does not elicit the special importance Heidegger attributes to historical understanding, nor the grounds for his own way of conceiving of it. But this intrinsic importance of historical understanding is illuminated in the preeminent insight of *Being and Time*, through which time emerges in its structural relation to the meaning of Being. Heidegger stipulates that *Dasein*'s choice of what it is is essentially drawn from its modes of being temporal. In this qualification, the claim that *Dasein is* its past in deciding its future acquires a unique significance, laying the temporal groundwork for Heidegger's reassessment of what it means to think historically.

For Heidegger, each of the aspects of *Dasein*'s fundamental constitution refers primarily to a mode of temporal Being. As he asserts in an elaborate line of argumentation, which cannot be recapitulated in detail here, existence is primarily oriented toward the future, facticity toward the past, and fallenness toward the present. The three modes of temporal Being—or *ekstases*—are always given in a unity; they owe the style of their unification to *Dasein*'s choices concerning what it means to be.[9] As inauthentic, *Dasein* confronts the future as a mere chronological waiting for events (*gewärtigen*); a simple expectation of a foreseeable future exactly modeled on the present, in which the eventuality of death is tacitly shunned. In this mode the past, too, is overlaid with the veneer of current events, a mere retention of occurrences in which the finite sense of past *Dasein*, and of the *Dasein* that retains it, escapes notice in the immediacy of present preoccupations.

In its authentic modes of temporalization, *Dasein* strives for transcendence of spontaneous presence of everyday Being-in-the-world. Temporal *ekstases* are unified, not on the basis of a current expectation of events to be retained at a later point, where a sense of what it means to be remains hidden in the face of pressing actuality (*Wirklichkeit*); the authentic unity of temporal modes, as Heidegger saw it, reveals this hidden meaning of Being as the explicit foundation of a choice. Placed primarily in the perspective of future anticipation (*Vorlaufen*) of death, this choice pierces through the veil of everyday actuality and illuminates possibilities ontologically specific to finite *Dasein*. The past, more than a mere former presence, or weighty precedent of present actuality, discloses itself for choice in a repetition (*Wiederholung*) of possibilities it bears. These possibilities (*Möglichkeiten*), projected as an "anticipatory repetition [*vorlaufende Wiederholung*]," unify the temporal *ekstases* as the decisive moment (*Augenblick*) when authentic choice is projected.

Dasein's dual possibilities of temporalizing, and of Being, had direct ramifications for the problem of historical meaning. The major nineteenth- and early-twentieth-century conceptions of history, from Hegel to the critical theorists, conceived of it in close relation to the objective development of national cultures in world history. The sequential order of history as an objectively unfolding process comprised a collective experience, founded in the past and lending coherence to present cultural development.

Heidegger's thinking about history started from a different premise. Heidegger did not interpret *Dasein*'s historical Being—or "historicity [*Geschichtlichkeit*]"—primarily in relation to the network of cumulative experience of the past, mediated by a sequential, objective coherence of culture.[10] Any possible sense of this network was traced back to what Heidegger viewed as the more primary source of historical meaning and coherence (*Zusammenhang*) in *Dasein*'s *choice* of a mode of temporalization in the projection of possibilities.

By rooting the source of *Dasein*'s historicity in a choice of temporal modes, Heidegger underlined an important proviso: historical theorists and historians had generally sought to induce historical meaning from the processes of historical development, assuming the spontaneous coherence of these processes in what objective analysis had proved to have once been actual. Reliance on objective standards, however, and on an overarching coherence of the historical process grounding their continuity, disregarded the essential moment of the modes of Being of *Dasein*.

As Heidegger makes clear in *Being and Time*, objective reality for *Dasein* is not the only source of past meaning, but corresponds to one mode of Being as appropriated by *Dasein* from a world of events, neglectful of the finitude of interpretation grounded in a sense of Being as Being toward death. The quest for objectivity and objective coherence misplaces this finitude, but is not able to overcome it. For Heidegger, it overlooks the authentic sense of the past, which is not revealed for any possible observer, but is grounded in *Dasein*'s *own* choice of a finite sense of what it means to be.[11]

Beyond a call to decision, Heidegger's approach to historical meaning has essential bearing on the way in which the past is revealed. Neglect of *Dasein*'s sense of Being issues from subservience to the weight of what has become actual, and veils the richness of original possibility that the authentic moments of the past embodied. This original possibility is intended by *Dasein*'s authentic projection of a meaning of Being in its modes of temporalization. Only such projection can free the past, as Heidegger viewed it, from its embalmment in the traditions of the present, for which a past moment of choice is forgotten in its primordiality and is confidently taken as an objective acquisition. The projection of authentic possibilities identifies an authentic past primarily in view of what can be retrieved for resolute repetition in the authentic future.[12]

Heidegger's philosophy thus retracted the authentic ground of history from historical concatenations, such as the objective development of national cultures or world history. This should not be taken to signify, however, that *Dasein's* authenticity is restricted to an isolated framework of action in which the individual has no ties to a larger collectivity. As a counterpart to the inauthentic collectivity characterized by *das Man*, Heidegger envisions the locus of authentic possibilities as implicit in "the people [*das Volk*]," which comprises the authentic community of individuals prepared to take upon themselves the responsibility for choice in light of the finitude of existence.

Das Volk, like *das Man*, remains empirically intangible. *Das Volk* is a community of authenticity, which has no necessary, direct counterpart in the political or cultural world. In the terse passages dealing with collective authenticity, Heidegger recounts that *Dasein's* authentic choice, projected in a singular fate (*Schicksal*), interweaves itself into the destiny (*Geschick*) of a people. The coincident interweaving of fates finds its locus in the generation (*Generation*):

> Destiny is not something that puts itself together out of individual fates, any more than Being-with-one-another can be conceived as the occurring together of several subjects. Our fates have already been guided in advance, in our being with one another in the same world and in our resoluteness for definite possibilities. Only in communicating and in struggling (*Kampf*) does the power of destiny become free. *Dasein's* fateful destiny in and with its "generation" goes to make up the full authentic historicizing of *Dasein*.[13]

From the standpoint of the problem of historical meaning (and in regard to the theme of *Being and Time* as a whole), Heidegger's elucidation of *das Volk* leaves undeniable gaps. Collective inauthenticity receives detailed description throughout the work, but the possibility of authentic community is described only in its last sections and in vague terms.

In dealing with the theme of the generation, which fills out the nexus between the authentic individual and the community of *das Volk*, Heidegger explicitly draws on Dilthey's use of the latter concept in "Über das Studium der Geschichte der Wissenschaften vom Menschen, der Gesellschaft, und dem Staat" (On the study of the history of the sciences of man, society, and state).[14] Although he much admired Dilthey's essay, Heidegger's treatment of communal authenticity is sketchy, perhaps due to the vacuum left by his distance from pre-World War I historical theory, within which Dilthey's thought had come to expression.

In applying the concept of generation, Dilthey sought a specifically historical unit of time. He considered the purely quantitative account of temporality in hours, minutes, and seconds to be inappropriate for this purpose, choosing instead a range of time that "reaches from the demarcation line of birth to that of old age."[15] In Dilthey's thought, the concept of generation represented the individual life span and, given a certain flexibility of interpretation, might be seen to anticipate Heidegger's notion of Being-toward-death.

Yet, in envisaging the life unity of the generation, Dilthey evidently did not claim to encompass an *ontological* unity. In descriptive and inductive terms, he attempted to account for a principle of unity interweaving the lives of con-temporary individuals. His conviction that the basis of such a principle lay in empirical reality had led him to reject the nominalistic conclusions of Heinrich Rickert, for whom the distance between meaning and reality itself precluded any possibility that a "generation" or "worldview [*Weltanschauung*]" might serve as the real, extraindividual context providing for meaning's preservation and transmission. For Rickert, the spirit of Goethe's generation, of the Italian Renaissance, or of any other such cultural unity might be applied as value re-lations only to certain great individuals. It would be erroneous to claim that the distinctive spirit of a generation or of an age might in any real sense refer to more than a few great individuals.

Dilthey's epistemology, which considered that meaning infused reality with-out ever exhausting its empirical plenitude, attributed the spirit of a generation to more than an atomistic collection of individuals, a conclusion Heidegger readily accepted. For Dilthey, the convictions of a generation or the spirit of an age did not touch all individuals in the same way; there nonetheless existed links between contemporary individuals, arising from the depths of a common past, through which an ideal meaning of life emerged in the limitless plenitude of a real present context. In this sense, "a generation then forms an interrelation of appearances into a whole, subject to explanatory study."[16]

It would be an oversimplification to see in Heidegger's use of the term "gen-eration" an extrapolation from Dilthey's insights, as Heidegger's comments might lead readers of *Being and Time* to believe. Unlike Dilthey—and in com-plete contradistinction to the Baden neo-Kantians—Heidegger is not referring to a generation as an "interrelation of appearances,"[17] but to the ontological preconditions universally underlying appearances. With ontological constructs such as *das Man* or the generations articulated in *das Volk*, Heidegger is refer-ring to the conditions of possibility of interrelation between individual and community concealed beneath the empirical flux of appearances.

Heidegger's notion of generation, as of communal authenticity in general, remains undeniably vague. A year after the publication of *Being and Time*, Karl Mannheim wrote a study of the concept of generation in which both Dilthey and Heidegger were analyzed. Dilthey's achievement, as Mannheim noted, was to have clearly expressed the idea of a qualitative cohesion (*Verbundenheit*) of specific styles of life interpretation among contemporaries, which could not simply be attributed to their quantitatively considered chronology. Given the vagueness of Heidegger's application of the notion of generation, is it any wonder that Mannheim, who was by no means unsympathetic to Heidegger's work, wrote that Heidegger "deepens precisely this problem of qualitative cohesion"?[18]

The distance of his thought from pre-World War I critical theories of history becomes clearest not only in its ontological theme, but in how Heidegger defines this ontology, notwithstanding its claim to universality. Given his attempt to conceive of a community interfused with authentic purpose, the thrust of Heidegger's analysis nonetheless focuses preponderantly on the fallenness of *Dasein* into an alienated (*entfremdete*), objectified world of inauthenticity. This aspect of his thinking would hardly seem to be free of the influence of historical circumstances: Heidegger's notion of authentic community remains sketchy to the extent that *Being and Time* itself emphasizes doubt in the collective world so often characteristic of his own generation. To that extent, it is informed by the factual circumstances of the times, in which the sense of worthiness of culture came into question in a manner that had been uncommon among members of the prewar generation. In this situation, is it any surprise that, for Heidegger, the dimensions of communal authenticity could inspire only the sparsest examination?[19]

For this reason, the claim that Heidegger's philosophy denies objectivity in history misses an important point. It is misleading to claim that, for Heidegger, the "real world of objective Being is dissolved."[20] The significant point is not an alleged dissolution of real Being; it lies rather in the manner of interpreting the historical world.

World history, heretofore taken as the objective totality of developing national cultures, represented, for Hegel, the invincible progression of the consciousness of freedom; for Ranke, the opaque habitat of Divine thoughts; for Rickert, the repository of ethereal transcendent values; and for Dilthey, the unique realm of crystallization of the human spirit. Not one of these thinkers questioned world history as a primary source of normative values and meaning.

For the Heidegger of *Being and Time*, by contrast, the objective coherence of world history *exists*, yet is reinterpreted in a way that denies its primary role as a source of *Dasein*'s authenticity. It is ultimately rooted in the temporal mode of existence that, under the hidden auspices of *das Man*, dissimulates the finitude of *Dasein* in an acquired, objectified actuality:

> The transcendence of the world has a temporal foundation; and by reason of this, the world-historical is, in every case, already "objectively" there in the historicizing of existing Being-in-the-world, *without being grasped historiologically*. And because factical *Dasein*, in falling, is absorbed in that with which it concerns itself, it understands its history world-historically in the first instance. . . .

> Blind for possibilities, it [*das Man*] cannot repeat what has been, but only retains and receives the "actual" that is left over, the world-historical that has been, the leavings, and the information about them that is present at hand.[21]

Once authentic historical meaning is displaced from objective world history and the nations or cultures composing it to *Dasein*, and to the unity of authentic *Dasein* achieved in a generation and in *das Volk*, there arises the problem of normative standards and values whose emergence and sustenance had previously been tied to an objective cultural context. Indeed, for the critical theorists of the previous generation, the objective historical process provided philosophers with material through which normative truths and the sense of human existence itself could be established. Let us therefore turn to Heidegger's reconsideration of the problem of normative truth, by way of his reformulation of the relation between philosophical truth and history.

* * *

The critical theorists—especially Windelband, Rickert, and Dilthey— attempted to establish broad principles of historical understanding in the humanistic disciplines, independent both of law-constructing methods of the natural sciences and of abstract speculation of metaphysical philosophy. Historical thinking, conceived as the study of the meaning of human existence through the comprehension of what humanity had been, proposed that elucidation of normative truths in human affairs had to depend on inductive comprehension of the development of human culture and of norms that had actually been manifested in it. The cardinal significance of historical methods in the humanistic disciplines presupposed a spontaneous coherence of the cultural world, where norms emerged and were refined in a continuous, unified process of development.

Heidegger's philosophy disagreed, not only with the principles of historical understanding that had been proposed as an autonomous method for the humanistic disciplines, but, above all, with the larger assumption that culture and world-historical development were primary sources of coherence (*Zusammenhang*). The appreciation of cultures as unique individualities constituting the epochs of world history and of human understanding as intertwined with the development of norms and values of a given culture, universal in implication but particular in concrete expression, found no significant echo in Heidegger's thought.

In view of this, it is hardly surprising that Heidegger failed to acknowledge the significance of the advent of the qualitative change in human historical understanding that arose with the modern appreciation for cultural diversity and the modern insight into the uniquely historical character of human existence. For thinkers like Windelband, Rickert, Dilthey, and Troeltsch, this insight had to be counted as one of the greatest theoretical fruits nurtured and sustained by the development of Western culture, liberating theoretical norms from the dogmatism of metaphysics. If, in his early writings, Heidegger had attributed a certain importance to that qualitative change in understanding, in *Being and Time*, this theme is entirely eclipsed. Evidently, he took this change as no salient development at all: his concern is with the unrecorded history of the forgetfulness of the ontology founded in the Being of *Dasein* and lying beneath the ontic level of culture and of individual diversity that is its dynamic principle.

Heidegger's retrieval of ontology was not tantamount to a resurrection of metaphysics in any traditional sense, precisely because it tried to open ontology to *Dasein*'s fluid temporalization of Being. In this role, transferring the ground of coherence of human existence from the objective realm of culture and world history into the temporalizing modes of *Dasein*'s understanding of Being meant redefining the aim of historical thinking and of the possibility of its grasp of truth.

This redefinition brings to the fore the confrontation with the problem of historical meaning that Heidegger subtly undertakes at the end of his section on temporality and historicity. Here, and in his course lectures of the period, the significance of Heidegger's attempt to root the sense of historical thinking in the fundamental ontology of *Dasein* finds its clearest relation to the issue of philosophical truth. Heidegger's thought on this matter is closely interwoven with his explicit rebuttal of the predominant ways in which historical theory had been articulated in the nineteenth and early twentieth centuries. His critique of the historians' specialized endeavor and of critical theories of historical knowledge calls into question the larger assumptions of previous styles of historical understanding, and leads directly to the theme of history and normative truth that concerns us most closely.

In the 1928 course lecture series "Die Grundprobleme der Phänomenologie" (Fundamental problems of phenomenology), Heidegger situated the special role of historical thinking in relation to philosophical knowledge:

> The history of philosophy is not a mere appendage to the philosophical teaching firm providing an opportunity to find oneself a comfortable and easy theme for the State examination. Nor is it there to enable one to look around and see how things once were. Rather, historical-philosophical knowledge constitutes a unity in itself, in which the specific kind of historical knowledge in philosophy, in accord with its topics, is distinct from every other kind of scientific historical knowledge.[22]

In *Being and Time*, it is obvious that Heidegger's concerns lie elsewhere than with these "other kinds of scientific, historical knowledge" claiming autonomy from philosophy. He rebuffs critical theories of history for their justification of the quest for historical meaning as it had been conceived in the historical sciences. Most explicitly, his comments touch on Heinrich Rickert's "logic with which the concepts of historiological presentation are formed" and on Simmel's "'epistemological' clarification" of historical matters; they anticipate his later, more detailed and explicit criticism of Dilthey's theory, orienting itself "toward the side of the object."[23] In opposition to these theories' quest for general validity (*Allgemeingültigkeit*) of historical meaning in the historical sciences, Heidegger counters that the place (*Ort*) of the historical problematic "is not to be sought in historiology [*Historie*] as the science of history."[24] Against any claim of an autonomous science of history, he asserts that all historical concepts presuppose an ontological interpretation of *Dasein*'s temporalizing modes, concretely expressed in its historicity: "But since the basic concepts of the historiological sciences—whether they pertain to the objects of these sciences or to the way in which these are treated—are concepts of existence, the theory of the human sciences presupposes an existential interpretation that has as its theme the *historicity* of *Dasein*."[25]

In the last section of the chapter on temporality and historicity, Heidegger investigates the contemporary claim to establish autonomous historical principles of understanding. His analysis proceeds by discussing the views of the late nineteenth-century figure Count Yorck von Wartenburg, who had remained beyond the pale of the academic institutions of his period. During the 1920s, after his death, when Yorck's correspondence with Wilhelm Dilthey was published for the first time, his letters caused a stir among the German intelligentsia, especially for the path of historical understanding he proposed as an alternative to the predominant critical ideas of his period.[26] Heidegger deftly cites passages from this extraordinary correspondence, often including Yorck's criticisms of Dilthey. [. . .]

Despite his admiration for him, Heidegger was convinced that Yorck had failed to penetrate to the ontological basis underlying a philosophy of life. Yorck's preliminary aim, as Heidegger indicated, lay in distinguishing between natural and historical styles of being. In this spirit, Yorck had made his celebrated separation between the "ontic" and the "historical"—between nature that "is" and the historical that "lives." Yorck's attempt to base a philosophy of history on this separation was taken by Heidegger as a sign of entanglement in the same presuppositions that ensnared the historians he criticized: the traditional neglect of the meaning of Being. This neglect obscured the ontological unity which is more fundamental than any distinction between nature and history, both of which Heidegger deemed "ontic" to the extent that this unity was not investigated.

Heidegger's criticism of Yorck's separating the ontic from the historical, by highlighting the broad conception of understanding (*Verstehen*) in Heidegger's philosophy, brings us closer to the problem of a relation between philosophical truth and its historicity. Yorck's thinking on this matter bore a marked resemblance to Dilthey's theory of interpretation, in which the relation maintained by consciousness that understands (*versteht*) other conscious life had to be sharply distinguished from any relation maintained by consciousness in its explanation (*Erklären*) of natural objects. Understanding of conscious life by other conscious life provided, for Dilthey and Yorck, a potential intimacy of apprehension that natural topics of explanation, because of their dissimilarity to consciousness, could never reveal.

Heidegger's ontology calls into question the distinction between understanding (*Verstehen*) and explanation (*Erklären*), which Heidegger views as a mere construct of the sciences.[27] For Heidegger, history and nature are both made possible by the fundamental unity constituted by *Dasein*'s modes of synthesizing time. As Heidegger points out in the concluding chapter of *Being and Time* (which follows the chapter on temporality and historicity), this synthesis of time does not have its roots in the abstract chronology of world time. Rather, world time—which *Dasein* attentively interprets in the movement of the planets—is itself made possible by *Dasein*'s finite projection of a meaning of Being. Without a projection of the meaning of Being in the structural unity of existence, facticity, and fallenness, the unification of temporal *ekstases* in any possible apprehension would have no coherence, and could be the source of no meaning.

Nowhere is the primordial unity of apprehension of nature and history in *Dasein* better illustrated than in the historicity of the most basic concepts of the natural and historical disciplines. For Heidegger, this historicity is rooted, not in a world time beyond *Dasein*, but in the temporalizing modes through which a world is approached and made meaningful. That the basic concepts of both the natural and humanistic disciplines are subject to historical modification through scientific revolutions attests to their unity in the temporalizing modes of *Dasein*'s historicity.[28] The *Dasein*-centeredness of this unity underscores the limited value of a distinction between inner understanding (*Verstehen*) and explanation (*Erklären*) of external natural objects.

Heidegger's exclusive application of the word *understanding (Verstehen)*—and his renunciation of the concept of explanation (*Erklären*)[29]—underlined a critical point about historicity and temporality in the ontology of *Dasein*. Natural and historical objects belong to the same synthetic structure of temporalizing and of Being, and access to them is afforded only by the finite aim toward Being that *Dasein* projects. On this basis alone, Heidegger allows for the primary historicity of normative truths serving as the criteria for all that *Dasein* understands.

Is not this fundamental grounding of the sciences in *Dasein*'s historicity tantamount to an embrace of relativism? If, for Heidegger, the historicity of *Dasein* and of the finite possibilities of understanding is undeniable, the universal claim of ontology nonetheless provides finitude with an affirmative aim.[30] As we have seen, *Dasein*'s historicity moves within the structural boundaries delimited by the fundamental constitution of its Being and its modes of temporalization. Finitude is not a mere limit to *Dasein*'s understanding but a mode of access to other finite *Dasein* and to the world it composes. In stark contrast to the absolute ground of truth that had been the legacy of traditional ontology, Heidegger is thus able to specify that "[o]ntology needs only a finite being."[31]

For Heidegger, relativism and skepticism have their source, not in a frank acknowledgment of the historicity of human existence, but in an impossible epistemological demand: "The theories of relativism and skepticism originate in a partly justified opposition against a distorted absolutism and dogmatism of the concept of truth."[32] Insofar as the historical sciences had employed this impossible epistemological demand as a theoretical buttress, it becomes clear why Heidegger in *Being and Time* can regard them as the source of "historicism."[33]

From Heidegger's perspective, the foundation of normative truths on the finitude of *Dasein* does not represent a surrender to relativism. On the contrary, this foundation leads, for Heidegger, to an interpretation of truth that genuinely transcends the temporal horizons of specific epochs and the barriers of given cultures. Beneath the criteria of truth characteristic of past epochs or foreign cultures, the existential analytic displays the universal claim of the criteria of finitude in its focus on the persistent *motives* governing *Dasein*'s quest for truth's absolute, ahistorical ground. In these motives, Heidegger discerns the tacit reiteration of *Seinsvergessenheit* (the forgetfulness of Being) amid the diversity of the criteria of truth predominant in Western intellectual traditions, from the emergence of Western metaphysics to the development of modern thought. From the vantage point provided by the broad articulation of

Western intellectual traditions, the debate surrounding historicism and relativism and the related quest for stable theoretical criteria emerge in a wholly new
light.

Heidegger's notion of the motives underlying the predominant Western ideas
of truth informs his attempt to adumbrate, on the ground of *Seinsvergessenheit,*
a transhistorical unity of Western intellectual traditions, leading up to the
quest for theoretical truth capable of surmounting historicism and relativism.
From the standpoint of *Being and Time,* the transhistorical unity of Western
traditions finds its source in an age-old presupposition. Rather than think that
the finite Being of *Dasein,* through which the question of Being emerges, is
essentially implicated in the understanding of Being per se, these traditions
presuppose that *Dasein,* as all Being revealed through it, *is* insofar as it can
be transposed into terms foreign to its finitude—into abiding presence and
subsistence (*Vorhandensein*). This "diversion from finitude [*Wegsehen von der
Endlichkeit*]"[34] was not only expressed in the determination of Being in terms
of the abiding idea or permanence of substance of Plato and Aristotle (and
their respective medieval successors); it left its mark on the great formative
influences of modernity, despite all further innovations. In each case, from the
Cartesian cogito to the Kantian "I think" (*ich denke*), to the Hegelian Spirit
(*Geist*), to name only the most fateful of these influences, the finite meaning
of *Dasein* "each time my own [*jemeiniges*]" disappeared before conceptual
structures in which consideration of finitude had been tacitly preempted.[35]
Each time, rather than Being in terms of the finite Being of *Dasein,* all Being
per se, including that of *Dasein,* had been posited in relation to criteria of
truth residing in what remained continually present and capable of becoming
a permanent acquisition of thought. Ephemerality, contingency, and finitude,
rather than being viewed as essential criteria of truth, were thus excluded from
its definition.

According to Heidegger's well-known thesis, the motives for this exclusion,
far from a disinterested search, have their seat in *Dasein*'s forgetfulness, spring-
ing from an unspoken quest to surmount the limits of its finite Being. Forgetfulness, as an essential moment in the uncovering of the truth of Being,
constitutes for Heidegger a subtle opacity at the heart of the normative criteria
that have determined Western metaphysics since antiquity.

Heidegger's claim about the unity of Western intellectual traditions applies
not only to traditional metaphysics but also to an essential criterion of truth
characteristic of modern intellectual traditions purporting to overcome the
dogmatism of metaphysics. The basis of Heidegger's claim and its general implications for the human sciences become clearer when we (once again) consider
his thought in relation to the aims of what he himself took to be the most radical critical reflection on the foundations of the human sciences—the thought

of Dilthey. Precisely because Dilthey, among all the critical philosophers, most nearly anticipated Heidegger's position in *Being and Time*, this point of contrast between Dilthey and Heidegger sets in relief Heidegger's appraisal of the human sciences—and the broader debate over historicism, relativism, and stable objective standards.

Like Heidegger, Dilthey had abolished recourse to an absolute starting point outside of history; truth was bounded by impenetrable limits that no finite being could surpass. Along with other critical philosophers, Dilthey concluded that the impenetrability of these limits precluded any possible overall vision of history claiming an ontological foundation, and that the decisive break with the dogmatism of traditional metaphysics lay precisely in the emergence of critical awareness of these limits.

Heidegger's considerations emerged from a very different vantage point. Beyond the limits that historical contingency necessarily imposed on truth, Heidegger emphasizes, above all, an opacity that deepens through *Dasein*'s everyday tendency to avoid the implications of its own finitude. Indeed, because *Dasein* is continually tempted to interpret itself in terms of a communal and instrumental world that encourages it to forget the meaning of its finitude, its understanding is partial and the hidden basis of its own ideations disguised.

Nowhere is this more evident than in what might be described, from Heidegger's standpoint, as the chief "noncritical" presupposition of the critical philosophies—the normative ideal of truth embodied in the criterion of "general validity [*Allgemeingültigkeit*]," which provided Dilthey and other critical philosophers the standard of objective truth par excellence in the historical methodology of the human sciences. For Heidegger, the criterion of "general validity" assumes that only what may be leveled down to an abiding acquisition, uniformly subject to verification, may be taken as true. From Heidegger's standpoint, this idea of the uniform objectivity of norms of truth implies that the primordial source of historical meaning is not *Dasein*, but the omnipresent coherence (*Zusammenhang*) of a historical process outside of human finitude and—in the guise of permanence of an acquisition—capable of offering a measure of compensation for the contingency of finite perception. For this reason, the criterion of "general validity"—encouraged by *das Man*'s diversion of *Dasein* from its finitude—is in Heidegger's words nowhere "less applicable than in the human historical sciences."[36]

All claims about the essentially historical character of humanity notwithstanding, Heidegger believed that modern historical methodologies depended on a notion of historical meaning that neglected the radical implications of human historicity. Rooted in the idea of a spontaneous coherence of history and the uniformity imposed by the criterion of "general validity," this modern methodology masks the true character of the historicity of human understanding, whose universality arises in its orientation of a plurality of finite choices (authentic and inauthentic) through which *Dasein* decides the meaning of its finite Being and illuminates a truth specific to that decision. In this manner, he displaced the primordial source of the contingency of truth from the level of perspectival worldviews and values to the facticity of *Dasein*.

From Heidegger's standpoint, reflection on the foundation of the human sciences in the critical philosophies of history thus did not break with, but profoundly extended the predominant conception of truth that had characterized Western metaphysical traditions. Despite their explicit renunciation of metaphysical assumptions, modern critical theories of truth obscured their deep roots in the metaphysical tradition stemming from ancient philosophy and Christian theology: they unwittingly appropriated from this tradition attributes of truth derived from the traditional "ontologies of presence."

For Heidegger, these ontologies presuppose that Being manifests itself as an abiding presence in the midst of change. In critical theory as in the Western metaphysical tradition in general, the characterization of truth illustrates *Dasein*'s tacit choice of a mode of Being, in which the consequences of its finitude are obscured but never overcome. *Seinsvergessenheit*, as the forgetfulness of the finite Being of *Dasein* in the disclosure of a meaning of Being, serves as a metahistorical leitmotiv linking in a silent unity the motives of a long tradition of reflection stretching back to antiquity.

Notes

1. Heidegger, *Sein und Zeit*, 12th ed. (Tübingen: Niemeyer, 1972), 7. I have modified Macquarrie and Robinson's English translation, *Being and Time* (New York: Harper & Row, 1962) where I have deemed it necessary.

2. Ibid., 20.

3. Ibid., 15; Heidegger, *Die Grundprobleme der Phänomenologie*, *Gesamtausgabe*, 24:16. The German pagination is also provided in *The Basic Problems of Phenomenology*, trans. Albert Hofstadter (Bloomington: Indiana University Press, 1982).

4. Heidegger, *Sein und Zeit*, 41–110, and *Prolegomena zur Geschichte des Zeitbegriffs*, *Gesamtausgabe*, 20:201–15. The German pagination is also provided in *History of the Concept of Time: Prolegomena*, trans. Theodore Kisiel (Bloomington: Indiana University Press, 1985).

5. In Heidegger's estimation, *Dasein* and its fellows find themselves in a publicly defined structure of roles in relation to a world of things they commonly dispose of. This collective environment reaches beyond a functional preoccupation with the environment to encompass a public style of interpretation that unavoidably saturates collective existence per se: "We take pleasure and enjoy ourselves as *they* [*man*] take pleasure; we read, see, and judge about literature and art as they see and judge; likewise

we shrink back from the 'great mass' as *they* shrink back; we find shocking what *they* find shocking. The 'they,' which is nothing definite, and which all are, though not as the sum, prescribes the kind of Being of everydayness." Heidegger, *Sein und Zeit,* 127.

6. Ibid., 301–31.

7. Heidegger, *Gesamtausgabe,* 21:233. This lecture series, "Logik: Die Frage nach der Wahrheit," was originally presented in the winter of 1925–1926. [The passage in question reads: "Dasein has factically fallen prey to its world; this fallenness into the world belongs to the facticity [*Faktizität*] of Dasein. I understand by facticity a specific determination of Dasein's Being; the expression is not meant in an indifferent sense that would be equivalent to the factuality [*Tatsächlichkeit*] of just any present-at-hand entity. Dasein, according to its sense, is never present-at-hand, and thus is never something like a fact [*Tatsache*]. Nevertheless, it is in a specific sense a fact [*Faktum*], and this specific [phenomenon] we designate as facticity." —Ed.]

8. Heidegger, *Sein und Zeit,* 348.

9. Ibid., 310–52. For a discussion of the aporias implicit in Heidegger's notion of time in relation to historicity and intratemporality in *Being and Time,* see Paul Ricoeur, *Time and Narrative,* vol. 3, trans. Kathleen Blamey and David Pellauer (Chicago: University of Chicago Press, 1988), 60–96.

10. John Macquarrie and Edward Robinson have translated Heidegger's "*Geschichtlichkeit*" as "historicality" and his "*Historizität*" as "historicity." Because "*Historizität*" rarely appears in the text, and the word *historicality* is by no means clear in English, I have translated Heidegger's "*Geschichtlichkeit*" as "historicity" instead. Cf. David Couzens Hoy, "History, Historicity, and Historiography in *Being and Time,*" in M. Murray, ed., *Heidegger and Modern Philosophy: Critical Essays* (New Haven: Yale University Press, 1978), 329n1.

It is curious that Heidegger hardly mentioned the theme of culture in *Being and Time.* In his 1929 debate with Ernst Cassirer at Davos, he remarked: "I can very well admit that if . . . one takes this analysis of *Dasein* in *Being and Time* as an investigation of people, and then asks the question how, on the basis of this understanding of people, it might be possible to understand culture and the realms of culture; . . . it is absolutely impossible to say anything from what is given here." Heidegger and Cassirer, "Davoser Disputation," in Heidegger, *Kant und das Problem der Metaphysik* (Frankfurt am Main: Klostermann, 1951), 256 = *Kant and the Problem of Metaphysics,* trans. Richard Taft, 5th ed. (Bloomington: Indiana University Press, 1997), 199. The broader implications of Heidegger's interpretation of culture are the central theme of Jeffrey Andrew Barash, *Heidegger et son siècle: Temps de l'être, temps de l'histoire* (Paris: Presses Universitaires de France, 1995), 105–49.

11. Heidegger, *Sein und Zeit,* 378–97.

12. Heidegger's discussion of objectivity in historical matters and the grounding of historical meaning in the *Dasein* that seeks to grasp it bear a striking resemblance to certain aspects of Nietzsche's thought. Later in Heidegger's chapter on temporality and historicity, he explicitly uses Nietzsche's philosophy, but not in relation to this specific theme, where certain points of congruence would seem to be most striking. In the second meditation of his *Untimely Meditations,* Nietzsche wrote: "Yes, one goes so far

as to suppose that he who has no relation to a moment of the past is called on to represent it . . . that is what one calls 'objectivity.' . . . Only in the strongest exertion of your most noble qualities will you discover what in the past is great and worthy of being preserved and known." Nietzsche, "Vom Nutzen und Nachteil der Historie für das Leben," in *Friedrich Nietzsche: Erkenntnistheoretische Schriften,* ed. J. Habermas et al. (Frankfurt am Main: Suhrkamp, 1968), 56 = Nietzsche, "On the Uses and Disadvantages of History for Life," in *Untimely Meditations,* trans. R. J. Hollingdale (Cambridge: Cambridge University Press, 1983), 93–94. On Heidegger's relation to Nietzsche in his critique of Dilthey, see Jeffrey Andrew Barash, "Über den geschichtlichen Ort der Wahrheit: Hermeneutische Perspektiven bei Wilhelm Dilthey und Martin Heidegger," in *Martin Heidegger: Innen- und Aussenansichten,* ed. Siegfried Blasche et al. (Frankfurt am Main: Suhrkamp, 1989), 58–74.

13. Heidegger, *Sein und Zeit,* 384–85.

14. Wilhelm Dilthey, *Die geistige Welt, Einleitung in die Philosophie des Lebens, Gesammelte Schriften,* vol. 5, 6th ed. (Stuttgart: Teubner, 1974), 36–41; Heidegger, *Sein und Zeit,* 384–85.

15. Dilthey, "Über das Studium," in *Geistige Welt,* 37.

16. Ibid.

17. Ibid.

18. Karl Mannheim, "Das Problem der Generationen," *Kölner Viertelsjahrhefte* 7:2 (1928), 164.

19. In his lectures of the late 1920s, Heidegger explicitly distanced himself from "bourgeois [*bürgerliche*]" styles of thinking, which he felt took comfort in the illusion of eternal truth. See, for example, Heidegger, *Gesamtausgabe,* 24:314, where after attacking the notion of eternal truth, he stated that "philosophical and scientific knowledge do not bother themselves at all about the consequences [of this], even if these consequences are still uncomfortable for bourgeois understanding." It was perhaps Hannah Arendt who best understood the deeper political implications of Heidegger's emphasis on collective inauthenticity. On this theme, see Jacques Taminiaux, *The Thracian Maid and the Professional Thinker: Arendt and Heidegger* (Albany: SUNY Press, 1998); Dana R. Villa, *Arendt and Heidegger: The Fate of the Political* (Princeton: Princeton University Press, 1996); Jeffrey Andrew Barash, "The Political Dimension of the Public World: On Hannah Arendt's Interpretation of Martin Heidegger," in Larry May and Jerome Kohn (eds.), *On Hannah Arendt: Twenty Years Later* (Cambridge, Mass.: MIT Press, 1996), 251–68; Jeffrey Andrew Barash, "Hannah Arendt, Martin Heidegger and the Politics of Remembrance," *International Journal of Philosophical Studies* 10:2 (May 2002): 171–82.

20. Georg Iggers, *The German Conception of History* (Middletown, Conn.: Wesleyan University Press, 1968), 244.

21. Heidegger, *Sein und Zeit,* 389, 391.

22. Heidegger, *Gesamtausgabe,* 24:31–32.

23. Heidegger, *Sein und Zeit,* 375.

24. Ibid., 375, 395.

25. Ibid., 397.

26. Alfons Degener, for example, noted the importance of this correspondence in highlighting the metaphysical implications of Dilthey's thought. Yorck seems to have encouraged the metaphysical tendency in Dilthey. See Degener, "Zwei Wege zu Diltheys Metaphysik" (Ph.D. diss., University of Münster, 1927), 9.

27. Heidegger, *Gesamtausgabe*, 20:2. Or, as Heidegger expressed this thought in his August 8, 1928, letter to Elisabeth Blochmann: "In the historical sciences ... there lies a specific understanding of existence; according to my conviction, indeed, the traditional separation of natural and human sciences is in every form a superficiality.... From a metaphysical standpoint there is only *one* science [*Wissenschaft*]." Heidegger and Blochmann, *Briefwechsel, 1918–1969*, ed. Joachim W. Storck (Marbach am Neckar: Deutsche Schiller-gesellschaft, 1989), 25.

28. Heidegger, *Sein und Zeit*, 8–11.

29. Heidegger, *Gesamtausgabe*, 24:390.

30. Notwithstanding his argument for the primary unity of natural and historical thinking in the ontology of *Dasein*, it is difficult to see any affirmative message in Heidegger's thought for the natural sciences. However much *Dasein*'s modes of Being may apply to the human sphere, it is difficult to envision how the choices of temporalizing that underlie *Dasein*'s authenticity or inauthenticity would have anything but a negative implication for natural sciences such as physics and astronomy. Although Heidegger suggested the contrary at various points in his writings of this period, and even that authentic science in general would be possible, when it came to defining what form authentic science would take, Heidegger sidestepped the question: "We shall not trace further how science has its source in authentic existence. It is enough now if we understand that the thematizing of entities-within-the-world presupposes Being-in-the-world as the basic state of *Dasein*, and if we understand how it does so." Heidegger, *Sein und Zeit*, 363.

31. Heidegger and Cassirer, "Davoser Disputation," in Heidegger, *Kant und das Problem der Metaphysik*, 252 = *Kant and the Problem of Metaphysics*, 197.

32. Heidegger, *Gesamtausgabe*, 24:316.

33. Heidegger, *Sein und Zeit*, 396.

34. Ibid., 424.

35. Ibid., 22.

36. Ibid., 395.

11

The Demise of *Being and Time*: 1927–1930

Theodore Kisiel

ALTHOUGH IT MAY WELL BE the most important book in twentieth-century philosophy, *Being and Time* remains a fragment. "This astonishing torso," as Herbert Spiegelberg called it, was judged by its own author to be an immature, premature thought-path. "The fundamental flaw of the book *Being and Time* is perhaps that I ventured forth too far too soon."[1] This remark alludes to the hastiness of the book's publication. Heidegger began to think through the issues in the "war emergency semester" of 1919,[2] began to write his book in 1923–1924 in the form of a long (and unpublished) journal article on the concept of time,[3] and presented the structure of its first division in his lecture course of the summer semester of 1925.[4] But he finished the final version of the first two divisions of the text in only a few months of 1926, under intense academic publishing pressure.[5] The "first half" of *Being and Time* appeared as a separate volume in April 1927, and one month later, together with only one other text (Oskar Becker's *Mathematische Existenz*) in Husserl's *Jahrbuch für Philosophie und phänomenologische Forschung*.

But why was the "second half" never published? Why was the text of this planned two-volume work, which Heidegger sketched in its entirety in an outline,[6] interrupted in the course of its composition, even before the appearance of the first volume? In the following decades, Heidegger often told the story of this interruption, and usually referred in this context to the various misinterpretations of *Being and Time* as anthropology, ontology of the human being, and existential philosophy. The failure to recognize the book's intention as fundamental ontology might well have been prevented or diminished with the timely appearance of the missing third division of Part One. We will cite the best-known story[7] along with some important supplements, in order to gain some anecdotal indications of the content of the missing division.

> Furthermore, the understanding of the "concept of existence" used in *Being and Time* is made difficult by the fact that the existential concept of existence appropriate to *Being and Time* [i.e., "man's being-a-self, insofar as it . . . relates to being and to the relation to being": GA 49, earlier on p. 39] was first developed in full in the division that as a consequence of the interruption of the publication was not communicated; for the third division of Part One, "Time and Being," proved during the typesetting to be unsatisfactory. ["And at the same time, external circumstances (the excessive length of the *Jahrbuch* volume) fortunately prevented the publication of this section."[8]] The decision to break up the text was made [in the first days of January 1927—T.K.] during a visit to Karl Jaspers in Heidelberg, where it became clear to me from our lively, friendly arguments based on the proof sheets of *Being and Time* that the elaboration I had attained thus far of this most important division (I.3) would have been unintelligible. The decision to break up the publication was made on the day that the news of the death of Rilke reached us. ["A conversation about Rilke on the same day made especially clear to me that the fundamental position of *Being and Time* was irreconcilably different from both Rilke and Jaspers."[9]] ["The attempt"—in its first execution, T.K.—"was 'destroyed,'[10] but a new start was made, on a more historical path, in the lecture course of summer semester 1927."[11]] Still, I was of the opinion at the time that I would be able to say everything more clearly over the course of the year. That was an illusion. So the succeeding years yielded some publications that attempted to raise the genuine question by circuitous routes. [GA 49, 40]

> *Being and Time* (1927) . . . originated . . . as an initial way of making the question of being visible, as far as possible, from the ground up and at the same time in an actual execution—in the form that essentially leads beyond all former ways of posing the question and yet leads back into the confrontation with the Greeks and with Western philosophy. [GA 66, 413]

> Precisely because the way of posing the question of the *meaning of being* (the truth of the projection of being—not of beings) is other than that of all of metaphysics up to now, this questioning could have shown what it achieves—although what was communicated often *says* what this questioning intends. For what was unsatisfactory in the section that was held back was not an uncertainty in the direction of questioning and its domain, but only an uncertainty in its proper elaboration. [GA 66, 414]

According to the outline, the final, "systematic," third division on "Time and Being" was supposed to carry out "the explication of time as the transcendental horizon for the question of being" (SZ 39). One could have expected that this final division of Part One of *Being and Time*, at least in the transition to the "historical" Part Two with its "phenomenological destruction of the history of ontology," would emphasize the completely different form of its question of being as opposed to "all of metaphysics up to now." Secure in its revolutionary direction of questioning, but inadequate in its proper elaboration—to the point of being unintelligible for intellects like Rilke and Jaspers: what exactly was unsatisfactory in the third division, which after repeated attempts to formulate it, was never to appear? Heidegger's explanation in the "Letter on 'Humanism'" strikes us as a final summary of these attempts. In this context Heidegger is trying to deflect the misinterpretation of the "projection" of the understanding of being as an achievement of subjectivity. It can be thought only as the ecstatic relation to the clearing of being:

> The adequate execution and completion of this other thinking that abandons subjectivity is surely made more difficult by the fact that in the publication of *Being and Time* the third division of the first part, "Time and Being," was withheld (cf. *Being and Time*, p. [SZ] 39). Here everything is reversed. The division in question was held back because thinking failed in the adequate saying of this turning [*Kehre*] and did not succeed with the help of the language of metaphysics. The lecture "On the Essence of Truth," thought out and delivered in 1930 but not printed until 1943, provides a certain insight into the thinking of the turning from "Being and Time" to "Time and Being." This turning is not a change of standpoint from *Being and Time*, but in it the thinking that was sought first arrives at the locality of that dimension out of which *Being and Time* is experienced, that is to say, experienced in the fundamental experience of the oblivion of being.[12]

The inadequacy of the withheld section lies in the way it speaks of the turn (*Kehre*). It fails in the attempt to carry out this turn with the help of the language of metaphysics, that is, the language of subject and object, which dominates the grammar of Western languages. That is why the later Heidegger seeks a transformation of the essence of language; he waits for a "language *of* being" that will indicate the appropriating event (*Ereignis*) of *Seyn* and *Zeyt*,[13] an event that does not lie at our disposal. The younger Heidegger was already aware of this problem in Western language. Just before he outlines the general plan of *Being and Time* he remarks, "For the . . . task [of grasping beings in their being] we lack not only most of the words but, above all, the 'grammar'" (SZ 39). From his review article on "Recent Research on Logic" (1912) to his *Habilitationsschrift* on the Scotist doctrine of categories and meaning (1915–1916),[14] the young Heidegger's interest revolves around a "logic of philosophy" (as the title of a book by Emil Lask has it),[15] which examines the peculiar phenomena at the margins of the ruling grammar of the subject-predicate relation, such as existential statements and impersonal sentences. The logic of philosophical concept formation, which for the neo-Kantian Lask is a transcendental logic, is developed by Heidegger into a phenomenological (hermeneutic-ontological) logic. Already in the war emergency semester of 1919 he replaces the well-known neo-Kantian impersonal expression for the transcendental difference—"It 'is' not, but it is valid (or more generally: 'it values')"—with newly coined impersonal expressions, which are now really supposed to express an ontological difference: "It 'is' not, but it's worlding, it's happening, it's appropriating itself [*es er-eignet sich*]."[16] Thus in *Being and Time* we find existential-ontological statements such as, "It [temporality] is not, but it *temporalizes* itself [*es zeitigt sich*]."[17] Likewise, the horizon of this temporality "simply 'is' not, but rather it temporalizes itself."[18]

Heidegger's search for a nonobjectifying language of being in the framework of a phenomenological logic of philosophical concept formation becomes particularly clear in the dramatic closing hours of the 1919 war emergency semester.[19] Here Heidegger tries to free the main methodological concept of phenomenology, the concept of intentionality, in its application to the primal-something (life in and for itself, lived experience), from all traces of a formal logical misinterpretation as a rigid dualism of subject and object. By objectifying life and handling it theoretically, this misinterpretation leads to a de-vivification, de-historicization, de-interpretation, and de-worlding of life. In its pure phenomenological formality, intentionality is simply a directing-itself-toward. As *comportment* as such, it is *indicated* in its pure moment of the *formal* "toward," which Heidegger considers the heart, the center, the middle, the origin, the concealed source of life—the inner happening of its being. The toward (*das Worauf*) of this comportment is initially described as a unitary intentional relation from motivation to tendency and back, in an intentional "circular" motion of "motivated tendency or tending motivation."[20] In *Being and Time*, "the toward-which [*das Woraufhin*] of the primary projection" is the *meaning* of Dasein qua temporality, whose circular motion is redescribed as a thrown projecting of a prestructured context "according to which something becomes comprehensible as something [and] conceived in its possibility" (SZ 324, 151).

Formal indication thus becomes the "methodological secret weapon" in Heidegger's logic of philosophical concept formation.[21] In the published fragment of *Being and Time* it is mentioned about a half-dozen times without further explanation (SZ 53, 114, 116f., 179, 231, 313–15; but also "provisional indication," 14, 16, 41). Formal indication, as hermeneutic phenomenology's guiding method for the phenomenology of the phenomenon in a distinctive sense (SZ 35), would have to become a main theme of the third division, to be explicated there in its hermeneutical logic. On the way to *Being and Time*,

Heidegger passes through a series of formal indications, but each should be seen as a formal deepening of the prestruction (*Praestruktion*) of intentionality, which is understood as pure directing-itself-toward: as an intentionality with the three dimensions of relation sense, content sense, and actualization sense (1920–1922), supplemented with a unifying temporalization sense in 1922; as Da-sein (1923), being-in-the-world (1924), to-be (*Zu-sein*, 1925), ex-sistence (1926), and transcendence (1927–1929). Thus the pure formula for the structure of care in *Being and Time*, "ahead-of-itself-being-already-in-(the-world) as being-amid (entities encountered within-the-world)" (SZ 192), is clearly *intentional*, in the broader (pretheoretical) sense. The "new start" on Division III "on a more historical path," in summer semester 1927, thus reaches the following conclusions by way of a series of formal indications: "Intentionality is the *ratio cognoscendi* of transcendence. Transcendence is the *ratio essendi* of intentionality in its diverse modes."[22] In Kantian terms, transcendence becomes the condition of the possibility of intentionality.[23] As the basic trait of the ontological structure of Dasein, transcendence belongs to the existentiality of existence.[24] "On a more historical path" one notices how strongly the features of the formal indications are expressed in a traditional "language of metaphysics."

Finally, the entire series of formal indications will prove to have "the condition of its possibility in temporality and temporality's ecstatic-horizonal character."[25] Intentionality, transcendence, existence: at their root they each indicate their temporal structure. What could be more formal in factical life than time? And as regards the function of indication: what could be more concrete and immediate in factical life, what could be nearer to us than time? Ecstatic time is both the ultimate formality of life (being) and the most intimate and immediate nearness of Dasein, facticity as such. In a note that belongs among the new attempts to begin Division III, Heidegger remarks: "temporality: it is not just a fact, but itself the essence of the fact: facticity. The fact of facticity (here the root of the 'reversal of ontology'). Can one ask, 'How does time originate?' ... Only with time is there a possibility of origination.... But then, what is the meaning of the impossibility of the problem of the origination of time?"[26]

I. Toward the Reconstruction of the Missing Third Division

"That the intentionality of 'consciousness' is grounded in the ecstatical unity of Dasein, and how this is the case, will be shown in the following Division" (SZ 363, note). This explicit reference to Division III is further evidence that it would have included a major methodological section on the sense-of-direction (*Richtungssinn*) of a formally indicative hermeneutics. The same §69 of *Being and Time* includes a similar reference, but this one refers not only to the "idea of phenomenology, as distinguished from the preliminary conception of it which we indicated by way of introduction [§7]," but also to the corresponding "existential conception of science" and its understanding "of the *ontological genesis* of the theoretical attitude." "Yet a fully adequate existential Interpretation of science cannot be carried out until the *meaning of being and the 'connection' between being and truth* have been *clarified* in terms of the temporality of existence" (SZ 357). And this clarification is the "central problematic" (SZ 357) of Division III. As a preparation for these tasks of the following division, §69c (SZ 364ff.) develops "the temporal problem of the transcendence of the world," that is, the problem of how the world temporalizes itself as the toward-which of the temporal ecstases into a horizonal unity in accordance with the "horizonal schemata"—the respective "whithers" of the ecstases. The temporal transcendence of the world is thereby founded ecstatically-*horizonally*. The ecstatical unity of temporality is also designated at the start of §69 as the cleared clearing of Dasein, which grounds the disclosedness of the there (cf. SZ 350f.). The clarification of the connection between being and truth thus begins with Dasein, whose fundamental characteristic is the understanding of being. In turn, the understanding of being is made possible by disclosedness, that is, disposed understanding—dynamically understood as thrown projecting (cf. §44c, SZ 230). The thrown projection that is Dasein in its ek-sistence is ultimately—and so finitely—grounded in ecstatical temporality, in the cleared clearing of the there. In this way time is used as the "preliminary name" for truth, which is now understood as disclosedness, clearing, and unconcealment. "Being [projected as time—T.K.] and truth 'are' equiprimordially" (SZ 230).

II. *The Basic Problems of Phenomenology* (Summer Semester 1927)

Placing it within the history of his development, Heidegger understands his lecture course of summer semester 1927 to be a "new elaboration of Division 3 of Part 1 of *Being and Time*" (1n).[27] The course completes only part of the path indicated in *Being and Time* toward the correlation of being and truth before it is broken off because of the great detour it takes through the history of ontology. The "first and last and basic problem" of a phenomenological science of being is: "How is the understanding of being at all possible?" (15). More explicitly, "Whence—that is, from which antecedently given horizon—do we understand the like of being?" (16). The presupposed analytic of Dasein gives a first answer: "time is the horizon from which something like being becomes understandable at all. We interpret being by way of time (tempus). The interpretation is a Temporal [*temporale*] one. The fundamental subject of research in ontology . . . is Temporality [*Temporalität*]" (17). Ontology is not only a critical and transcendental science (cf. 17), but also a Temporal one (cf. 228), which is hence quite different from all other, so-called positive sciences. But it is like the positive sciences in one way. A positive science must objectify the entities that lie before it upon the latent horizon of their particular being,[28] upon the whither of the "projection of the ontological constitution of a region of beings" (321)—their being what and how they are. Similarly, ontology must objectify being itself "*upon the horizon of its understandability*" (322)—that is, upon Temporality. Ontology becomes a temporal science "because Temporal projection makes possible an objectification [*Vergegenständlichung*] of being and assures conceptualizability, and thereby constitutes ontology in general as a science" (323). The fundamental act by which ontology constitutes itself as science is the objectification of being as such (cf. 281). This act has "the function of *explicitly* projecting what is antecedently given upon that toward which it has *already* been projected [and unveiled] in pre-scientific experience or understanding" (282). The explicit objectification "thematizes" (281), and "thematization objectifies" (SZ 363). This articulation of the basic concepts of a science, or explicit interpretation of its guiding understanding of being, determines the distinctive conceptual structure of the science, the possibility of truth that pertains to it, and its manner of communicating its true propositions (SZ 362f.). The true propositions of scientific ontology are a priori, transcendental, and Temporal (cf. 323f.). The phenomenological language of being as such is the language of Temporality, which is properly "the transcendental horizon for the question about being" (324). With this, the explicit goal of Division III, "the explication of time" as such a "horizon," has been reached (SZ 39). Temporality (*Temporalität*) is the transcendental horizon of the understanding of being, especially when this understanding overtly questions being and thus itself becomes worthy of questioning.

Temporality (*Temporalität*) is the temporality (*Zeitlichkeit*) that is interpreted in the existential analytic, when it is thematized in its function as condition of possibility of the pre-ontological and ontological understanding of being, and thus of ontology as such (cf. 324, 388). In this function, Temporality is "the most original temporalizing of temporality as such" (302). As the most original temporality, it is the most radical—the temporality that is fundamentally factical down to its abyssal ground, that is, the "appropriating event" (*Er-eignis*), if we may here use the later Heidegger's favorite word. But in 1927 Heidegger hesitates to push forward into the concealed depths of temporality, "above all with regard to its Temporality," and even to enter "the problem of the finiteness of time" (307f.).

> To what extent is a negative, a not, involved in Temporality in general and, conjointly, in temporality? We may even inquire to what extent time itself is the condition of possibility of nullity in general. . . . Closer consideration shows that the not and also the essential nature of the not, nullity, likewise can be interpreted only by way of the nature of time and that it is only by starting from this that the possibility of modification—for example, the modification of presence into absence—can be explained. . . . We are not well enough prepared to penetrate into this obscure region. [311f.]

A reason for this lies in the incompleteness of the analyses of Temporality as a whole as "*temporality with regard to the unity of the horizonal schemata belonging to it*" (307). The horizon of ecstatic temporality is understood more precisely as the horizonal schema of the corresponding ecstasis. For every ecstasis, as a removal-to, also has in it an anticipation of the formal structure of the "whither" of the removal, which is never an indefinite removal into nothingness. This anticipated whither of the ecstasis is the horizonal schema that belongs to it (cf. 302). In *Being and Time* (SZ 365), the horizonal schemata are expressed prepositionally, that is, in a meaninglike way, following the model of meaning as the pre-structured toward-which (SZ 152): the for-the-sake-of (the ecstasis of the future as coming-toward), the in-the-face-of-which of thrownness or the to-which of abandonment (past, *Ge-wesenheit*), the in-order-to (present). But in Summer Semester 1927, Heidegger intends to designate the horizonal schemata with the Latin expressions for the "tenses" (*Tempora*) of time. "Here, in the dimension of the interpretation of being via time, we are purposely making use of Latinate expressions for all the determinations of time, in order to keep them distinct in the terminology itself from the time-determinations in the previously described sense" (305). *Praesens* is used instead of "present" (*Gegenwart*), and *praesens* now means the horizonal schema of the present. More precisely, *praesens* (instead of the in-order-to) is supposed explicitly to "constitute the condition of possibility of understanding handiness as such" (305).

> As the condition of possibility of the "beyond itself," the ecstasis of the present has within itself *a schematic prefiguration* of the *where out there* this "beyond itself" is. . . . Praesens is not identical with present, but, as *basic determination of the horizonal schema of this ecstasis*, it joins in constituting the complete time-structure of the present. Corresponding remarks apply to the other two ecstases, future and past (repetition, forgetting, retaining). [306]

But Heidegger treats only the ecstasis of the present in regards to *praesens*, and says nothing at all about the other ecstases in regards to their presumably

Latinized tenses and schemata, the *futurum* and *praeteritum*. Yet *praesens* in particular is not independent; it stands in an inner Temporal connection with the other Temporal schemata. "In each instance the inner Temporal interconnections of the horizonal schemata of time vary also according to the mode of temporalizing of temporality, which always temporalizes itself in the unity of its ecstases in such a way that the precedence of one ecstasis always modifies the others along with it" (307). In a summary of the prepositional nexus of *Being and Time*, Heidegger had already emphasized that the relations of the in-order-to can be understood only "if the Dasein understands something of the nature of the for-the-sake-of-itself" (295). An in-order-to (present) can be revealed only insofar as the for-the-sake-of (future) that belongs to a potentiality-for-being is understood.

But the *futurum*, as the condition of possibility of understanding the self of Dasein, does not come under consideration at all, not even in its inner connection to *praesens*. With his exclusive treatment of *praesens*, Heidegger apparently leaves room for the domination of a metaphysics of constant presence, which understands the being of beings only "in the horizon of productive-intuitive comportment" (165) and which is interpreted up to its epochal conclusion in the contemporary age of technology. In this way the most brilliant insights of the analytic of Dasein, for example, insights into the existential priority of the future and into the historicity of Dasein, are not followed further, up to the fundamental horizon of the most radical temporality. Heidegger's break with the Platonic thesis of recollection had been indicated in his transformation of Pindar's saying, "become what you [always already] are," into "become what you have to be"; in *Being and Time* the directive is "be what you will be" (cf. SZ 145), "become what you yourself are not yet at all" (cf. SZ 243), or "become what you can be" (cf. the statements on "resoluteness," SZ 305f.). But this transformation is not taken farther, into the uttermost Temporal horizon and into its abyssal implications. The levels of Dasein's historicity—for example, how, in the resolute repetition of the destiny of the change of generation, the past perfect of precedented Dasein takes the form of the future perfect of a community—remain uninvestigated in the Temporality of their modes of being.

Hence the historiological-practical science of Christian theology, which takes as its object the traditional and repeated happening of revelation for the community of faith, is corrected only in a formally indicative way by philosophical concepts and is no longer understood in a philosophically scientific way, that is, Temporally.[29] With the renunciation of the language game of Temporality, the dream of philosophy as Temporal science—that is, the objectification of being itself on the horizon of time—comes to an end. The thought that philosophy cannot be a science at all thus becomes the main theme of *Introduction to Philosophy*, the lecture course of Winter Semester 1928–1929.

III. *The Metaphysical Foundations of Logic*
(Summer Semester 1928)

But already in the course of his final Marburg lectures, concerning Leibniz's logic and the principle of sufficient reason, it becomes gradually clear to Heidegger that philosophy itself is more originary in its logic and ontology than any science, due to its radicalization on the basis of originary temporality, and is thus completely different from science. With its new elaboration of ecstatic-horizonal temporality as *nihil originarium* (cf. 196, 210),[30] one could see *The Metaphysical Foundations of Logic* as the second (and last) "start on a more historical path" toward "the problem of 'Time and Being' indicated in *Being and Time*" (208). But Heidegger no longer speaks of the third division, but rather of the not yet published "second part" (168) of *Being and Time* as the place where the tasks projected in §69, in particular the radical turnabout from intentionality to transcendence, are carried out. For "on a more historical path" the tasks have now multiplied in their scope and extent. After *The Basic Problems of Phenomenology*, the analytic of the Temporality of being now includes the Temporal exposition of the problem of being, that is, the distinction of the basic problems of phenomenological ontology that are comprised in the question of being: the problems of (1) the ontological difference; (2) the regionality of being and the unity of the idea of being; (3) the basic articulation of being; (4) the veridical character of being (cf. 154, 158, 152f.). But the Temporal analytic, which constitutes fundamental ontology along with the analytic of Dasein and its temporality, becomes in its execution "at the same time the turning-around, where ontology itself expressly turns back to the metaphysical ontic in which it implicitly always remains" (158). This overturning pertains to the inescapable ontical founding of ontology, which Aristotle had already recognized in his double concept of ontology as first philosophy and theology.[31] Relying on Max Scheler's concept of metasciences, such as metanthropology, Heidegger designates metaphysical ontic as "metontology." The double concept of philosophy as fundamental ontology and metontology "is only the particular concretion of the ontological difference, i.e., the concretion of carrying out the understanding-of-being. In other words, philosophy is the central and total concretization of the metaphysical essence of existence" (158). On the basis of fundamental ontology, metontology poses the basic ontical-existentiell questions of concrete Dasein in its particular world, in the midst of beings as a whole, as in Kant's *metaphysica specialis* "according to the concept of the world": What can I know? What should I do? What may I hope? (178f.). Metontology, as a metaphysics of the ontical primal phenomenon of human existence in its exceptional position in the cosmos, does not only thematize the global questions of "life conduct" and "worldview" in ethics, politics, practice, technique, and faith (cf. 157). Metontology also considers the regional questions of the difference between human existence and non-Dasein beings, such as the "worldless" stone and the animal, which is "poor in world";[32] particular questions concerning Dasein, such as its "being factically dispersed into bodiliness and thus into sexuality" (137); historical questions, such as a metaphysics of myth (209) and the metaphysics of other worldviews.[33]

To what extent does the new elaboration of ecstatic-horizonal temporality in *The Metaphysical Foundations of Logic*, in which Temporality is never mentioned, point to this conversion of the Temporal analytic into the new task of a metontology? In contrast to the presentation in *The Basic Problems of Phenomenology*, originary temporality is ruled by the ecstatic being-toward-itself in the mode of the for-the-sake-of-itself (cf. 213). "This approaching oneself in advance, from one's own possibility, is the primary ecstatic concept of the *future*" (206). The for-the-sake-of is thus the distinguishing mark of Dasein, "that it is concerned with this being, in its being, in a specific way. Dasein exists for the sake of Dasein's being and its potential-to-be.... It belongs to Dasein's essence to be concerned in its being about its very being" (186). The for-the-sake-of-itself formally determines an ontological circuit that transcends beings—the "circle" (215) of self-understanding, of freedom, of selfhood and its binding obligations. "Freedom gives itself to understand, freedom is the primal understanding, i.e., the primal projection of that which freedom itself makes possible" (192). But what does freedom make possible? The world, "the wholeness of beings in the totality of their possibilities" (180), which gets its specifically transcendental form of organization from the particular for-the-sake-of in each case (cf. 185). The world temporalizes itself primarily from the for-the-sake-of, from the ecstasis of the future, and is grounded in the ecstatic unity and wholeness of the temporalized horizon (cf. 211f.). Heidegger now speaks of an "ecstematic" unity of the horizon, that is, a systematic unity that is temporalized by the unity of the ecstases (cf. 208). This horizonal unity weighted toward the future is the "temporal condition for the possibility of *world*" (208). Because this horizon is not an entity, it cannot be localized anywhere. It shows itself only in and with the ecstases as their *ecstema*. It is "not at all primarily related to looking and intuiting, but by itself means simply that which delimits, encloses, the *enclosure*.... It 'is' not as such, but it temporalizes itself" (208). Or better: it's worlding!—to use an expression that Heidegger revives now, having coined it in 1919 (cf. 170–73). With this formulation, Heidegger wants to convey that the world is not an entity, but a temporal How of being. The world, the unity of the temporal horizon, is "nothing that is, yet something that 'is there' [*etwas, was es gibt*]. The 'it' that gives this non-entity is itself no being, but is the self-temporalizing temporality. And what the latter, as ecstatic unity, temporalizes is the unity of its horizon, the world ... that which simply arises in and with temporalization. We therefore call it the *nihil originarium*" (210).

It's worlding, it's giving, it's temporalizing itself: these are the impersonals of sheer facticity. "The primal fact, in the metaphysical sense, is that there is anything like temporality at all" (209). Sheer facticity is the *nihil originarium*, and the product of the "peculiar productivity intrinsic to temporality" is "precisely a peculiar nothing, the world" (210). Thus the primal fact of temporality is no *factum brutum*, but rather "primal history pure and simple" (209), "the primal event [*Urereignis*]" (212). The impersonal sentence "it's appropriating itself [*es er-eignet sich*]" already makes an appearance in 1919 as the *principium indi-viduationis*, that is, the principle of facticity as such.[34] But in *The Metaphysical Foundations of Logic*, Heidegger emphasizes the ontical aspect of the "happening of transcendence," in which "beings are already discovered as well" (217). The metaphysical primal history of Dasein as temporality also documents the completely "enigmatic" tendency to understand beings as intratemporal, extratemporal, and supratemporal (212). Of course, "the event of the world-entry of beings" happens only as long as there exists historical Dasein, which as being-in-the-world gives beings the opportunity to enter the world. "And only when [being-in-the-world] is existent, have [present-at-hand] things too already entered world, i.e., become intraworldly" (194). "There is time, in the common sense, only with the temporalization of temporality, with the happening of world-entry. And there are also intratemporal beings, such that transpire 'in time,' only insofar as world-entry happens and intraworldly beings become manifest for Dasein" (210). The thorough elaboration of world-entry is in part Heidegger's answer to the basic metaphysical problem of the ontological relation between realism and idealism (SZ §§43, 44c) in his confrontation with Max Scheler (131f.), which he inserts in this lecture course on the occasion of Scheler's death. Intraworldliness and intratemporality do not belong to the essence of the present-at-hand in itself, which remains the same entity that it is and as which it is, "even if it does not become intraworldly, even if world-entry does not happen to it" (194). The happening of the world-entry of beings is only the transcendental condition of possibility for the fact that extant entities reveal themselves in their in-itselfness, and thus "for [extant] things announcing themselves in their not requiring world-entry regarding their own being" (195; cf. 153). The fact that we are called to let beings be what and how they are is another sign of the facticity and thrownness of temporal Dasein, whose powerlessness in the face of beings is disclosed in transcendence and in world-entry (cf. 215). The freedom of transcendence is at the same time the binding character of the ground.

To sum up what we have said in temporal terms: "The ecstematic temporalizes itself, oscillating as a worlding. *World entry* happens only insofar as something like ecstatic oscillation temporalizes itself as a particular temporality. . . . The entrance into the world by beings is primal history pure and simple" (209). The explication of the oscillating vectors of world-entry is not completely new in Heidegger. In a decisive closing statement in the war emergency semester of 1919, he said, "But this means that the sense of the something as the experienceable implies the moment of 'out towards,' of 'direction towards,' '*into* a (particular) world,' and indeed in its undiminished 'vital impetus.'"[35] The oscillating rhythm of the primal spring of life, in its motivated tendency or tending motivation, is to be found in the oscillation of time.[36] In the summer semester of 1928, Heidegger recognizes Bergson's ontical language of the *élan* of time as the source of ontologically directed expressions—for example, the being of the ecstases "lies directly in the free ecstatic momentum. . . . Temporality is the free oscillation of the whole of primordial temporality; time expands and contracts itself. (And only because of momentum is there throw, facticity, *thrownness*; and only because of oscillation is there *projection*)" (207f.). Thrown projection, instead of motivated tendency, is now the basic movement of Dasein. The basic projection of transcendence, which finds its possibility in the unity of ecstatic oscillation, now becomes "the upswing, regarded as [swinging] toward all possible beings that can factically enter there into a world" (209). World-entry is, to begin with, an ecstatic happening of worlding, that is, the unitary oscillation of the removal (*raptus*) of the ecstases into a unitary horizon. Oscillating or swinging from the ecstatic unity of time, the horizon is not an objectification; it may not be represented as "anything thing-like, present at hand" (cf. 208).

The transcendence of Dasein is an upswing into the possibilities of the world, which itself is "the free surpassive counter-hold of the for-the-sake-of" (193). Transcendence means leaping over the beings that in each case factically and factually exist, to "an excess of possibilities, within which Dasein always maintains itself as free projection" (192). Dasein is always "farther" than any factual entity. In its "domain" of the understanding of being there lies the inner possibility of enrichment: "Dasein always has the character of being-richer-than, of outstripping" (211). It is, in its originary temporalizing, an effusive exuberance of possibilities. Transcendence, according to Plato, is *epekeina tes ousias*: "The for-the-sake-of, however, (transcendence) is not being itself, but surpasses being, and does so inasmuch as it outstrips beings in dignity and power" (219, Heidegger's rendition of *Republic* 509b). "The freedom toward ground is the outstripping, in the upswing, of that which carries us away and gives us distance" (221). Yet we must also emphasize the unfreedom of finite transcendence: "On the basis of this upswing, Dasein is, in each case, beyond beings . . . but it is beyond in such a way that it, first of all, experiences beings in their resistance, against which transcending Dasein is powerless" (215).

IV. The Break Begins: *Introduction to Philosophy*
(Winter Semester 1928–1929)

Since 1919, when Heidegger characterized philosophy as the pretheoretical primal science of originary life, he gave a vacillating answer to the question of whether phenomenological philosophy should be a primal science, or even any science at all. For philosophy, as primal science, is unlike any other science, because it is supposed to be *supra*theoretical or *pre*theoretical—a nontheoretical science, which seems to be a square circle. Already in the Winter Semester of 1919–1920 (according to unpublished student transcripts) Heidegger remarks that philosophy, as "originary science," is not a science at all "in the real sense," for every philosophy presumes to do more than mere science. And in the next semester he traces this "more" back to the original motive of philosophizing, that is, the disquieting of life itself.

This pre- and supratheoretical "more" is "thematized" again in the Winter Semester of 1928–1929, at the end of the phenomenological decade of Heidegger's development (1919–1929). As the successor of Husserl, Heidegger takes up anew the theme of the scientificity of philosophy in this first of the later Freiburg lecture courses, which bears the title *Introduction to Philosophy*. Philosophy is not a science among others, but is more originary than any science. "Philosophy is indeed the *origin* of science, but for this very reason it is *not* science—not even a primal science" (18).[37] Because it gives science its possibility, philosophy is something more, something else, something higher and more originary. This "something else" is related to transcending, of which science as such is incapable. Or better: philosophy is something deeper, more radical, and more essential because philosophizing is "an existing from the essential ground of Dasein, [i.e.] becoming essential in transcendence" (218).[38] It is not a science at all—not out of lack, but out of excess, because through the understanding of being it is a constant inner friendship (*philia*) with things, and is thereby truer to the matters at stake and "more scientific than any science can ever be" (219). Therefore the expression "scientific philosophy" is not just superfluous, like the term "round circle," but also a deceptive misunderstanding (cf. 16, 22, 219, 221).

Philosophizing as explicit transcending, as explicitly letting transcendence happen, is grounded in the "primal fact" (223, 205) of the understanding of being, the thrown projection of being. Transcending is, first, the surpassing of beings, which happens in science on the basis of the prior, nonobjective, background projection of the ontological constitution of beings; on this basis, beings in themselves come to appear and can be articulated as openly lying before us (*positum*). "Against the background [this means horizon!] of the being that is projected in the projection, the entity that is thus determined first comes into relief" (196). But in this projection of the fundamental, positive concepts of the sciences, being itself remains unconceived, and at first even inconceivable. Nevertheless, the understanding of being is "nothing other than the possibility of carrying out the distinction between beings and being—in short, the possibility of the ontological difference" (223). There remains the radical possibility of developing the understanding of being into a conceiving of being, that is, into a question about what being itself is, and how such things as the understanding of being and transcendence become possible. This self-articulating transition from the preconceptual understanding of being to the questioning will to conceive is philosophy as explicit transcending.

Philosophy is now sharply delimited from science, which is the cognition of beings as *positum* in a demarcated domain. "Neither being as such nor beings as a whole and as such, nor the inner connection between being and beings [in transcendence—T.K.] is ever accessible . . . to a science" (224). "Transcendence is nothing that could lie before us like an object of science" (395). Being itself is no *positum*, but is like a nothing, and is close to the nonentities of the world and freedom. What, then, is the language of being, *onto-logos* (200f.), if it is not scientific language? For the propositional truth of science is founded "on something more originary that does not have the character of an assertion" (68). Philosophy as onto-logy, "the thematic grasping and conceiving of being itself" (200), in essence becomes a problem that cannot be solved until we can "unveil the full, inner direction of the essence of philosophizing" (217). Significant in the edition of these 1928–1929 lectures is a single paragraph on time as the transcendental horizon of the question of being, that is, on the schematic-phenomenological construction of the concept of being by way of time at the heart of Division III. This paragraph, as the editors note, was *not* read out loud in the lecture course (218n).[39] Even the discussion of the "construction of the problem of being" or the "construction of transcendence" (cf. 394, 396, 400), which occasionally surfaces in Heidegger's lecture-manuscript (the basis for GA 27), is not to be found in the more extensive student transcripts of the course. Instead, philosophizing as questioning about the concept of being becomes an everlasting, ever failing, inexhaustible task—a task that "leads us again and again into situations from which there seems to be no exit" (216). And the question of being, which "leads us anew into abysses" (205), is only one path to philosophy, the path via science. But in order to make the full concept of philosophy intelligible, this path must be supplemented by two further paths: via worldview and via history.

A goal common to both paths is important for our purposes. *Being and Time* had already expressed the transcendence of being-in-the-world and thereby the transcendence of the world (cf. SZ §69c). "If transcending means being-in-the-world, and if this in each case means taking a stance in the world, a worldview, then explicit transcending—philosophizing—means an explicit development of a worldview" (354f.). Philosophy as worldview is a stance, in the distinctive sense of what the Greeks called *ethos* (cf. 379), and which the later Heidegger will identify with the hermeneutic relation of *being*-human as the *Brauch* (tradition, custom, usage, practice) that develops from our dwelling in the world, the habit of a habitat.[40] "Philosophy is not *one* worldview among others, not one stance among others, but the stance that comes from the ground of transcendence, *the* grounding stance pure and simple" (SM 678; cf. GA 27, 397). In philosophizing, as explicitly letting Dasein's transcendence happen *from its ground*, the most originary possible stance takes place (396). "Only in explicitly letting transcendence happen, in the breaking-open of the inner breadth and originality of transcendence, do the concrete possibilities of the [concrete] stance [of factical existing] open up. But these concrete possibilities for the stance [of factical worldviews] are not determined on the path of philosophy, but [in each case] from the particular Dasein itself" (397; cf. SM 679). Developing a particular stance and promulgating it as a standard is not the task of philosophy as the fundamental stance, which expresses the conditions of possibility and the presuppositions of the primal act of taking a stand in the world, that is, the "form" of its actualization (cf. 390). At the most, and at best, philosophy can be the "occasion" for the possibilities of a stance to break open for the factically existing human being in their basic traits, in a free and nonbinding way; the individual's own coming to a stance and attaining a stance can then be sharpened in free choice and decision (SM 679 = GA 27, 397; also 381). The more originary the fundamental stance of philosophizing Dasein, the freer and less binding is each act of allowing a stance to take place in the Dasein of others. And the less bindingly the fundamental stance takes place, the better it can awaken the stance in others.

Philosophy as a wake-up call and as the occasion for free decision and interpretation—this is philosophy's exhortative function, which Aristotle already designated as protreptic. This function of philosophy is connected to two temporally determined and interwoven features of the transcendence of Dasein: its freedom and its historical particularity. Philosophizing—letting transcendence happen from its ground—

means precisely the development of that transcendence of Dasein which we call freedom. . . . The essence of philosophizing consists in its development of the leeway and space of free movement [*Spielraum*] into which concrete, historical Dasein, which is in each case guided by a particular stance, can enter. The fact that philosophy develops the leeway [=freedom] for the particular attainment of a stance means that philosophizing is essentially linked to the future. Just as myth is an essential and necessary recollection for philosophy, the future of its questioning is its real strength. But the present disappears, for the present is always only the tip of the moment that takes its power and its wealth from futural recollection.... With futural remembrance, we indicate the distinctive historical position that the metaphysical essence of philosophy bears within it. [SM 680f.; cf. GA 27, 398]

Philosophy is the liberation of the particular Dasein (401). Philosophizing, as letting the particular leeway happen for the moment of decision and the possibilities that are temporalized at this moment, is itself the primal action of letting-be (cf. 205), of release (*Gelassenheit*)—"a primal action of the freedom of Dasein—yes, the happening of the space for the freedom of Dasein itself" (214), "a 'deed' of the highest and most originary sort, which is possible only on the basis of the innermost essence of our existence—freedom" (103). "In the letting-happen of transcendence as philosophizing there lies the originary release of Dasein, man's trust in the Da-sein within him and in its possibilities" (401). "This entity [called] Da-sein...in and through its being, lets such a thing as a 'there' [a field of openness and disclosure] first be" (136).

And this "there" is always particular, in each case mine, in each case ours, and this means in each case historical. Dasein never exists in general, so "philosophy does not occur in general, as such, somewhere, in some indefinite Dasein or in itself" (SM 682 = GA 27, 399). "Dasein never exists in general; as concrete, it exists in a particular circumstance and, depending on these circumstances, in each case secures for itself the essential and inessential situations [of action]" (227; cf. SM 407). The explicit and decisive leap into worldview as a stance is necessarily the leap into one's own historicity, into concrete historical circumstances, into the specific historicity of one's own questioning from the whole of one's own historical situation (cf. 400). In a radical sense, philosophy leaps into the historicity of its factical Dasein, in order to attain originality and strength and to be what is essential (cf. SM 682f.). The fact that the essential and originary is revealed only in historical concretion is a difficulty that is considered along the third path to the full essence of philosophy. This difficulty is nothing other than the problem of the essence of philosophical truth as opposed to scientific truth, and thus the problem of the essence of truth as such. This problem of truth belongs together with the problem of being (in the first path) and the problem of the world (in the second path) within the architectonic of philosophy. More precisely, each of these problems constitutes the whole of philosophy (cf. SM 683).

In this first of the late Freiburg lecture courses, in the Winter Semester of 1928–1929, Heidegger breaks off some old directions of his path of thinking. But the course also forges the way for new directions that Heidegger's development will follow in the coming decade:

1. First, this lecture course documents the first signs of the often halting and even silent abandonment of the conceptual constellation "horizon—transcendence—Temporality," which had formed the original core of the projected third division of *Being and Time*. In December 1928, Heidegger begins tentatively and provisionally to distance himself from the book *Being and Time* and to interpret its thought-path as a dead end. In "On the Essence of Ground" (his article for the Husserl *Festschrift*, composed October 1928, around the time of the first draft of *Introduction to Philosophy*) he speaks, without explicitly mentioning Division III, of *Being and Time*'s "*sole* guiding intention . . . the *entire thrust*, and the *goal* of the development of the problem": "what has been published so far of the investigations on 'Being and Time' has no other task than that of . . . attaining the '*transcendental* horizon of the *question* concerning being' [on the basis of time—T.K.]."[41] Yet he still emphasizes that "in the present investigation, the Temporal interpretation of transcendence is intentionally set aside throughout."[42] This even though Heidegger's personal copy of the 1929 edition includes two handwritten marginalia that still recognize Temporality as the condition of possibility of temporality: "the essence of the 'happening'—temporalization of Temporality as preliminary name for the truth of be-ing [*Seyn*]."[43] In the *Contributions to Philosophy* (1936–1938) temporality, or "the originary unity of the ecstatic remotion that clears and conceals itself,"[44] is understood as the first beginning's transition to the grounding of the time-play-space of the site of the moment (cf. GA 65, 18, 29, 294). In order to complete this passage of transition, it was necessary "above all to avoid any objectification of be-ing, both by *withholding* the 'Temporal' interpretation of be-ing and by attempting to make the truth of be-ing 'visible' independently of this interpretation (freedom toward ground in 'On the Essence of Ground')."[45] In the Summer Semester of 1930, for example, freedom and not the unitary horizon of Temporality is designated as "the condition of the possibility of the manifestness of the being of beings, of the understanding of being."[46] Nevertheless, one could always still "identify" freedom and temporality by means of mediating concepts such as "possibility."

As we noted, in *Introduction to Philosophy* the objectifying language of the "transcendental horizon of time" is mostly held back. It is not without critical questions and reservations that Heidegger introduces the long-familiar, "commonplace piece of self-evidence"[47] of the single yet threefold "horizon" of time in his phenomenological interpretation of the essence of radical boredom, in Winter Semester 1929–1930. According to this self-evident notion, if we wish to gather all beings together at once, in all three perspectives—respect (present), retrospect (past), and prospect (future), "the perspectives of all *action and in-action* of Dasein"[48]—then in order to do this, we introduce and assume an original, unifying, and fully disclosed horizon of time.

> Let us concede for a moment... that the full horizon of time is the condition of possibility for the manifestness of beings as a whole... What does it mean to say that time is a horizon?... It is hard to say what horizon means here, or how this—namely functioning as a horizon—is possible in terms of the essence of time.... The temporal horizon is in each case playing a role in every manifestation of beings as a whole... Yet this then entails that the temporal horizon can play a role in manifold ways which are still entirely unfamiliar to us, and that we do not have the slightest intimation of the abysses of the essence of time.... *How does time come to have a horizon?* Does it run up against it, as against a shell that has been placed over it, or does the horizon belong to time itself? Yet what is this thing for, then, that delimits (*horizein*) time itself? How and for what does time give itself and form such a limit for itself? And if the horizon is not fixed, to what is it held in its changing? These are central questions. [49]

The assumption of a temporal horizon will become still more questionable in the basic experience of the most radical boredom. The mood of radical boredom is precisely the oscillation between the empty expanse of the tempo-ral horizon and the peak of the moment of vision (*Augenblick*). The moment is the acute vision of Dasein's resoluteness toward being-there, which in each case, as existing, is in the fully grasped situation of action, as this particular, singular, and unique being-there.[50] "The moment of vision ruptures the en-trancement of time, and is able to rupture it, insofar as it is a specific possibility of time itself. It is not some now-point... but is the look of Dasein in the three [temporal—T.K.] perspectival directions."[51] The entrancement of time is ruptured, and can be ruptured only by time itself, by the moment of vision that belongs to temporality. Thereby time itself has now become still more enigmatic for us, "when we think of the horizon of time, its expanse, its hori-zonal function—among other things as entrancement—and finally when we think of the way in which this horizon is connected to what we call moment of vision."[52]

> Whence the necessity of this relation between expanse and peak, between horizon and moment of vision, between world and individuation, and why does it arise? What kind of "and" is it that links these terms? Why must that expanse of the entrancing horizon ultimately be ruptured by the moment of vision? And why can it be ruptured only by this moment of vision, so that Dasein attains its existence proper precisely in this rupture? Is the essence of the unity and structural linking of both terms ultimately a *rupture*? What is the meaning of this *rupture within Dasein itself*? We call this the finitude of Dasein and ask: *What does finitude mean?*[53]

These questions reach in their origin back to the question of the essence of time.[54] As the basic question of metaphysics, it is the question about being and time. Is time itself finite, and is a being that is finite in its ground and essence still a question that belongs to metaphysics? A note from around the time of the *Contributions* (1936–1938), written by Heidegger in the copy of *Being and Time* that he kept in his cabin, in the section on the "Design of the Treatise" (SZ 39), gives the third division on "Time and Being" a new direction. This note lists three tasks that must be carried out regarding "the difference bound to transcendence": "The overcoming of the horizon as such. The return into the source. The presencing out of this source."[55] But it was not until the *Feldweg-Gespräche* (1944–1945, GA 77) that Heidegger thoroughly overcame and deconstructed the transcendental-horizonal construction of metaphysics: beyond the horizon and the objects that stand opposed to it, the objects that the horizon embraces, there comes toward us the free expanse of an enveloping open, a "regioning region" in whose "while" things come to last for a while, instead of appearing as objects.[56]

2. Philosophy is not a science, but a directing, exhorting protreptic. The course of Winter Semester 1929–1930 emphasizes this point from a unique perspective in Heidegger's very last treatment of formal indication. In contrast to scientific concepts, all philosophical concepts are formally indicative. "The meaning-content of these concepts does not directly intend or express what they refer to, but only gives an indication, a pointer to the fact that anyone who seeks to understand is called upon by this conceptual context to undertake a transformation of themselves into their Dasein [into the Da-sein within them—T.K.]."[57] A formally indicative concept "merely directs us toward our proper and peculiar task."[58] But when concepts are generic and abstract, rather than proper to the unique occasion on which they are to be interpreted, "the interpretation [is deprived] of all its autochthonous power, since whoever seeks to understand would not then be heeding the directive that lies in every philosophical concept."[59] Yet the kind of interpreting that seeks out one's own facticity in each case is not "some additional, so-called ethical application of what is conceptualized, but . . . a prior opening up of the dimension of what is to be comprehended."[60] The concepts and questions of philosophizing are in a class of their own, in contrast to science. These conceptual questions serve the task of philosophy: not to describe or explain man and his world, "*but to evoke the Dasein in man.*"[61]

Among Heidegger's still unpublished "Supplements to *Being and Time*" is found a preface to the third edition of the book, drafted in the middle of 1930, which announces a completely new elaboration of the published first half of *Being and Time* and, furthermore, a second half which would contain only the third division of Part One. But in 1931, the third edition of the first half appeared unchanged. The book project titled *Being and Time* had now finally failed, although Heidegger communicated his decision of a definitive break only to a few confidants in personal letters:

November 14, 1931, Heidegger to Rudolf Bultmann: "My own attempts, especially in the midst of these baseless times, become even pettier than they already are. In the meantime, I wear the mask of someone who 'is writing his second volume.' Behind this shield I can do whatever I like, that is, what I feel an inner necessity to do."[62]

September 18, 1932, Heidegger to Elisabeth Blochmann: "People think that I am writing SZ II, and are even talking about it. That's all right with me. SZ I was once a path for me that led me somewhere, but now this path is no longer trodden and has become overgrown. That is why I can no longer write SZ II. I am not writing any book at all."[63]

December 16, 1932, Heidegger to Bultmann: "It is difficult for me to say anything about my own efforts. My inner bearing has become much more ancient, the more clearly I see over the passing years that the task posed for me in SZ is the task of contesting the ancient question of being."

An overgrown path that can no longer be traveled, yet a necessary path full of tasks for further thought. "The path through SZ [is] unavoidable, yet it is a dead end [*Holzweg*]—a path that suddenly stops. . . . SZ—only a transition, which [stands] undecided between 'metaphysics' and the event of appropriation."[64] With the *Contributions* (1936–1938), Heidegger begins increasingly to apply a fundamental critique or "destruction" to the publication *Being and Time.* Correspondingly, in 1941 he could write:

> We take "Being and Time" as the name for a meditation whose necessity lies far beyond the activity of an individual, who cannot "invent" this necessity but cannot master it either. We thus distinguish the necessity named "Being and Time" from the "book" with this title. ("Being and Time" as the name for an appropriating event in be-ing itself. "Being and Time" as the formula for a meditation within the history of thinking. "Being and Time" as the title of a treatise that tries to carry out this thinking.)[65]

Appendix: The References to the Earliest Draft of the Third Division

1. *Textual references.* In the earliest editions of *Being and Time* (until the sixth edition) one finds a footnote to §68d on "The Temporality of Discourse" (SZ 349) that gives us an insight into the thematic structure of the very first draft of Division III—that is, the "systematic" draft that was supposedly completely

unintelligible to intellects like Rilke and Jaspers. The footnote reads, "Cf. Division Three, Chapter II of this treatise" and refers to problems that in part are already indicated in §69 as substantive themes to be treated in Division III, such as the development of the problem of the connection in principle between being and truth on the basis of the problematic of temporality. But in §68d the elaboration of this basic problem of phenomenology now becomes the presupposition for "the analytic of the temporal Constitution of discourse and the explication of the temporal characteristics of language-structures." Central to an ontological explication is the widely dispersed grammar of the verb "to be" in the articulation of the variations of its conjugation. For discourse does not primarily temporalize itself in one particular ecstasis. The verb is grounded in the whole of the ecstatic unity of temporality. Furthermore, the three tenses are mingled with "the other temporal phenomena of language—'aspects' and 'temporal stages.'" In particular, contemporary linguistics, which is obliged to carry out its analyses with the help of the vulgar concept of time, cannot even pose the "problem of [the] existential-temporal structure of the aspects [*Aktionsarten*]" (SZ 349).

Verbal action is grammatically divided into three basic types: 1) momentaneous, instantaneous, iterative; 2) continuous, ongoing, lasting, imperfect; 3) perfect, complete, perfecting. Above we have already encountered an experiential variant of this division: the three types of boredom, variously based on a limited constant time, a wavering-fleeting time, and the time of Dasein as a whole, which is entranced as a horizon. For horizonal time as Temporality is an ontological, transcendental, or a priori perfect "which characterizes the kind of being belonging to Dasein itself" (SZ 85).[66] "Each ecstasis as such has a horizon that is determined by it and that first of all completes that ecstasis' own structure."[67] The open horizon where each ecstasis ends is a perfective sign of the finitude of temporality, for "this end is nothing but the beginning and starting point for the possibility of all projecting."[68] The enabling of the transcendental perfect has the character of a prior letting-be (*Seinlassen*) (SZ 85), or better, releas*edness* (*Gelassenheit*), where the perfective suffix is both active and passive, in the ambiguity of the middle voice: it means both already-having-let-be-in-each-case and letting-be. Thus we have a series of perfective existentials in *Being and Time*: thrown*ness*, dis-posed*ness*,[69] discovered*ness*, fallen*ness*, resolute*ness*, etc. The perfect expresses an action that has somehow become definitive and that is always still in the further process of becoming. The perfect is used only when the effect of earlier activity is still at work. Heidegger comments, for example, that in perception, understood in terms of intentionality, what is central is neither perceiving nor the perceived; instead, *perceivedness* is the enabling center of the intentionality of perception, the sense of its intentional direction, which is neither subjective nor objective and which, as what makes perception possible, can ultimately be understood only on the basis of the essence of time.[70]

2. *Archival reference.* Along with the manuscript of the lecture course of Winter Semester 1925–1926 in the Heidegger Archives in Marbach, there is a file of some 200 pages wrapped in a sheet marked "I.3." A selection of about 30 pages from this text has been published,[71] but these include none of the many pages—and an entire file—that are marked with the number "69." For the entire folder is a collection of notes that refer to the themes, and even to particular chapters, of the unpublished Division III, and which were probably written in 1926–1927. A summary of the classification of the notes indicates a division into about six chapters in the missing division. Chapter 1 would have probably borne a title such as "Phenomenology and the Positive Sciences" and would have treated the method of ontological (as opposed to ontical) thematization. "Temporality (*Zeitlichkeit*) and Worldliness" is the explicit title of Chapter 4, which would have taken its themes primarily from §69c of *Being and Time.* One also finds remarks, expressions, and turns of phrase throughout this text that do not appear in Heidegger's known lectures and publications: for example, the division of awaiting into "expectative—presentative—perfective"; "moments of existence" such as "the formally futural" and "the formally perfect"; the claim "time is a self-projection upon itself (its horizonal [aspect], its ecstatic [aspect])." A thorough study of the entire file can deepen our knowledge of the direction and goals of the missing Division III, and enrich the attempt to reconstruct it.[72]

—translated by Richard Polt in consultation with the author

Notes

1. Heidegger, "A Dialogue on Language," in *On the Way to Language,* tr. Peter D. Hertz (New York: Harper & Row, 1971), 7. (This translation and others have occasionally been modified; such modifications will not be noted individually.)

2. Heidegger, *Towards the Definition of Philosophy,* tr. Ted Sadler (London: Athlone, 2000).

3. Cf. Theodore Kisiel, "Why the First Draft of *Being and Time* was Never Published," *Journal of the British Society for Phenomenology* 20 (1989): 3–22. Heidegger's 70-page journal article entitled *Der Begriff der Zeit* was finalized in November 1924 and appears in *Der Begriff der Zeit,* GA 64. ("GA" will refer to volumes of Heidegger's *Gesamtausgabe,* published in Frankfurt am Main by Vittorio Klostermann.)

4. Heidegger, *History of the Concept of Time: Prolegomena,* tr. Theodore Kisiel (Bloomington: Indiana University Press, 1985).

5. Cf. Theodore Kisiel, *The Genesis of Heidegger's "Being and Time"* (Berkeley: University of California Press, 1993), esp. 477–89.

6. Heidegger, *Being and Time*, tr. John Macquarrie and Edward Robinson (New York: Harper & Row, 1962), 63f. (German page 39f.). Henceforth cited as "SZ" followed by the German pagination.

7. *Die Metaphysik des deutschen Idealismus*, GA 49, 39f.

8. *Besinnung*, GA 66, 413.

9. *Zur Erläuterung von SZ*, manuscript, 1941.

10. Substantial notes pertaining to this first draft were however preserved. See the Appendix to this chapter.

11. *Besinnung*, GA 66, 413f. The lecture course in question is *The Basic Problems of Phenomenology*, tr. Albert Hofstadter (Bloomington: Indiana University Press, 1982).

12. Heidegger, "Letter on 'Humanism,'" tr. Frank A. Capuzzi, in *Pathmarks* (Cambridge: Cambridge University Press, 1998), 249f.

13. These obsolete spellings of *Sein* (being) and *Zeit* (time) are used by Heidegger in some texts, beginning in the later thirties, to indicate his nonmetaphysical understanding of being and time. (Trans.)

14. "Neuere Forschungen über Logik" and *Die Kategorien- und Bedeutungslehre des Duns Scotus*, both in Heidegger, *Frühe Schriften*, GA 1.

15. Emil Lask, *Die Logik der Philosophie und die Kategorienlehre: Eine Studie über den Herrschaftsbereich der logischen Form* (Tübingen: J. C. B. Mohr, 1911).

16. Cf. Kisiel, *The Genesis of Heidegger's "Being and Time,"* chapter 1.

17. SZ 328; cf. Heidegger, *The Metaphysical Foundations of Logic*, tr. Michael Heim (Bloomington: Indiana University Press, 1984), 204.

18. *The Metaphysical Foundations of Logic*, 208.

19. *Towards the Definition of Philosophy*, 90–99.

20. *Towards the Definition of Philosophy*, 99.

21. Cf. Theodore Kisiel, "Die formale Anzeige: Die methodische Geheimwaffe des frühen Heideggers," in Markus Happel (ed.), *Heidegger—neu gelesen* (Würzburg: Königshausen & Neumann, 1997).

22. *The Basic Problems of Phenomenology*, 65.

23. Cf. ibid., 314f.

24. Cf. ibid., 162.

25. Ibid., 268.

26. Heidegger, "Unbenutzte Vorarbeiten zur Vorlesung vom Wintersemester 1929/1930: *Die Grundbegriffe der Metaphysik: Welt, Endlichkeit, Einsamkeit,*" *Heidegger Studies* 7 (1991), 9.

27. Within this section, parenthetical references are to *The Basic Problems of Phenomenology* unless otherwise indicated.

28. Heidegger never speaks of a horizon of being; the term is reserved in this context for a horizon of time or of the world. But a *horizonal* temporality is mentioned for the very first time in *Being and Time* in relation to the horizonal schema of the as-structure, the "if-then" schema (SZ 359), that is, the what and how of the *being of an*

entity, in accordance with which the genesis of theoretical comportment occurs by way of a modification of the understanding of being.

29. Cf. "Phenomenology and Theology," a lecture held in 1927–1928, in *Pathmarks*.

30. Within this section, parenthetical references are to *The Metaphysical Foundations of Logic* unless otherwise indicated.

31. Cf. *The Metaphysical Foundations of Logic*, 158, 178; *The Basic Problems of Phenomenology*, 19f.

32. Cf. Heidegger, *The Fundamental Concepts of Metaphysics: World, Finitude, Solitude*, tr. William McNeill and Nicholas Walker (Bloomington: Indiana University Press, 1995), 261f.

33. Cf. Heidegger, *Einleitung in die Philosophie*, GA 27. A translation of this text, *Introduction to Philosophy*, is forthcoming from Indiana University Press.

34. *Towards the Definition of Philosophy*, 63; cf. *The Metaphysical Foundations of Logic*, 209.

35. *Towards the Definition of Philosophy*, 97.

36. Cf. ibid., 99, 80–83, 51.

37. Within this section, parenthetical references are to GA 27 unless otherwise indicated.

38. Cf. *The Metaphysical Foundations of Logic*, 221.

39. The two sentences about a "transcendental horizon" before the paragraph in question were not read out loud, either. I have compared the GA 27 edition with a much more extensive transcript by Simon Moser, and have supplemented and improved my citations from the edited version using explanatory expressions from the Moser transcript (henceforth "SM"). (A copy of this Moser transcript is to be found in the Simon Silverman Phenomenology Center at the Duquesne University Library.)

40. "A Dialogue on Language between a Japanese and an Inquirer," in *On the Way to Language*, trans. Peter D. Hertz (New York: Harper & Row, 1971), 32–33.

41. Heidegger, "On the Essence of Ground," tr. William McNeill, in *Pathmarks*, 371, note 66.

42. Ibid., note 67.

43. Ibid., 123, note a; cf. 132, note a.

44. Heidegger, *Beiträge zur Philosophie (Vom Ereignis)*, GA 65, 234. Cf. *Contributions to Philosophy (From Enowning)*, tr. Parvis Emad and Kenneth Maly (Bloomington: Indiana University Press, 1999), 165.

45. *Beiträge zur Philosophie*, GA 65, 451. Cf. *Contributions to Philosophy*, 317.

46. Heidegger, *The Essence of Human Freedom: An Introduction to Philosophy*, tr. Ted Sadler (London and New York: Continuum, 2002), 205.

47. *The Fundamental Concepts of Metaphysics*, 145.

48. Ibid.

49. Ibid., 146.

50. Cf. ibid., 169, 149.

51. Ibid., 151.

52. Ibid., 152.

53. Ibid., 170.

54. Cf. ibid., 171.

55. Heidegger, *Being and Time*, tr. Joan Stambaugh (Albany: SUNY, 1996), 35.

56. Cf. Heidegger, *Discourse on Thinking*, tr. John M. Anderson and E. Hans Freund (New York: Harper & Row, 1966), 65ff.

57. *The Fundamental Concepts of Metaphysics*, 297; and on p. 296: "our understanding must first twist free from our ordinary conceptions of beings and properly transform itself into *the Da-sein in us*."

58. Ibid., 293.

59. Ibid., 298.

60. Ibid., 296.

61. Ibid., 174.

62. The letters to Bultmann are to be published in *Rudolf Bultmann / Martin Heidegger: Briefwechsel*, ed. Andreas Großmann and Klaus Müller (Frankfurt am Main: Vittorio Klostermann, forthcoming).

63. *Martin Heidegger, Elisabeth Blochmann: Briefwechsel, 1918–1969*, ed. Joachim W. Storck (Marbach am Neckar : Deutsche Schillergesellschaft, 1989), 54.

64. *Der Weg: Der Gang durch SZ*, unpublished typescript, 1945.

65. Heidegger, *Die Metaphysik des deutschen Idealismus*, GA 49, 27.

66. Cf. Heidegger's handwritten note on SZ 85: *Being and Time*, tr. Stambaugh, 79.

67. *The Basic Problems of Phenomenology*, 306.

68. Ibid., 308.

69. *Befindlichkeit*, translated by Macquarrie and Robinson as "state-of-mind" and Stambaugh as "attunement." (Trans.)

70. *The Basic Problems of Phenomenology*, 68ff.

71. Heidegger, "Aufzeichnungen zur Temporalität (Aus den Jahren 1925 bis 1927)," *Heidegger Studies* 14 (1998): 11–23.

72. Cf. Dietmar Köhler, *Martin Heidegger: Die Schematisierung des Seinssinnes als Thematik des dritten Abschnittes von "Sein und Zeit"* (Bonn: Bouvier, 1993).

12

Being and Time in Retrospect: Heidegger's Self-Critique

Dieter Thomä

IN 1941 MARTIN HEIDEGGER EXPLAINED, "I think I myself know something about the fact that this book [*Being and Time*] has its flaws. It's like climbing an unascended mountain. Because it is both steep and unknown, whoever travels here sometimes falls. The wayfarer suddenly loses his way. At times he even falls down without the reader noticing."[1] If we follow this saying, there turn out to be four tasks involved in interpreting Heidegger's "self-critique."[2]

First, one must find the passages in *Being and Time* where, according to the author's later assessment, he undertook "false paths"(GA 66, 411), "detours and retreats,"[3] or even fell down. These falls need not, of course, be fatal; the later Heidegger believes that in *Being and Time* he pulled himself back to his feet every time, and partially conquered the rest of the ascent. Nevertheless, at the end of his work on *Being and Time*, that is, at the end of his "half attempts,"[4] he lost his way. As is well known, this work remained unfinished; in particular, the third division of Part One, which, according to Heidegger's report in 1928, was supposed to describe a "turn" (*Kehre*),[5] is missing. "The attempt failed along the way," Heidegger remarks.[6] He did not, however, attribute this failure to the fundamental direction of *Being and Time* itself, but rather to the still insufficient circumspection of the author (or the mountain climber). For the author could not go any further—not, however, because there had not been any path at all, but rather because he did not see it and in a certain way he was "walking blind."

The *second* point forms a counterpoint to the first. As a contrasting figure to that mountain climber who is afflicted by setbacks, one can imagine someone who knows how to avoid headlong falls and is on the right path. Heidegger thinks he is able to find such a figure in the course of carrying out an "immanent critique" in the form of a "purifying" of *Being and Time*.[7] The genuinely correct path, "the *one* track" (GA 66, 411), should be elaborated from *Being and Time*. The question is how exactly this *direttissima* should have developed from the point of view of the late Heidegger.

This question leads immediately to the *third* problem that lies hidden in the citation given at the beginning. Imagine that ideal path Heidegger traces in retrospect as an isolated line in space. Whether it is in fact a philosophical "royal road" depends on the region over which it is supposed to pass. For example, it would be inappropriate to make hairpin turns on a level plain. The pressing question is what sort of "mountain" Heidegger later attributes (or imputes) to the expedition of *Being and Time*. It is only if this "mountain" in fact corresponds to the target he had set for himself at that time that what he later deplores as a false path or a headlong fall can be rightly seen as a shortcoming, according to the inner logic of *Being and Time*. In turn, it is possible that what seemed to Heidegger according to his later revision to be a purified movement through the region appeared from his own earlier viewpoint as a path in another landscape which leads to a dead end, or where one loses the ground beneath one's feet or meets with granite. In this third point the question, generally speaking, is whether what Heidegger says in retrospect about *Being and Time* may be valid as "immanent critique" or whether he addresses his early major work from a foreign perspective and paints a distorted picture. The problem is that there are two perspectives—an early and a late—whose relation must first be clarified.

Fourth, along with his internal attempts at clarification and delimitation, there is the issue of Heidegger's efforts to defend *Being and Time* from external attacks, or as he puts it, against a "confusion of misinterpretation."[8] His own self-critique is joined by the rebuttal of external critiques and certain interpretations which, from his point of view, conceive of *Being and Time* in misleading ways. To stay within the framework of our metaphors, then, these misleading ways set the author of *Being and Time* on a track which does not appeal to him.

With these four points the course is laid out which I want to travel along in the following four sections. As a preliminary note, one remark is in order: there may be a decisive answer to the question of whether Heidegger's late texts in comparison with *Being and Time* should be seen as the purified, freer unfolding of his thinking or as a step backwards. But the concern of this commentary is not to deliver such an answer. Here it is rather a question of giving, on the basis of Heidegger's "self-critique," the clearest possible description of the relationship between *Being and Time* and his later writings.

1

What Heidegger in hindsight finds "awkward"[9] are first and foremost the titles under which he placed his early enterprise. He considers it unavoidable that at first he had to think "in the tracks" from which he frees himself. Thus he uses concepts like "phenomenology," "metaphysics of Dasein" (in the Kant book), and "fundamental ontology" (GA 49, 28). Accordingly a weakness in *Being and Time* is that the garment in which his philosophy was clothed at the time consisted of old fabric. On the one hand, *Being and Time* was "metaphysically articulated and presented," and on the other hand, it was "nonetheless *thought otherwise*" (GA 66, 321). In this distinction lies the thesis that what is traditional remained external to the thinking of *Being and Time*—and it can thus be shaken off—so that the "other thinking" comes to the fore all the more purely. That he still had difficulty at the beginning establishes the authenticity with which he labored under the burden of the past, which was not so easily cast off.[10]

But why did Heidegger reject the titles under which he placed his early enterprise? He explains this in the most detail in regard to "fundamental ontology," which now appears to him as something "provisional."[11] His reference point is here a sentence from the introduction to *Being and Time*: "Therefore *fundamental ontology* ... must be sought in the *existential analytic of Dasein*" (SZ 13).[12] The later Heidegger rejects the idea that it is through such an existential analytic that "the foundation for ontology itself which is still lacking, but is to be built upon that foundation" can be erected.[13] This idea appears to him as misleading because he sees Being itself already engaged in that analytic—so there is nothing left that would still have to be built on the foundation. Accordingly the analytic of the inner constitution of Dasein does not precede ontology; rather it should already be nothing other than the thinking of Being. In a marginal note from his own copy of *Being and Time* Heidegger thus finds fault with the fact that his earlier presentation remains "misleading, above all in relation to the role of Dasein" (SZ 439).[14] To the extent that "Dasein's horizon of understanding" is itself already indebted to Being, this horizon cannot "endure"—as it is now put—"any construction thereupon" that would thematize for the first time the Being of beings as understood by Dasein; the horizon does not serve as Being's "condition" or "foundation."[15] On account of this, in a later marginal note Heidegger strives for the "overcoming of the horizon as such" (SZ 440) and "forbids" himself without hesitation to use this word.[16] The early definition of "horizon" is bound to that which projects itself and looks out upon something, and not to that which makes possible this regard in some way. Therefore he later says, "That temporality which was termed in *Being and Time* ecstatic-horizontal is in no way the sought for most unique characteristic of time that corresponds to the question of Being."[17]

Heidegger sees himself in *Being and Time* as searching for a bridge between two questions: the question about the temporality of Dasein and the question about truth. To the extent, namely, that Dasein "endures" its temporal constitution or is able to "displace" itself into it (cf. SZ 325, 445), beings should be accessible in their unconcealment, in other words in their "truth"; they become "cleared." It is exactly this transition from temporality to truth[18] that Heidegger, as he explains in retrospect, "suspected, but did not master" in *Being and Time.*[19]

According to the intention Heidegger attributes to himself in hindsight, the self-discovery of Dasein in *Being and Time* should proceed with the opening or clearing (*Lichtung*) of a world in which beings in their Being come to appearance for Dasein. Indeed Dasein itself "belongs to the world" (SZ 65) or even, as is clarified in a marginal note, "obeys and listens to the world" (SZ 441). But this connection was not adequately expressed at first, if we follow the later self-critique. Heidegger sees the reason for this, in a word, in a subjectivistic contamination of *Being and Time.* He confirms this analysis through different examples, and three of these critical points will be treated here briefly: they have to do with *space, language,* and the *I*. In the *first* example we will discuss *space.*

As Heidegger remarks concisely in 1962, "The attempt in *Being and Time,* section 70, to derive human spatiality from temporality is untenable."[20] This self-critique—rarely as candid as here—is directed against the thesis from *Being and Time* according to which time has a "founding function for spatiality" (SZ 368, translation modified). At that point it was said that "something such as *place*," and thus "space," first arises out of the temporally conceived Dasein, the "self-directive discovery," thus "*on the basis of its ecstatico-horizonal temporality*" (SZ 368f.). But what Heidegger cannot delete in these earlier views is precisely the authentic action of Dasein, to whom a unique temporal dimension belongs. What is interesting in this self-critique at this point is that even the later Heidegger is not concerned with strictly separating space from time. According to his later positions, furthermore, it falls to time to "make room, that is, provide ... the self-extending, the opening up, of future, past, and present."[21] Thus space is also here derived from time. Time is of course no longer assigned to Dasein as "thrown projection," but it makes its appearance rather as the successor to that "Temporality [*Temporalität*] of Being" of which Heidegger had spoken in *Being and Time* and also in the lectures from summer semester 1927.[22] Previously it was declared that this "Temporality" was a (merely "turned" around) aspect of the temporality (*Zeitlichkeit*) of Dasein. The failure of this conjunction is now attested to indirectly in that Heidegger in his later self-critique repudiates the derivation of space from the temporality of Dasein and instead ascribes it to time as a movement in the "event of appropriation" or "enowning" (*Ereignis*). He thereby breaks apart the temporality of

Dasein and the Temporality of Being—contrary to the program of *Being and Time*. The failure to unite these two sides is nothing other than the failure of the completion of *Being and Time*.

The persistent self-sufficiency of Dasein is also noticeable in relation to a *second* critical point: the concept of language, which in *Being and Time* is introduced in connection with the concept of "involvement" (*Bewandtnis*). There it is said that the "Being of innerworldly beings" with which Dasein is concerned consists in their "involvement" for Dasein, more precisely in the "'towards-which' of serviceability and the 'for-which' of usability" (SZ 84). Along with this "involvement" goes the "signification" that an entity has. Dasein is "familiar" with the world as "significance" (*Bedeutsamkeit*), and the significations that are thereby opened up to Dasein "found," says Heidegger, "in turn the [possible] Being of word and language" (SZ 86f.). He notes at this point in the margin of his personal copy: "Untrue. Language is not imposed, but *is* the primordial essence of truth as there [*Da*]" (SZ 442). The interweaving into pragmatic relations that marked Heidegger's analysis of the world displaces, according to Heidegger's later judgment, the primordiality of language, which precedes all doing and letting. (Moreover, the question of whether this primordiality is conceived as fidelity to the soil or structural priority opens up the entire spectrum of Heidegger interpretations from "the Black Forest" to Michel Foucault.) That interweaving of language with actions was, however, an expression of the self-sufficiency of Dasein, which is later rejected as residual subjectivism.

Heidegger now sees the very same residual subjectivism—this is the *third* critical point—at work in the talk of the "I" itself. The procedure by which Dasein itself came to itself was described in *Being and Time* as a running toward death, by which it was thrown back upon itself and was first put into the position to be itself. "Saying I" belonged to this Being-one's-self: "With the 'I,' this entity has itself in view" (SZ 318). Indeed Heidegger already proceeded cautiously in these statements, with quotation marks. Nevertheless, later this "I" had to appear to him as a deviation from that "self" which "refers not to the self as an entity [*das seiende Selbst*] but rather to Being and the relation to Being" (GA 49, 39). In 1934 he says, "It is precisely the bursting of I-hood and of subjectivity through temporality that conveys Dasein as it were away from itself and dedicates it to Being, compelling it in this way to Being-one's-self."[23] In a marginal note to *Being and Time* there is a warning: "clarify more precisely: *saying-I* and being a self" (SZ 445).

According to Heidegger's summary, "the attempt and the path [in *Being and Time*] ... confront the danger of unwillingly becoming merely another entrenchment of subjectivity ... the attempt itself hinders the decisive steps; that is, hinders an adequate exposition of them in their essential execution."[24]

In retrospect he sees his earlier conception in danger of a "fall . . . into a merely modified subjectivism."[25] The question is now how he describes a path from *Being and Time* that leads directly to the later thought.

2

Heidegger may have recognized parts of *Being and Time* that rendered difficult the overcoming of subjectivity, the task he had made his own. These are the "false paths" or "falls" of which he speaks in retrospect. At the same time he vehemently defends himself against the interpretation according to which his early major work should be considered a direct contribution to the theory of subjectivity. This self-defense is carried out so apodictically that it appears as a defiant reaction to his own critique of the residual subjectivism of his early major work when he declares in 1941, "In *Being and Time* the essence of the selfhood of man is not determined by 'I-hood,' not as personality and not at all as the 'subjectivity' of a 'subject'" (GA 49, 60). More generally he says in 1949: "It"—namely the substance of *Being and Time*—"remains valid."[26] But wherein consists this substance? Or more precisely, what is later defined as the substance which may remain valid as an improved, purified version of *Being and Time*? With subtle conceptual displacements Heidegger attempts to liberate what he sees as its essential content from deficiencies and to guard it against misunderstandings.

In the center of these displacements there stands nothing other than the principal concept of *Being and Time*, "Dasein": "Because Being-in-the-world belongs essentially to Dasein, its Being towards the world is essentially concern" (SZ 57). In a marginal note to this sentence Heidegger writes: "being-human here equated with being-here [*Da-sein*]" (SZ 441, translation modified), and this comment is nothing but a self-reproach. This reproach presses itself upon Heidegger in the course of his self-critique because he wants to overcome the active self-will of Dasein as man. In contrast to the equation of Dasein and man he considers in a subsequent marginal note the formulation "being-here, wherein man essentially happens [*west*]" (SZ 442, translation modified). The reinterpretation implied here—and in the end the abolition of the concept of Dasein—proceeds in several steps.

The *first* step occurs at the end of *Kant and the Problem of Metaphysics* with the talk of the "Dasein in man."[27] Here Dasein changes from an apparently constitutive condition of man into a condition to which man is related. This difference is sharpened in a *second* step in the middle of the 1930s.

Now it is man who, insofar as he allows himself into his Dasein, enters at the same time into the world as the play of Being. Heidegger claims that in

Being and Time the "essence of man's selfhood" had already been determined "by the insistence in the projection of Being, i.e., by being-here."[28] Should that imply that this "being-here" is identical with the Dasein from *Being and Time*? That would be misguided. For while the "old" Dasein had to endure in itself the ambivalence of being able to exist in the mode of inauthenticity as well as authenticity, there appears here by contrast a "new" being-here, a "site"[29] into which man can displace himself or "in" which he can "stand" (GA 49, 50 and 54; cf. GA 69, 57). The later interpretation of being-here can make sense only if this "new" being-here is reserved for a particular (authentic) form of the "old" Dasein. By contrast, the latter receives in the course of this revision a modest designation: it is nothing but "man," who can either become "insistent in the [new] being-here" (GA 49, 61) or remain forgetful of Being. "Therefore it remains misleading," as Heidegger puts it in 1941, "when in *Being and Time* the talk is about 'human Dasein.' The term 'being-here' absolutely must be used because it names something that never coincides with being-human, but is rather of a 'higher' essence than man" (GA 49, 62). This new difference between man and Dasein reaches its sharpest point in Heidegger's remark that his "*thinking*" is "*in-human*" in the sense that it "does not rely upon standards and goals and motives of mankind up to now," to which he adds: "Such thinking is—*being*-here" (GA 69, 24). One could say that in this tension between man and Dasein the old alternative of inauthenticity and authenticity returns. Of course according to *Being and Time* it was, ontologically speaking, unimportant which specific individuals attained authenticity, but now Heidegger rejects this indifference. The respective distance from or nearness to being-here and thus to Being becomes, as it is now put, "determined through Being itself" (GA 49, 62f.): "Not every historical mankind is expressly assigned to the insistence of being-here; in history up until now absolutely none, due to the forgetfulness of Being that is to be thought in terms of the destiny of Being" (GA 49, 61). But Heidegger now thinks he can hear when, in the sense of that nearness of Being, "the hour of our history . . . has struck" (GA 39, 294). (Of course he misheard on occasion, for example in 1933.)

As a result of the separation from man, the concept of Dasein as distinguished from Being becomes superfluous, and in the course of this *third* step it disappears from the later work. Now it suffices to see "man's distinctive feature" in his standing "open to Being, face to face with Being; thus man remains referred to Being and so answers to it."[30] Heidegger's discourse now concerns the "belonging together of Being and man."[31] But because this doubling still brings with itself the illusion of the "objectification" of Being (*Seyn*)[32] and motivates the deceptive impression that here two different things have to be brought together, that pair of concepts is finally given up. In order not to stray from *Being and Time,* at this point I would like to leave unexplained this last step toward the "event" and the "fourfold," in which man is already involved.

Despite these incisive redescriptions Heidegger insists that he remains faithful to his first undertaking, *Being and Time*—except for the contaminations discussed above in the first section. The question in the following section will be whether his retrospective interpretation remains immanent, that is, whether the task that he retroactively assigns to *Being and Time* coincides with what he had first attempted. If we follow the metaphor which Heidegger himself used for his undertaking, the question now becomes: is the "mountain" that he climbed in *Being and Time* in fact the same mountain that he ascribes to his retrospectively described path?

3

Heidegger's self-critique of *Being and Time* pursues a double strategy: he excludes certain subjectivistic errors (see above, section 1) in order to blaze a path through this work that leads directly to the late thought (see above, section 2). This of course raises the question of whether he does justice to his early main work with this separation of disruptive externals and a positive core. For the sake of intelligibility I would like to discuss this question starting from a single short passage, which runs: "That *Present* which is held in authentic temporality and which thus is *authentic* itself, we call the '*moment of vision*' [*Augenblick*]. This term must be understood in the active sense as an ecstasis. It means the resolute rapture with which Dasein is carried away to whatever possibilities and circumstances are encountered in the Situation as possible objects of concern, but a rapture which is *held* in resoluteness" (SZ 338).

First of all I will briefly explain the context of this passage in *Being and Time*. The "moment of vision" was introduced there as "authentic present." The "present" on the other hand was assigned in general to "falling" as one of the structural forms of "disclosedness" (SZ 334f. and 346). This "falling" attains the "authentic" form of the "moment of vision" insofar as the present does not render itself independent at the expense of the other temporal dimensions of that which will come and that which has been. It is precisely for this reason that the "rapture" should be held in "resoluteness" (see above), and thus remain related to the temporal totality of Dasein (cf. SZ 298 and 305).

Despite the danger of being fastidious, I would now like to pursue the interpretations to which the above cited passage, as a "test case" from *Being and Time*, is subjected in the course of Heidegger's further development. I restrict myself thereby above all to the idiom of the "rapture of Dasein which is *held* in resoluteness" and ask what happens to the two concepts that are juxtaposed in it.

The first explanations of *rapture* are found in the lecture course of summer 1928. According to this course it means a "stepping out [from] itself," the "upswing" (*Überschwung*), the "ecstasis," to which the "transcendence" of Dasein is linked.[33] Rapture as ecstasis is clarified as what is characteristic of "*Ek-sistenz.*" But rapture's standing-outside has already been conceived at this point—so Heidegger says in 1941—in the orbit of the questioning of *Being and Time* as "standing-in" or "insistence" (GA 49, 53f. and 76). This reversal of perspective is summarized in 1949: "The stasis of the ecstatic consists—strange as it may sound—in standing in the 'out' and 'there' of unconcealedness, which prevails as the essence of Being itself. What is meant by 'existence' . . . could be most felicitously designated by the word 'insistence.'"[34] Summing up this terminological interplay, we find that the concept that we first discussed, namely, "rapture," turns out to be *insistence*—this is so not on the basis of a subsequent revision, but rather as an allegedly faithful exposition of *Being and Time*.

And what happens to the second concept, that of *resoluteness*? Notwithstanding its martial undertone Heidegger wants to show precisely with this concept the consistency of his work. The new spelling as resolute openness (*Ent-schlossenheit*)[35] makes it clear that it is supposed to be a matter of an unlocking (*Aufschliessen*) of oneself, and thus a "self-opening" or "keeping-open." As an idiom opposed to inauthenticity this was understood in *Being and Time* as a being-open for oneself, for one's own Being; what also belonged entirely to this "resoluteness towards [Dasein] itself" (SZ 298) were energy and zest for action, as is made clear in *Being and Time* and the texts from around 1933. In the following years Heidegger opposes "resoluteness" to the "decided action of a subject" and interprets it as "the opening up of Dasein out of its captivity in beings toward the openness of Being."[36] "Resoluteness" is indeed defined as "will";[37] to will oneself is, however, nothing but an affirmation of that which one is, and because one's own Being is already embedded in the world, when man wills himself he really wills nothing but Being.[38] "Resoluteness" then becomes explicitly identified with "insistence," into which, as we saw, "rapture" had also already changed: "What is essential to resoluteness lies . . . in the . . . openness to the truth of Being as such. . . . It is the insistence in the exposure to the here [*Da*]: Being-here."[39] In this way the talk in the *Contributions to Philosophy* of the "will to enowning [*Ereignis*]" and of "the insistence in enowning"[40] can amount to the same thing. The second concept to be discussed here, "resoluteness," also turns out at the end of Heidegger's explication to be *insistence*.

If we now allow ourselves to be led back from this late insight to the passage which I cited at the beginning of this section as a "test case," then something troubling results. If in *Being and Time* what he means by "moment of vision" is "the resolute rapture . . . but a rapture which is *held* in resoluteness" (SZ 338), then on the basis of Heidegger's later interpretation there now arises the thesis that the moment of vision is "the insistent insistence, but the insistence which is *held* in the insistence of Dasein." This is unfortunately rather nonsensical. Whereas in *Being and Time* the opposition between resoluteness (to one's own self) and rapture (toward the world) is expressed by the "but," this opposition now collapses with the general expansion of "insistence"—and the sense of that statement thereby breaks down.

One may find the opposition between resoluteness and rapture in *Being and Time* questionable or not—that is irrelevant here. What is decisive is that Heidegger expressly makes the claim to have remained faithful to the genuine concern of *Being and Time* in his later interpretations; but according to my "test case" this claim is untenable. When it comes to the statement discussed here, the strategy to overcome contaminations and sustain a true core fails. Heidegger does not do justice to what is treated in *Being and Time*. He attempts rather to polish it up in such a way that it fits into his later thought. Contrary to his own testimony he does not practice an "immanent critique" of *Being and Time* (see my introduction), but rather he steps out of the immanence of that work.

What is lost in the later mistaken interpretation of *Being and Time* is the independent dimension in which Dasein had to deal with itself. In this dimension man was summoned to an engagement with himself. As late as in the lectures of summer 1928 we can read the following: "Existing is precisely this being towards oneself."[41] Accordingly the "concept of subjectivity and of the subjective [ought to be] . . . fundamentally transform[ed]," thus retained in another form.[42] This subjectivity is anchored more deeply in *Being and Time* than Heidegger later wants to believe—so deeply that it cannot be eliminated as a contamination.

The revisionary reading, according to which in *Being and Time* the subject has indeed already been "overcome,"[43] gains a certain plausibility if one starts from a concept of the subject as it is laid out in Heidegger's own critique of metaphysics. According to this critique the subject is driven by the tendency to posit itself and to dominate the world. The Dasein of *Being and Time* does not of course succumb to this power fantasy, despite all of its "control" over beings; it exists on a ground which it itself has not posited. This encourages the late Heidegger to declare that at bottom, Dasein was actually already far from the subject. Thus the later question of whether the Dasein of *Being and Time* is still to be attributed to the philosophy of the subject functions purely rhetorically: "How should something ever be 'subjective' which precisely does *not* arise from a subjectivity?" (GA 49, 50).

The problem is only that this question is not at all rhetorical, but misleading. Of course that which is "subjective" need not also "arise from a subjectivity." It belongs rather to the fundamental structure of subjectivity to experience itself in a self-relation about whose origin there is no sufficient information. When this subject does not make itself into its own origin, it surely does not cease to be a subject. A common problem in the history of modern philosophy—from Descartes and Montaigne to Kant, Rousseau, and Schelling—is that the subject has encountered its self-referential nature and self-determination in ever-recurring ways. This is in no way something that the subject makes "arise" from itself. One may submit this structure of subjectivity to critique; Heidegger prefers, however, to provide a caricature of self-control, and so it becomes easy for him to exclude the Dasein of *Being and Time* from this caricature.[44] This Dasein belongs, nonetheless, together with the problem of self-relation, in the framework of a theory of subjectivity which retains its validity while keeping its distance from the idea of the power-obsessed subject. This problem, which in Heidegger's later reading remains unnoticed, cannot be conceived as a mere contamination of *Being and Time*. Rather it belongs to the independent systematic core of this book, which becomes unrecognizable in his revisionary attempt to arrange the early main work in such a way that it appears as a still clumsy ascent on the "mountain" of Being. For this reason Heidegger's conjunction, according to which one can only "gain access" to the later thought starting out from *Being and Time* and *Being and Time* must be understood as "contained" in the later thought, is untenable.[45] A fitting statement at this point is one originally aimed at Karl Marx: "Such fundamental and flagrant contradictions rarely occur in second-rate writers; in the work of the great authors they lead into the very center of their work."[46]

The opposition in *Being and Time* between "resoluteness" and "rapture" thematizes a gulf between self and world, the Being of Dasein and Being as such—a separation which prevented Heidegger from completing within the logic of *Being and Time* the self-enclosed movement within the "same" that he later titles "the turn."[47] After the completion of *Being and Time* failed, Heidegger first had to make the gulf between self and world disappear in order to prepare for the "turn" from a new, simulated starting point. But with this, *Being and Time* as a factical starting point is lost and Heidegger's work breaks apart. It does not make available the reference points which could be related to each other strictly under the title "turn." This concept causes confusion because it presupposes the immanence and closedness of a movement that turns itself to itself and comes back to itself, whereas there never really was any such movement.

In view of the difficulties with this "turn," the passage from *Being and Time* by which I let myself be guided in this section as a "test case" is enlightening in two respects. First, as we saw, the passage gives evidence that *Being and Time* still provided for a "relation" of man that was not a direct relation to "Being," but related on the one hand to one's own Being-oneself and on the other hand to the world. Second, as we will show, the passage gives evidence that that to which man relates himself there is conceived in *Being and Time* otherwise than in the later work.

Dasein was "enraptured" by "whatever possibilities and circumstances are encountered in the Situation as possible objects of concern" (SZ 338). This pragmatic transition to the "object of possible concern" would have a strange effect if one tried to transfer it to "insistence" in the later context. In the background of this difficulty there is a concept that now—like its conceptual pair, Dasein (see above, section 2)—is subject to reinterpretations: namely, the "world." Just as Dasein as "resolute" in *Being and Time* became capable of acting, so too the world by which it was "enraptured" had pragmatic features; how Dasein was conceived there was mirrored in the world. Thus later on, at the same time as Dasein, its "world" must also be held at abeyance. Therefore, Heidegger writes that the "analyses of the environment" in sections 14–24 of *Being and Time* are "on the whole and with respect to the *guiding goal* of secondary signification."[48] On the other hand he introduces the new concept of "earth" as that into which "Dasein, as historical, is already thrown";[49] in *Being and Time* precisely this would still have been the "world," but Heidegger gives no more precise information about the change of concepts effected here.

When one takes a step back and compares the late to the early Heidegger, the following alternatives open up. If one turns to *Being and Time*, then one confronts the problem of how a Dasein entangled in its concerns comes to itself in such a way that it enters into a free relationship to the world, in other words, in such a way that the world opens itself to it. However, *Being and Time* obviously lacks a satisfactory solution to this problem. The widely divergent interpretations which find in Heidegger on the one hand the decisionist, and on the other hand the contextualist, are merely a symptom of this problem. If to the contrary one concentrates on the later texts, then one brings that problem brusquely to a standstill: "resoluteness" on the one hand and "rapture" on the other become transformed into the very same "insistence."

How one should decide this question in view of these alternatives is not this commentary's business. But in neither way can *Being and Time* be accommodated under the roof of a "proper and singular question"[50] that slowly purifies and clarifies itself. Heidegger's claim, on the one hand, merely to purify (see section 1) and on the other hand, merely to interpret his early masterwork (see section 2) is misleading; in the course of his interpretation he turns away from it.

4

Heidegger's attempt to extract from *Being and Time* the core which contains the seed for his further thought is accompanied by efforts to defend his early masterwork from interpretations which retain, instead of this core, merely the husks, that is, the externals. His self-critique is therefore accompanied by a defense against external critique, and if necessary, even against false friends (as is perhaps the case with Jaspers, whose *Existenzphilosophie* is stigmatized as the "emptiest leveling" of his thought: GA 69, 9). Heidegger takes up and tackles two misunderstandings above all: the first leads to the anthropologizing and the second to the ethicizing of *Being and Time*. I would like briefly to deal with both these points.

It is obvious from Heidegger's point of view that the "differentiation from every kind of philosophical anthropology" (GA 49, 33) is decisive for the correct understanding of *Being and Time*: with Dasein's Being-in-the-world the specialized treatment of man, in which his essential traits are investigated, is disposed of. In his view, precisely this isolation is fateful. If Heidegger had to distinguish himself from an anthropology of Arnold Gehlen's sort, he would say: human life is not already endowed with characteristics which determine its ambitions in relation to the environment into which it then falls. If he had to distinguish himself from a pragmatism of John Dewey's sort (at the basis of which there is an anthropology implicitly directed against Gehlen), he would say: the world is not utterly exhausted in the experiences that human life has in its dealings with it.

Heidegger's reservation with respect to anthropology can easily be retraced: for him what is ultimately in question is not man at all—or at most, it is man only insofar as man is opened for Being. Of course this remains unclear in *Being and Time* because the "world" in which Dasein is involved does not yet possess the independence which is granted to it later in the leeside of the "earth," when man is conceived as one of the players, so to speak, in a "fourfold of the world,"[51] a "world play."[52] So Heidegger's critique of the anthropologizing of *Being and Time* contains something irritating. He indeed defends himself against a separate treatment of man, but this does not hinder him from making assertions about man in the framework which he constructs: about the structures of his everyday life, about the constitution of his Being-in-the-world, etc. One could say that the critique of the isolated treatment of human peculiarities itself contains an anthropological assertion about the worldliness or contextuality of human life.

Heidegger now defends this assertion in a second step directed against an ethicizing interpretation. The decisive key word in his interpretations after 1927 is that of the "neutrality" of the analytic of Dasein.[53] Accordingly the priorities and tendencies in it, and how they are connected to the ethical questions of obligation and will, play no more of a role than "prophesying and heralding world-views."[54] In the background of this aversion to morals and ethics, found already in Heidegger's earliest texts, there stands a critique inspired by Nietzsche of "values" that are distant from life.

No objection to *Being and Time* has been made with such popularity as that according to which Heidegger has sketched here, a separate world that is "not everyone's affair." Following this objection, the question becomes what then speaks on behalf of living "as Dasein does," and why then one should or would want to live "in this way." But nothing so aroused Heidegger's polemical verve as this objection concerning the separate world. He was encouraged to engage in this polemic because the images drawn of his idiosyncrasies were so varied that they could easily be stigmatized as caricatures. Thus he saw himself during the Nazi period exposed to the reproach that in *Being and Time* he succumbed to the "influence" of a "'metropolitan' conception" of life (GA 66, 327). On the other hand he was amused by the reproach that for him "the world [consisted] only of cooking pots, pitchforks, and lampshades," and that he had "no relationship at all to 'higher culture' . . . and to 'Nature,'" for all this "does not come to the fore in *Being and Time*." Heidegger saw the "genuine ground" for such "misinterpretations . . . in the fact that one ascribes as it were self-evidently to the author the wish to establish here a 'system of the world,' whereas something completely different is in question" (GA 49, 44).

Just as little as he tolerates the reproach that the world he describes is one-sided does Heidegger accept that Dasein is prejudiced in its way of world-disclosure. He defends himself against the reproach of the "philistine" that "human Dasein must not be laid out so gloomily and exclusively as care,"[55] because then "gloom and grief" would be demanded.[56]

When he speaks of the "neutrality" of his analytic of Dasein, Heidegger could have two different things in mind. *On the one hand*, it could be a matter of exhibiting a constitution of Dasein that underlies all of its behaviors and of which one can become certain in the mode of authenticity. In this respect what one does would not be decided in advance, but rather only the way in which one comes to and stands toward this doing would be modified. According to this reading, the "authentic" existence in *Being and Time* favors a particular way of life no more than, say, "falling" is meant in a disparaging way.[57] This argument comes to light especially forcefully in the claim that Dasein, despite its often reviled "neuter" state, opens up "the intrinsic possibility for being factically dispersed into bodiliness and thus into sexuality."[58]

On the other hand, Heidegger could entirely join a modifying claim to his analytic and all of its "neutrality." It would be "neutral" then not because it allows diverse deviations, but rather because the grounding for "authentic" Dascin is neither tendentiously designated nor positively asserted. Accordingly, a determinate form of life is very much worked out in *Being and Time*, but it does not originate from an ethical, non-neutral, tendentious decision; it has nothing to do with moral obligation and will. It discloses itself in the insight into the constitution of Dasein, to which it merely corresponds.

In his later writings Heidegger follows the second of the above mentioned variants. On the basis of his now strictly drawn distinction between Dasein and man he sees the latter exposed to an "errancy" which can be put to an end only through its "transformation."[59] In 1946 he repeats his critique of "ethics" as a baseless construction. Nevertheless at the same time he clarifies that a "peremptory directive" as to how man "ought to live"[60] is to be found in an "originary ethics" which "ponders the abode of the human being," how man "determines himself from the . . . belongingness to Being."[61] From this there should arise "directives," "law and rule" in a new sense.[62] The question about the good life is here replaced by the question about life in accordance with Being—and this is a fundamental characteristic of his thought, which is in fact already found in Heidegger's earliest texts onward.

In his interpretation of *Being and Time* Heidegger wants to claim for himself such uniformity throughout. Nonetheless, our overview of his "self-critique" has shown that the attempt to present *Being and Time* as the first and still unsure step on a path that later was trodden farther brings with it distortions and confusion. This is of course not surprising; it is well-known that authors are not predestined to be their own most competent interpreters.

Heidegger was occasionally pained by the deficiencies which appeared in *Being and Time* when his later standards were applied to it. In view of the misunderstandings which he considered resolved by these later standards which corrected *Being and Time*, he arrived at the conclusion that it "would be good if one were to let *Being and Time*, the book and the matter, finally repose for an indeterminate future" (GA 49, 34). But insofar as this conclusion implies the recommendation that one now abide only by the less "misleading" later thought of Heidegger, one should not follow it.

—translated by Daniel J. Dwyer

Notes

1. GA 49, *Die Metaphysik des deutschen Idealismus*, 27. [Translator's note: "GA" will refer to volumes of Heidegger's *Gesamtausgabe*, published in Frankfurt am Main by Vittorio Klostermann. Where existing English translations are available, they will be cited first, followed by the corresponding volume and pagination of GA or another specified German edition. Subsequent references to untranslated GA volumes will be parenthetical. All references to *Sein und Zeit* will be indicated parenthetically by "SZ" and the German pagination of the seventh and later editions (Tübingen: Max Niemeyer, 1953–). Unless otherwise indicated, the English translation of this text is *Being and Time*, trans. John Macquarrie and Edward Robinson (New York: Harper and Row, 1962).]

2. Heidegger designates his text "Auseinandersetzung mit 'Sein und Zeit'"—a text which dates from 1935 to 1936 and will appear in GA 82, *Zu eigenen Veröffentlichungen*—as a "self-critique" (cf. GA 66, *Besinnung*, 420); this text was not available to me. Heidegger's "critique" must be understood in a neutral sense, that is, as an attempt at delimitation and clarification. The classic texts containing self-interpretations—including the "Letter on 'Humanism,'" in *Pathmarks*, ed. William McNeill (Cambridge: Cambridge University Press, 1998) = *Wegmarken* (Frankfurt am Main: Klostermann, 1967), the letter to Richardson in William Richardson, *Heidegger: Through Phenomenology to Thought*, 4th ed. (New York: Fordham University Press, 2003), and the lecture "Time and Being," in *On Time and Being*, trans. Joan Stambaugh (Chicago: University of Chicago Press, 2002) = *Zur Sache des Denkens* (Tübingen: Max Niemeyer, 1976)—have now been supplemented by detailed comments in GA 49 and GA 66.

3. Hannah Arendt and Martin Heidegger, *Letters 1925–1975*, ed. Ursula Ludz, trans. Andrew Shields (Orlando, FL: Harcourt, 2004), 84 = *Briefe 1925 bis 1975 und andere Zeugnisse*, ed. Ursula Ludz (Frankfurt am Main: Vittorio Klostermann, 1998), 104; GA 49, 40.

4. *On Time and Being*, 44 = *Zur Sache des Denkens*, 47.

5. *The Metaphysical Foundations of Logic*, trans. Michael Heim (Bloomington: Indiana University Press, 1984), 158 = GA 26, *Metaphysische Anfangsgründe der Logik im Ausgang von Leibniz*, 201.

6. Letter to Jan Aler, November 1970, in *Zeitschrift fur Ästhetik und allgemeine Kunstwissenschaft* 18 (1973): 5. Details concerning this third division can be found in GA 49, 39f. and GA 66, 413f.; cf. also Theodore Kisiel's contribution in this volume.

7. *On Time and Being*, 55 = *Zur Sache des Denkens*, 61; *Contributions to Philosophy (From Enowning)*, trans. Parvis Emad and Kenneth Maly (Bloomington: Indiana University Press, 1999), 154 = GA 65, *Beiträge zur Philosophie (Vom Ereignis)*, 221.

8. GA 69, *Die Geschichte des Seyns*, 9.

9. *Pathmarks*, 288 = *Wegmarken*, 209.

10. Cf. *On Time and Being*, 30 = *Zur Sache des Denkens*, 32; *Contributions to Philosophy*, 246 = GA 65, 351.

11. *Contributions to Philosophy*, 215 = GA 65, 305.

12. Cf. *On Time and Being*, 31 = *Zur Sache des Denkens*, 34; *Pathmarks*, 288–89 = *Wegmarken*, 209.

13. *On Time and Being*, 31 = *Zur Sache des Denkens*, 33f.

14. In *Sein und Zeit* (Tübingen: Max Niemeyer, 1977), 439. [Translator's note: all subsequent parenthetical references to Heidegger's marginal notes will be to this German edition's pagination and the translations will be those found in *Being and Time*, trans. Joan Stambaugh (Albany: SUNY Press, 1996).]

15. *On Time and Being*, 31–32 = *Zur Sache des Denkens*, 34.

16. Cf. Georg Picht, "Die Macht des Denkens," in *Erinnerung an Martin Heidegger*, ed. Günther Neske (Pfullingen: Neske, 1977), 204.

17. Letter to Richardson, in Richardson, *Heidegger: Through Phenomenology to Thought*, xii.

18. Cf. Jean Grondin, *Le tournant dans la pensée de Martin Heidegger* (Paris: PUF, 1987), 32ff.

19. GA 69; cf. GA 66, 300; *Contributions to Philosophy*, 246 = GA 65, 351.

20. *On Time and Being*, 23 = *Zur Sache des Denkens*, 24.

21. *On Time and Being*, 14 = *Zur Sache des Denkens*, 15.

22. SZ 19 and 39; *The Basic Problems of Phenomenology*, trans. Albert Hofstadter (Bloomington: Indiana University Press, 1982), 228 = GA 24, *Die Grundprobleme der Phänomenologie*, 324.

23. GA 38, *Logik als die Frage nach dem Wesen der Sprache*, 163; cf. GA 39, *Hölderlins Hymnen "Germanien" und "Der Rhein,"* 101.

24. Heidegger, *Nietzsche*, vol. 4, ed. David Farrell Krell, trans. Frank A. Capuzzi (San Francisco: Harper and Row, 1982), 141 = *Nietzsche*, Band II (Pfullingen: Neske, 1961) 194–95.

25. Arendt and Heidegger, *Letters 1925–1975*, 84 = *Briefe 1925 bis 1975 und andere Zeugnisse*, 104.

26. Cited from Roger Munier, "Todtnauberg 1949," in *Martin Heidegger*, ed. Michel Haar (Paris: l'Herne, 1983), 154.

27. *Kant and the Problem of Metaphysics*, 5th ed., trans. Richard Taft (Bloomington: Indiana University Press, 1997), 164 = GA 3, *Kant und das Problem der Metaphysik*, 234.

28. GA 49, 60; cf. GA 66, 144f. [Translator's note: "insistence" will translate *Inständigkeit*, which means standing steadfastly in the truth of Being. This is not to be confused with *Insistenz* as Heidegger uses it in 1930 to mean "hold[ing] fast to what is offered by beings, as if they were open of and in themselves": "On the Essence of Truth," in *Pathmarks*, 150.]

29. *On the Way to Language*, trans. Peter D. Hertz (San Francisco: Harper and Row, 1971), 159–60 = *Unterwegs zur Sprache* (Pfulligen: Neske, 1959), 156; *Contributions to Philosophy*, 171 = GA 65, 242.

30. *Identity and Difference*, trans. Joan Stambaugh (Chicago: University of Chicago Press, 2002), 31 = *Identität und Differenz* (Pfullingen: Neske, 1957), 22.

31. *On Time and Being*, 42 = *ZurSache des Denkens*, 45.

32. *Contributions to Philosophy*, 317 = GA 65, 451.

33. *The Metaphysical Foundations of Logic*, 205–9 = GA 26, 265ff.; *Pathmarks*, 108 = *Wegmarken*, 34.

34. *Pathmarks*, 284, translation modified = *Wegmarken*, 203.

35. *Pathmarks*, 151f. = *Wegmarken*, 93f.

36. *Off the Beaten Track*, ed. and trans. Julian Young and Kenneth Hayes (Cambridge: Cambridge University Press, 2002), 41 = *Holzwege* (Frankfurt am Main: Klostermann, 1950), 55.

37. *Introduction to Metaphysics*, trans. Gregory Fried and Richard Polt (New Haven: Yale University Press, 2000), 22f. = *Einführung in die Metaphysik* (Tübingen: Niemeyer, 1953), 16f.

38. *Nietzsche*, vol. 1, trans. David Farrell Krell (San Francisco: Harper and Row, 1979), 51 and 136 = *Nietzsche*, Band I, 63 and 161.

39. GA 66, 144f.; cf. GA 38, 162f.; *Discourse on Thinking*, trans. John M. Anderson and E. Hans Freund (NY: Harper and Row, 1966), 82–83 = *Gelassenheit* (Pfullingen: Neske, 1959), 61.

40. *Contributions to Philosophy*, 40 and 50, translation modified = GA 65, 58 and 72.

41. *The Metaphysical Foundations of Logic*, 189 = GA 26, 244; cf. SZ 325; *Nietzsche*, vol. 1, 51 = *Nietzsche*, Band I, 63.

42. *The Metaphysical Foundations of Logic*, 195 = GA 26, 252.

43. *Off the Beaten Track*, 76 = *Holzwege*, 104 and *Pathmarks*, 249 = *Wegmarken*, 159; GA 49, 50 and 60.

44. Heidegger's caricature has several disagreeable consequences. Those who start from Heidegger and think further along deconstructionist lines take over his late critique of the subject all too lightly and fall thereby into the misleading schema depicted above. Then there are those who, under a reversal of these premises but still beholden to this schema, blame Heidegger for eliminating the subject in its autonomy and rationality. They thereby overlook the intrinsic difficulties with which this subject must still struggle. A further problematic consequence of Heidegger's caricature of the subject manifests itself in the interpretation of his engagement with National Socialism: it is in retrospect interpreted as an errant path in which subjectivism as the "bad side" of *Being and Time* has rendered itself independent. Yet Heidegger's Nazi engagement, as a version of the "will to enowning" (see above), stands quite close to his own counterpart to the so-called subject. Thus, the context of Heidegger's encounter with *Being and Time* also includes his confused interpretation of National Socialism.

45. Letter to Richardson, in Richardson, *Heidegger*, xxii.

46. Hannah Arendt, *The Human Condition*, second edition (Chicago: University of Chicago Press, 1998), 104–5.

47. Cf. Grondin, *Le tournant dans la pensée de Martin Heidegger*; Thomas Sheehan, "'Kehre' and 'Ereignis': A Prolegomenon to *Introduction to Metaphysics*," in *A Companion to Heidegger's "Introduction to Metaphysics*," ed. Richard Polt and Gregory Fried (New Haven: Yale University Press, 2001); Dieter Thomä, *Die Zeit des Selbst und die Zeit danach: Zur Kritik der Textgeschichte Martin Heideggers 1910–1976* (Frankfurt am Main: Suhrkamp, 1990), 444–65; Dieter Thomä, "Stichwort: Kehre. Was wäre, wenn es sie nicht gäbe?" in *Heidegger-Handbuch*, ed. Dieter Thomä (Stuttgart: J. B. Metzler, 2003), 134–41.

48. *Pathmarks*, 121, translation modified = *Wegmarken*, 52.

49. *Off the Beaten Track*, 47 = *Holzwege*, 62; cf. GA 39, 88.

50. *Pathmarks*, 287 = *Wegmarken*, 207.

51. *On Time and Being*, 42 = *Zur Sache des Denkens*, 45.

52. *On the Way to Language*, 106 = *Unterwegs zur Sprache*, 214.

53. *Pathmarks*, 122 = *Wegmarken*, 54; *Metaphysical Foundations of Logic*, 136ff. = GA 26, 171ff.; cf. Jean Greisch, *Ontologie et temporalité: Esquisse d'une interprétation intégrale de "Sein und Zeit"* (Paris: PUF, 1994), 499ff.

54. *The Metaphysical Foundations of Logic*, 137 = GA 26, 172; cf. *Pathmarks*, 253 = *Wegmarken*, 163; GA 66, 144f.

55. GA 38, *Logik als die Frage nach dem Wesen der Sprache*, 162.

56. GA 69, 213; cf. GA 69, 57 and *Kant and the Problem of Metaphysics*, 165–66 = GA 3, 236.

57. *Pathmarks*, 253 = *Wegmarken*, 163.

58. *The Metaphysical Foundations of Logic*, 137 = GA 26, 173.

59. Cf. *Contributions to Philosophy*, 58 and 163 = GA 65, 84 and 230; *Off the Beaten Track*, 40ff. = *Holzwege*, 53f.

60. *Pathmarks*, 268 = *Wegmarken*, 183.

61. *Pathmarks*, 271, translation modified = *Wegmarken*, 187f.

62. *Pathmarks*, 274 = *Wegmarken*, 191; cf. Dieter Thomä, "Existenz," in *Ethik: Ein Grundkurs*, ed. Heiner Hastedt and Ekkehard Martens (Reinbek: Rowohlt, 1994).

Selected Bibliography

This bibliography is only a small selection from the extensive literature by and on Heidegger, with an emphasis on recent work in English.

The plan of the *Gesamtausgabe*, or complete edition of Heidegger's writings, can be found at the publisher's website: www.klostermann.de.

Each volume of the yearly journal *Heidegger Studies* contains an update on the texts that have been published in the *Gesamtausgabe* and their translations into English, French, Italian, and Spanish.

The most complete and up-to-date international bibliography of secondary literature on Heidegger since 1990 can be found on the Web site of the library of the University of Freiburg: www.ub.uni-freiburg.de/referate/02/heidegger/heidgg90.html.

Editions and Translations of *Being and Time*

Being and Time. Trans. John Macquarrie and Edward Robinson. New York: Harper & Row, 1962.

Being and Time. Trans. Joan Stambaugh. Albany: State University of New York Press, 1996.

Sein und Zeit. Gesamtausgabe, vol. 2. Ed. Friedrich-Wilhelm von Herrmann. Frankfurt am Main: Vittorio Klostermann, 1977.

Sein und Zeit. 15th ed. Tübingen: Max Niemeyer, 1984. Later Niemeyer editions are reprints of this one, which has been corrected in light of the *Gesamtausgabe* edition. Both this Niemeyer edition and the *Gesamtausgabe* edition include Heidegger's marginal notes from his personal copy of *Sein und Zeit*; these notes are included in the Stambaugh translation but not the Macquarrie and Robinson translation.

Other Texts by Heidegger Especially Relevant to *Being and Time*

The Basic Problems of Phenomenology. Composed 1927. Trans. Albert Hofstadter. Bloomington: Indiana University Press, 1982.

Der Begriff der Zeit. Gesamtausgabe, vol. 64. Composed 1924. Ed. Friedrich-Wilhelm von Herrmann. Frankfurt am Main: Vittorio Klostermann, 2004.

Einleitung in die Philosophie. Gesamtausgabe, vol. 27. Composed 1928–1929. Ed. Otto Saame and Ina Saame-Speidel. 2nd ed. Frankfurt am Main: Vittorio Klostermann, 2001.

The Fundamental Concepts of Metaphysics: World, Finitude, Solitude. Composed 1929–1930. Trans. William McNeill and Nicholas Walker. Bloomington: Indiana University Press, 1995.

History of the Concept of Time: Prolegomena. Composed 1925. Trans. Theodore Kisiel. Bloomington: Indiana University Press, 1985.

Kant and the Problem of Metaphysics. Composed 1929. Trans. Richard Taft. 5th enl. ed. Bloomington: Indiana University Press, 1997.

Logik: Die Frage nach der Wahrheit. Gesamtausgabe, vol. 21. Composed 1925–1926. Ed. Walter Biemel. 2nd ed. Frankfurt am Main: Vittorio Klostermann, 1995.

The Metaphysical Foundations of Logic. Composed 1928. Trans. Michael Heim. Bloomington: Indiana University Press, 1984.

Ontology: The Hermeneutics of Facticity. Composed 1923. Trans. John van Buren. Bloomington: Indiana University Press, 1999.

Reference Works

Bast, Rainer A., and Heinrich P. Delfosse. *Handbuch zum Textstudium von Martin Heideggers "Sein und Zeit,"* vol. 1, *Stellenindizes, philologisch-kritischer Apparat.* Stuttgart-Bad Cannstatt: Frommann-Holzboog, 1979.

Denker, Alfred. *Historical Dictionary of Heidegger's Philosophy.* Lanham, Md.: Scarecrow, 2000.

Feick, Hildegard, and Susanne Ziegler. *Index zu Heideggers "Sein und Zeit."* 4th ed. Tübingen: Max Niemeyer, 1991.

Thomä, Dieter, ed. *Heidegger-Handbuch: Leben—Werk—Wirkung.* Stuttgart: J. B. Metzler, 2003.

Single-Author Commentaries and Studies

Blattner, William D. *Heidegger's Temporal Idealism.* Cambridge: Cambridge University Press, 1999.

Carman, Taylor. *Heidegger's Analytic: Interpretation, Discourse, and Authenticity in "Being and Time."* Cambridge: Cambridge University Press, 2003.

Dahlstrom, Daniel O. *Heidegger's Concept of Truth.* Cambridge: Cambridge University Press, 2001. Chapter 4.

Dastur, Françoise. *Heidegger and the Question of Time.* Trans. François Raffoul and David Pettigrew. Atlantic Highlands, N.J. : Humanities, 1998.

De Boer, Karin. *Thinking in the Light of Time: Heidegger's Encounter with Hegel.* Albany: State University of New York Press, 2000.

Dreyfus, Hubert. *Being-in-the-World: A Commentary on Heidegger's "Being and Time,"* Division I. Cambridge: MIT Press, 1991.

Gelven, Michael. *A Commentary on Heidegger's "Being and Time."* Rev. ed. De Kalb: Northern Illinois University Press, 1989.

Greisch, Jean. *Ontologie et temporalité: Esquisse d'une interprétation intégrale de "Sein und Zeit."* Paris: Presses Universitaires de France, 1994.

Guignon, Charles. *Heidegger and the Problem of Knowledge.* Indianapolis: Hackett, 1983.

Herrmann, Friedrich-Wilhelm von. *Subjekt und Dasein: Interpretationen zu "Sein und Zeit."* 2nd ed. Frankfurt am Main: Vittorio Klostermann, 1985.

———. *Hermeneutische Phänomenologie des Daseins: Eine Erläuterung von "Sein und Zeit,"* vol. 1, *Einleitung: Die Exposition der Frage nach dem Sinn von Sein.* Frankfurt am Main: Vittorio Klostermann, 1987.

———. *Heideggers "Grundprobleme der Phänomenologie": Zur zweiten Hälfte von "Sein und Zeit."* Frankfurt am Main: Vittorio Klostermann, 1991.

Kaelin, Eugene. *Heidegger's "Being and Time": A Reading for Readers.* Tallahassee: University Press of Florida, 1988.

Kisiel, Theodore. *The Genesis of Heidegger's "Being and Time."* Berkeley: University of California Press, 1993.

Kockelmans, Joseph J. *Heidegger's "Being and Time": The Analytic of Dasein as Fundamental Ontology.* Lanham, Md.: University Press of America, 1989.

Luckner, Andreas. *Martin Heidegger: "Sein und Zeit": Ein einführender Kommentar.* 2nd ed. Paderborn: Schöningh, 2001.

Polt, Richard. *Heidegger: An Introduction.* Ithaca: Cornell University Press, 1999. Chapters 3–4.

Vogel, Lawrence. *The Fragile "We": Ethical Implications of Heidegger's "Being and Time."* Evanston: Northwestern University Press, 1994.

Zimmerman, Michael E. *Eclipse of the Self: The Development of Heidegger's Concept of Authenticity.* Athens: Ohio University Press, 1981.

Collections of Essays Largely about *Being and Time*

Dreyfus, Hubert L., and Mark Wrathall, eds. *Heidegger: A Critical Reader.* Oxford: Blackwell, 1992.

———, eds. *Heidegger Reexamined,* vol. 1, *Phenomenology, Dasein, and Truth;* vol. 2, *Authenticity, Death, and the History of Being.* New York: Routledge, 2002.

———, eds. *A Companion to Heidegger.* Oxford: Blackwell, 2005.

Elliston, F., ed. *Heidegger's Existential Analytic.* New York: Mouton, 1978.

Guignon, Charles, ed. *The Cambridge Companion to Heidegger.* Cambridge: Cambridge University Press, 1993.

Kockelmans, Joseph J., ed. *A Companion to Martin Heidegger's "Being and Time."* Washington, D.C.: Center for Advanced Research in Phenomenology and University Press of America, 1986.

Macann, Christopher, ed. *Martin Heidegger: Critical Assessments,* vol. 1, *Philosophy.* London: Routledge, 1992.

Rentsch, Thomas, ed. *Martin Heidegger, "Sein und Zeit."* Klassiker Auslegen, vol. 25. Berlin: Akademie, 2001.

Scharff, Robert C., ed. *The Blackwell Guide to Heidegger's "Being and Time."* Oxford: Blackwell, forthcoming.

Index

239

About the Contributors

Jeffrey Andrew Barash (Université de Picardie, Amiens) is the author of *Martin Heidegger and the Problem of Historical Meaning*, *Heidegger et son siècle: Temps de l'Être, temps de l'histoire*, and articles on Heidegger, Arendt, Strauss, Levinas, and the philosophy of history. His latest book is *Politiques de l'histoire: L'historicisme comme promesse et comme mythe*.

Steven Crowell (Rice University) is the author of many articles on phenomenology and Continental philosophy, some of which are collected in *Husserl, Heidegger, and the Space of Meaning: Paths toward Transcendental Phenomenology*. He is coeditor of *The New Yearbook for Phenomenology and Phenomenological Philosophy*.

Daniel O. Dahlstrom (Boston University) is the author of *Heidegger's Concept of Truth* and of numerous articles on Heidegger, Kant, Hegel, and other German thinkers. He has edited several philosophical anthologies and the *Philosophical Writings* of Moses Mendelssohn.

Karin de Boer (University of Groningen) is the author of *Thinking in the Light of Time: Heidegger's Encounter with Hegel* and of articles on Heidegger, Hegel, and Derrida.

Hubert L. Dreyfus (University of California, Berkeley) is the author of numerous essays and books on Heidegger, technology, and Continental philosophy, including *Being-in-the-World*, *What Computers Still Can't Do*, and *On the Internet*.

Günter Figal (University of Freiburg) is the author of *Martin Heidegger: Phänomenologie der Freiheit* and *Heidegger zur Einführung* as well as books on Adorno, Nietzsche, and Socrates. Some of his essays are collected in *For a Philosophy of Freedom and Strife: Politics, Aesthetics, Metaphysics*.

Jean Grondin (University of Montréal) has published numerous books and articles on Heidegger, hermeneutics, and Kant, including *Introduction to Philosophical Hermeneutics*, *Sources of Hermeneutics*, and *Hans-Georg Gadamer: A Biography*. His latest books are *Du sens de la vie* and *Introduction à la métaphysique*.

Charles Guignon (University of South Florida) is the author of *Heidegger and the Problem of Knowledge* and *On Being Authentic*, as well as articles on Heidegger, hermeneutics, and psychotherapy. His edited volumes include *The Cambridge Companion to Heidegger*, *Richard Rorty*, and *The Existentialists: Critical Essays on Kierkegaard, Nietzsche, Heidegger, and Sartre*.

Theodore Kisiel (Northern Illinois University) is the author of *The Genesis of Heidegger's "Being and Time"* and numerous articles on Heidegger, some of which are collected in *Heidegger's Way of Thought*. He is the translator of Heidegger's *History of the Concept of Time* and coeditor of *Reading Heidegger from the Start*.

William McNeill (DePaul University) is the author of *The Glance of the Eye: Heidegger, Aristotle, and the Ends of Theory*, editor of Heidegger's *Pathmarks*, and cotranslator of Heidegger's lecture courses *Hölderlin's Hymn "The Ister"* and *The Fundamental Concepts of Metaphysics*. He is preparing translations of two more lecture courses on Hölderlin.

Graeme Nicholson (University of Toronto, emeritus) is the author of *Illustrations of Being*, *Seeing and Reading*, *Plato's "Phaedrus,"* and articles on Heidegger, Gadamer, Plato, and other topics. He has coedited anthologies of articles on Gadamer and Emil Fackenheim.

Richard Polt (Xavier University, Cincinnati) is the author of *Heidegger: An Introduction* and *The Emergency of Being: On Heidegger's "Contributions to Philosophy."* With Gregory Fried, he has translated Heidegger's *Introduction to Metaphysics* and edited *A Companion to Heidegger's "Introduction to Metaphysics."*

Dieter Thomä (University of St. Gallen, Switzerland) is the author of *Die Zeit des Selbst und die Zeit danach: Zur Kritik der Textgeschichte Martin Heideggers 1910–1976* and editor of *Heidegger-Handbuch*. He has also authored philosophical books on parenthood, autobiography, Americans, and happiness.